Quantum Ops

Milankumar Rana · Bishwajeet Pandey
Editors

Quantum Ops

Bridging Quantum Computing and IT Operations

Springer

Editors
Milankumar Rana
University of the Cumberlands
Williamsburg, KY, USA

Bishwajeet Pandey
GL Bajaj Institute of Technology
and Management
Greater Noida, Uttar Pradesh, India

ISBN 978-3-032-10774-9 ISBN 978-3-032-10775-6 (eBook)
https://doi.org/10.1007/978-3-032-10775-6

This Springer imprint is published by the registered company Springer Nature Switzerland AG
The registered company address is: Gewerbestrasse 11, 6330 Cham, Switzerland

Preface

The meteoric emergence of quantum computing has marked a significant turning point in the history of computing. In contrast to the binary bits that are utilized in conventional computing, the fundamental components of quantum computing are referred to as qubits, entanglement, and superposition. Because of this, it can perform tasks with data that were previously thought to be extremely difficult to accomplish. The purpose of this book is to attempt to satisfy the growing demand for a comprehensive resource that explores the fundamentals of quantum computing as well as the potential applications of this technology across a variety of fields.

Within the first few chapters of the book, the fundamental concepts of the area are discussed. In the Chapter "Quantum Computing Fundamentals: Beyond Classical Bits", which was written by Swati Karni, offers a concise introduction to the function of quantum physics in computing and explains how it is distinct from traditional paradigms. In her extensive explanation of "Qubits, Quantum Gates, and Quantum Circuits", Saraswati Mishra lays the groundwork for understanding how to manipulate quantum states to carry out logical operations. Ashwin Prakash Nalwade presents the practical aspects of programming in "Quantum Programming: Languages and Frameworks", establishing a connection between theory and practice.

Having built a solid foundation, the book transitions to quantum algorithms and error prevention, two crucial areas propelling contemporary research. Khan Shariya Hasan Upoma's chapter, "Key Quantum Algorithms: Shor's, Grover's, and Applications", emphasizes the significant ramifications of quantum accelerations for cryptography, search, and optimization. Omkar Bhalekar focuses on "Quantum Error Correction and Noise Mitigation", tackling the significant challenge of maintaining coherence in delicate quantum states—a critical issue for the practicality and reliability of quantum computer.

The ensuing chapters illustrate the growing accessibility and integration of quantum computing into practical systems. Monika Malik's "Quantum Cloud Services: Getting Quantum Power" presents the swiftly expanding landscape of cloud-based quantum platforms, facilitating universal access for academics and developers globally. Keshav Kumar offers an in-depth examination of "Quantum Simulation and Emulation Techniques", illustrating how simulations facilitate the investigation of quantum phenomena and the evaluation of algorithms on classical systems.

The book thereafter transitions to the realms of transdisciplinary innovation. Sakhita Sree Gadde's "Quantum Machine Learning: Merging Quantum and AI" examine how quantum principles could transform artificial intelligence, perhaps leading to advancements in pattern identification and optimization. Anurag Reddy, in "Quantum Security—Cryptography and Threat Landscape", delineates the dual function of quantum technology in jeopardizing existing cryptographic systems while simultaneously facilitating the development of novel, more secure paradigms. Anticipating industrial applications, Varun Awasthi's the Future of Quantum processes in Enterprises examines how companies might achieve quantum readiness and incorporate it into commercial processes.

The collection ends with paradigm shifts and disciplinary convergence. In "Quantum Computing as a Paradigm Shift in Mechanical and Allied Engineering", Vipul Kumar Sharma explains how quantum methods could change how engineers' model, simulate, and optimize things. Keshav Kumar's last chapter, "Quantum Without Hardware: Cloud Services and the New Computing Paradigm", goes back to the theme of accessibility. It shows how people who don't have direct access to quantum computing hardware can still use its capabilities. This is a big step forward in making advanced computation available to everyone.

Together, these contributions provide a single story, from the beginnings of algorithms and applications to the current possibilities and future paradigm shifts. This book has a lot of different points of view and talents, which shows how quantum computing is both interdisciplinary and collaborative. Each chapter stands on its own but is also connected to the others. This makes it easy for both professionals and beginners to follows along.

This book is for scientists, engineers, and computer scientists who want to be a part of the quantum revolution. We hope that this collection will serve as both an introduction and a visionary guide, encouraging more research, collaboration, and creativity. We want to thank the writers for their hard work, dedication, and ideas, as well as the people in the community whose curiosity and tenacity are moving the quantum age forward.

Williamsburg, USA — Milankumar Rana
Greater Noida, India — Bishwajeet Pandey

Contents

Quantum Computing Fundamentals: Beyond Classical Bits

Swati Karni and Arun Kumar Rajamandrapu

Abstract

The new technique to solve the problems is quantum computing, which involves the use of the laws of quantum physics that are completely dissimilar to the laws used in normal (classical) computers. The potential possibilities of quantum computers are that they would provide a solution to the problems, e.g., in the fields of finance, designing new materials, and medical research, so much faster than any other computer in current use. The researchers are, however, making good progress to take advantage of the superior hardware and the brainier codes, going by the fact that the field of quantum computers is not complete yet. Quantum can no longer be called a theory since it is soon going to be viable and powerful. In 2019, Google reported having cracked a problem on its quantum computer in 200 s that would require an ordinary supercomputer approximately 10,000 years [3]. The 433-qubit Doppelganger development of more powerful quantum computers, referred to as the so-called Osprey, was released by IBM as evidence of the major progress in development [11]. There are some examples that explain why quantum computers are slightly closer to offering some help in solving some practical problems to contribute to the strengthening of cybersecurity, the development of new medications, and the optimization of complex systems. This chapter shows big ideas that characterize quantum computing. It provides qubits (that can possess more than one value at a certain moment in

This chapter is co-authored by **Ms. Swati Karni** and **Mr. Arun Kumar Rajamandrapu**, both distinguished professionals in the fields of cloud computing and quantum computing.

S. Karni (✉)
Department of Information Technology, University of the Cumberlands, Williamsburg, KY, USA
e-mail: skarni70360@ucumberlands.edu

A. K. Rajamandrapu
Solution Architect OTA - Information Technology, General Motors, Detroit, MI, USA
e-mail: Arunkumarrajamandrapu@ieee.org

M. Rana and B. Pandey (eds.), *Quantum Ops*,
https://doi.org/10.1007/978-3-032-10775-6_1

an effect known as superposition). It can also give entropy and interference that enables the quantum computers to perform complex activities in a more coordinated way. We also compare the work of both classical and quantum computers and give basic comparisons of their capabilities to illustrate various things that have already been accomplished with the quantum computers, like molecule simulation or hard math problems solved. The basics leave the readers prepared to read the upcoming chapters, in which it will be discussed further on how the quantum systems can be built and how they can be implemented in the world. Once the reader gets to the end of this chapter, he/she will have an opportunity to understand why quantum computing is a wonderful and thrilling field of investigation, and that to take advantage of this superb technology, one should be aware of the fundamentals.

Keywords

Quantum computing • Qubits • Superposition • Entanglement • Quantum algorithms • Quantum computer error correction • Quantum gates • Quantum artificial intelligence

1 Introduction

Today's computers use small electronic switches called transistors to process information using binary digits (0s and 1s). These systems work by following the rules of classical physics, doing one step at a time to complete tasks. While these computers are fast, they are reaching their limits. As transistors become smaller—almost as small as individual atoms—classical physics can no longer explain or control how they behave.

This challenge shows that traditional computing is hitting a wall, and we need a new way to continue making progress. This is where quantum computing comes in. Quantum computers use the rules of quantum physics, which are very different from classical physics. This special ability is called superposition. Qubits can also be entangled, meaning they can be connected in ways that let them share information instantly.

Because of these abilities, quantum computers could become much faster and more powerful than today's best computers. They could help with:

- Medicine: Finding new drugs by simulating how molecules interact.
- Materials science: Creating new materials with special properties.
- Finance: Making better investment decisions and spotting fraud.
- Cybersecurity: Breaking current encryption and creating stronger, quantum-proof systems.
- Artificial intelligence: Speeding up learning and making AI smarter.

Scientists have been working on quantum computers since the 1980s. The idea that quantum computers could solve problems that classical computers can't was first suggested by physicist Richard Feynman. Since then, progress has been steady. For example:

- In 1999, D-Wave built a basic quantum computer.
- By 2007, they reached 28 qubits.
- In 2010, they had 128 qubits.
- By 2013, they reached 512.
- And in 2018, they achieved over 2,000 qubits.

Even with these advances, quantum computers are still mostly found in research labs, and many challenges remain, like making them more stable and less error-prone. Still, major companies like IBM, Google, Microsoft, and Intel are investing heavily in making quantum computers practical.

Different types of qubits are being tested. Some use superconductors (materials with no electrical resistance), while others use spin qubits in silicon, which could work well with existing computer chip technology.

A global study using Scopus, a database of research papers, shows that interest in quantum computing is growing quickly. Researchers have studied where this research is coming from, what topics are being covered, and which countries are leading the way.

This first chapter introduces the most important ideas in quantum computing. It explains how qubits, superposition, and entanglement work and how they are different from regular computer bits. Understanding these basics is important before moving on to more advanced topics.

By learning these essentials, readers will be ready to explore how quantum computing can change the future of technology, science, and everyday life. This chapter is the starting point for understanding one of the most exciting and powerful technologies of our time.

2 Conceptual Foundations and Theoretical Framework

This section clearly explains the basic ideas that make quantum computing different from regular (classical) computing. It covers important concepts like quantum bits (qubits), superposition, entanglement, interference, and measurement. It also looks at how quantum computers are built in the real world and compares how classical and quantum computers work.

2.1 Computing Foundations

2.1.1 Bits and Binary Logic

Classical computers are built on the binary system, where all information is stored using bits. Each bit can be either a 0 or a 1 [4]. This simple system is the base of today's digital technology and helps computers handle numbers and symbols effectively [4]. The binary nature of bits allows for deterministic processing, where a specific input always yields the same output, which is a hallmark of classical computing systems [18].

2.1.2 Classical Gates and Circuits

To process binary information, classical computers rely on Boolean logic gates such as AND, OR, NOT, NAND, and XOR. These gates are implemented through electronic components like transistors and are arranged into logic circuits that perform operations varying from basic arithmetic to complex decision-making [26]. A well-known model underpinning classical computers is the von Neumann architecture, which features a centralized processing unit, a control unit, and a memory unit connected via a shared communication bus [4]. Instructions and data are fetched from memory sequentially, leading to a predictable but linear flow of execution.

2.1.3 Computational Limitations

Despite its widespread adoption, classical computing encounters inherent limitations, especially when dealing with problems of exponential complexity. Tasks such as large-scale optimization, prime factorization, or simulating quantum physical systems often require resources that scale beyond feasible computational limits. Furthermore, the shared data bus in von Neumann systems introduces a performance constraint known as the von Neumann bottleneck, where the transfer rate between memory and processor becomes a limiting performance factor [26]. Additionally, the deceleration of Moore's Law—the trend of doubling transistor density every two years—due to physical limitations such as heat dissipation, atomic-scale barriers, and power constraints signals the plateau of classical computational scalability [14]. These challenges are among the key motivations driving research into alternative paradigms like quantum computing, which operates beyond the binary logic model.

2.2 The Rise of Quantum Computing

Over the years, computer systems have become faster and more powerful. This progress started with cluster computing and later included grid, cloud, and fog computing. These technologies helped improve processing power, data sharing, and security. Today, researchers are focused on a new area called quantum computing. Their goal is to make computers even faster, strengthen networks, and improve system security. Many believe that using ideas from quantum physics can help build better computing systems that are both secure and reliable [2].

From 2016 to 2023, quantum computing made major progress, reaching key breakthroughs. These advances had a big impact on areas like cryptography and opened the door to solving problems that traditional computers can't handle [16]. The years 2016 to 2018 were especially important for laying the foundation for this progress. During this time, scientists made big improvements in designing new quantum algorithms and ways to fix errors in quantum systems. A major moment came in 2016 when IBM introduced its first publicly available quantum computers—the IBM Q 5 series [21]. These early models only had a few qubits, but they were very useful for testing quantum programs and learning how to control quantum systems. In 2017, researchers at the University of Southern California proposed a new method of error correction called the surface code, which became a key step toward making reliable, large-scale quantum computers [7].

In 2019, Google informed the world about one of the most significant achievements, called quantum supremacy. Their Sycamore quantum processor ran through a task in a few minutes that would otherwise take a classical supercomputer thousands of years to complete [3]. This feat was largely notional, but it demonstrated that quantum computers could, in the future, be more effective at performing certain tasks than a classical computer. At the same time, quantum computing was also implemented in cloud computing. Web-enabled platforms such as Amazon Braket, IBM Quantum, and Microsoft Azure Quantum enabled individuals to traverse quantum experiments via the internet without necessarily requiring a quantum computer. Big tech firms joined in, and startups entered this race, too. Firms such as Rigetti Computing and IonQ developed new qubits, such as trapped-ion qubits, to enhance the efficiency and decrease the restrictions [13]. These trends created greater strides and innovation.

Over the past two years, attention has begun to stretch upward and outward to enlarge and precisely define quantum computers. In 2022, IBM released its Osprey processor that, with 433 qubits, was nothing short of amazing compared to previous machines [11]. Researchers also persisted with the error correction protocols, which are a prerequisite to engineering useful and robust quantum computers such as the surface code. Big intergenerational projects started coming into existence. As an example, the European Union announced an ambitious program, the Quantum Flagship program, within which it planned to invest heavily to take a leading position globally in quantum technology in 2023 (The Quantum Flagship Initiative). Other initiatives by both governments and businesses globally signify the relevance of quantum computing. Despite the fact that numerous problems are still ahead, including enhancing the reliability of hardware and engineering it at a more affordable price, between the years 2016 and 2023, the groundwork was laid for a possible future where quantum computing might revolutionize numerous fields in science and technology.

Quantum computing relies on quantum theory, which describes the behavior of very small particles, such as atoms. Contrary to classical computers, whose processing system is based on bits that can either be 0 or 1, quantum computers are based on qubits, which can simultaneously be 0 and 1. This property, which is known as superposition, allows quantum computers to be much faster than standard computers at solving a given problem. Provided it is successful, a quantum computer will be able to perform better than the most developed classical systems that are now accessible [15].

But coming up with a workable quantum computer is not a walk in the park. Qubits are extremely fragile, and they may lose their quantum state when disturbed. This issue is what is referred to as decoherence. When decoherence occurs, the qubit behaves as a normal bit, at which point the computer ceases to have an advantage. Researchers are developing the means to avoid decoherence by ensuring better qubit fabrication and error correction during calculations [29].

In spite of the fact that quantum computing is at the stage of development, contributors globally are advancing it. They are making hardware design, developing software, and also making systems that are likely to be used by ordinary users. A lot of questions remain unresolved, but the discipline is expanding. Researchers are also investigating how quantum computing should enhance fields such as secure communication and encryption [17].

2.3 Understanding Qubits

The technology of quantum computing is a formidable new form of computation, and it is constructed on the counterintuitive and yet really interesting principles of quantum mechanics. Computers have a unit of information known as a bit, which could be a 0 or 1, which is the minimal data unit used in traditional computers. All jobs in a normal PC are performed with combinations of these two values. This is very different in quantum computers, however, which use special bits called qubits. A qubit may be either a 0 or a 1 or both simultaneously. This special power is named superposition. Think of a coin that is wobbly in the air; it is both heads and tails until it falls. Similarly, a qubit is in a mixed state before it is measured [12, 16].

Quantum computers can search simultaneously through a very large number of potential solutions since qubits simultaneously store many different values. The advantage of this is that they are able to find solutions to some problems much quicker than a classical computer [16]. As an example, issues such as the breaking of complex codes, molecule simulation to discover drugs, or analyzing huge sets of data can be done with far easier quantum computers.

Qubits have been found to have roughly the same properties as small particles in the natural world; thus, quantum computers are very effective at modeling the real world. Instead of resolving problems, as generally done by computers, quantum computers have the capability of investigating numerous options simultaneously, and this makes them more efficient and faster [25]. Simply put, quantum computing is a large leap into technology. It exploits some of the weird yet potent capabilities of quantum mechanics to complete things that would otherwise take normal computers years, maybe even centuries [16].

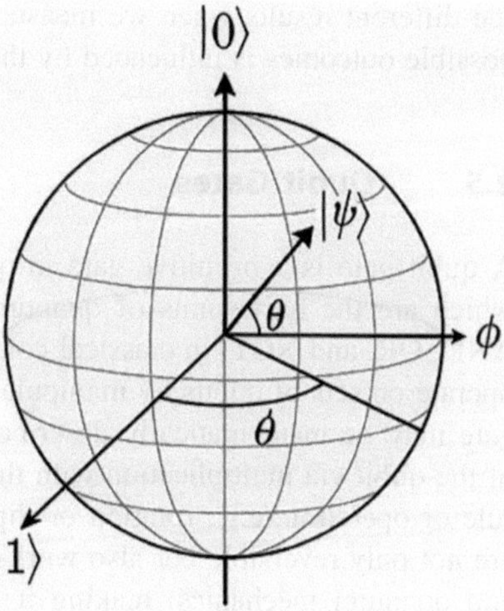

Fig. 1 Bloch sphere diagram

Table 1 Comparison between classical bits and qubits across key computational features

Feature	Classical bit	Qubit
State	0 or 1	Superposition of $
Representation	Single value	Vector in a two-dimensional Hilbert space
Measurement	Definite value	Probabilistic

2.3.1 Classical Bits Versus Qubits

The Bloch Sphere, shown in Fig. 1, provides a useful visualization of a qubit's state. The top of the sphere (the north pole) represents the qubit in the $|0\rangle$ state, while the bottom (the south pole) represents the $|1\rangle$ state. Any point on the sphere's surface corresponds to a superposition, or mixed state, of these two basis states. The qubit's position on the sphere is defined by two angles: θ, indicating its vertical position, and ϕ, indicating its rotation around the sphere. This representation helps illustrate how a qubit can encode more complex information than a classical bit, which can only exist as 0 or 1 (Table 1).

2.4 Measurements

Measurement in quantum computing is the set of operations to translate the quantum information, i.e., stored in quantum states, into classical bits, processed by a conventional computer, or read by classical observers. The importance of this step is that quantum systems are said to be in superposed states, and it is measurement that actually collapses the superpositions to definite classical states, i.e., a 0 or a 1. One fundamental fact in quantum mechanics is that the outcome of a measurement is not found to be guaranteed but random. In these words, it is meant that we may prepare a quantum system identically on successive occasions, but we may still see different results when we measure it. The probability of attaining any of the possible outcomes is influenced by the state in the quantum system [1].

2.5 Qubit Gates

A qubit gate is a primitive gate in quantum computing that operates on qubits, which are the basic units of quantum information. Just as logic gates (such as AND, OR, and NOT) in classical computing consume a set of bits, so qubit gates operate on sets of qubits by manipulating their probability amplitudes. Each qubit gate may be mathematically described by a square matrix that acts on the state of the qubit via multiplication with the matrix. That is, the gate implements some rule or operation, e.g., rotation or flipping, to the state vector of the qubit. They are not only reversible but also work according to the principles of linear algebra and quantum mechanics, making it possible to do complex computations with sequences of gates in a quantum circuit.

2.6 Quantum Superposition

The significant characteristic of quantum computing is superposition. In a classical computer, every bit is a 1 or a 0. However, in a quantum computer, both states, 0 and 1, are possible simultaneously due to the existence of qubits in these computers. That is referred to as superposition [12]. In turn, due to this, quantum computers are able to examine multiple solutions simultaneously. The more qubits there are, the faster and more powerful the computer will be. This contributes to the resolution of intricate issues significantly faster as compared to ordinary computers [28].

Superposition may be applied in numerous situations, such as locating records in a huge database or other mathematical tasks, such as decomposing larger numbers into several variables [20]. It can also assist with machine learning models to understand patterns and make more decisions. It is, however, challenging to maintain qubits in superposition. When a qubit is put to a measurement or influenced by the surroundings, it loses this unique status and is simply either 0 or 1. It is referred to as decoherence [16]. Simply, the superposition allows quantum computers to accomplish numerous processes simultaneously, which is why these computers are significantly stronger than classical ones [16].

Example. Think of a coin that is spinning in the air. It is either a tail or a head until one of the two possibilities is realized after application of the coin. Not till it lands do we know the definite outcome. In the same manner, before being measured, a qubit is in a superposition of eigenstates.

2.7 Quantum Entanglement

The entanglement is an unusual and potent component of quantum physics [5]. It implies that two qubits can be correlated so that a happening to one will immediately change the other as well—even in the event when they are separated by distance. Such an atypical connection endows quantum computers with peculiar powers [3].

Entanglement is a unique characteristic of quantum systems that incorporates two or more qubits in an inseparable manner such that the occurrence of an event on one qubit is relative to the condition of the other qubit, despite the distance between them. This implies that when two qubits are entangled, we can access their collective state immediately, even when they are located at a vast distance. This weird entanglement, or what Einstein referred to as spooky action at a distance, enables quantum computers to synchronize qubits in a manner not accessible to normal computers. Due to this, quantum computers have a significant advantage in performing some sorts of calculations as compared to conventional systems [22].

What made entanglement surprising and counterintuitive is pointed out in the Einstein–Podolsky–Rosen paradox. Einstein, Podolsky, and Rosen reasoned that in the case that the measurement of one particle can have an instantaneous effect on a distant particle, it would mean that we can communicate at a speed faster than light, which is not true in the theory of relativity. But entanglement cannot possibly permit faster-than-light communication since the measurement result is random.

Applications
Quantum Teleportation. Transference of the condition of one qubit to another.

Quantum Cryptography. Creating secure communication channels that are impossible to eavesdrop on without detection.

Qubit A ○ — ○ Qubit B

2.8 Classical Versus Quantum Computation

Tasks processed via the normal computers using the binary code are executed step by step. They occur at a very high speed, and the process can take only milliseconds, but it may appear that the computer does numerous things at the same time. In real life, every single calculation or decision is executed sequentially. It conducts small procedures very well and is slow and less effective when addressing huge or otherwise intricate issues. However, quantum computers pursue an absolutely different model, thanks to which they can solve some tasks much faster [9].

The main distinction is the way both systems treat information. A classical computer makes a search by going through every solution possible at a time, just as going through pages to arrive at the correct page in a book. However, a quantum computer can look at multiple possibilities simultaneously due to such quantum properties as superposition and entanglement. It will allow reducing the correct answer faster, namely, without going through every option. As an illustration, the quantum computer developed by Google has managed to address more complicated problems in a few seconds, which is a much shorter time compared to doing the same in a normal supercomputer [16].

Although quantum computers have this potential, they have not yet become mature enough to be used daily. A big problem is that they require quite particular conditions to operate. The majority of quantum computers need to operate at such low temperatures that they are near absolute zero, i.e., 0–5 Celsius. When they become any warmer, the qubits no longer have their fragile quantum state, and the computer might keep coming to a halt [16].

Quantum computers are highly mismatched with regular computers. Due to this reason, they are able to work out certain issues much more quickly. The new form of artificial intelligence, or AI, also creates opportunities to enhance it through this special ability. AI is already applied to most spheres where machines are supposed to think and to learn in a way similar to humans. Due to quicker computers, additional information, and improved learning techniques, it has grown more potent. Nevertheless, despite all these advancements, regular AI still finds it difficult to deal with truly difficult challenges that require extensive computing resources. That is where the Quantum AI arrives. It integrates the AI intelligent learning with the speed and power of quantum computers. There are quantum computers, and quantum computers have something called qubits, and quantum computers can simultaneously perform a lot of things [22]. It implies that they are capable of processing massive information in a significantly shorter time frame in comparison to ordinary computers.

Using a combination of AI and quantum computing, Quantum AI might enable machines to learn quickly, identify patterns more effortlessly, and solve quantifiably challenging problems that are out of the range of current AI. The comparison of the two types is presented below.

Table 2 suggests that while quantum AI offers groundbreaking advances in speed, efficiency, and security, its real-world implementation remains limited by current technological hurdles.

3 Architecture of Quantum Computers

The qubits, or a number of qubits, need to be at very low temperatures to do the operations on them over a long period. Whenever heat is added to the system, it is very likely to make an error; that is a quantum error, and so quantum computers are meant to operate in low temperatures to ensure that such errors are avoided [12]. The quantum computer, called the dilution refrigerator, has more than 2,000 components so that the properties of mixing two helium isotopes can be used to produce an environment that suits the qubits. This is done in one of the stages,

Table 2 Run classic totopall versus run totopall quantum

Aspect	Classic totopall	Run totopall quantum
Processing power	Operates on traditional binary systems with limited scalability	Leverages quantum principles like superposition and entanglement for vastly superior performance
Data processing	Processes data sequentially using bits	Uses qubits to process multiple data states simultaneously, boosting speed
Optimization techniques	Depends on heuristics or exhaustive search methods	Employs quantum algorithms (e.g., Grover's) for significantly faster optimization
Pattern detection	Needs large datasets and extended training times	Can identify patterns more efficiently with fewer data due to quantum parallelism
Security and cryptography	Susceptible to quantum-based attacks	Can both break classical encryption and support quantum-resistant cryptographic methods
Machine learning impact	Constrained by classical computing capabilities	Enables advanced ML models (e.g., quantum neural networks) with faster and deeper learning
Development status	Well-developed with mature tools and platforms	Still in early stages, with active research in both hardware and algorithm design

and the cooling is done to around 4 Kelvin. When the control and readout signals are transferred to the processor, attenuation may take place on every possible stage within the refrigerator in order to make the qubits resistant to being influenced by the thermal noise. Superconducting materials are used to manufacture the coaxial wires used to transmit signals between stages of amplification in order to minimize energy loss [19]. Cryogenic isolators make sure that qubit signals advance without noise obstructing their quality (Fig. 2).

Fig. 2 Example of a quantum computer system [6]

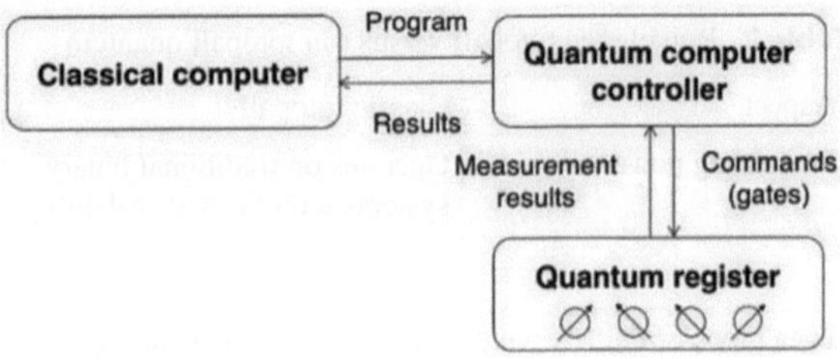

Fig. 3 Simple structure of a quantum computer [6]

The quantum processor is encapsulated with shielding to prevent electromagnetic interference, whereas the quantum amplifiers trigger processor readout as well as amplify them and reduce noise. The bottom of the refrigerator mixing chamber provides cooling requirements necessary to cool the processor and its attached parts to approximately 15 millikelvin, which is colder than the space vacuum. Such low temperatures, usually lower than 250 millikelvin, are necessary to prevent the inadvertent excitation of the quantum states of superconducting qubits by heating [24]. A quantum computer will have classical and quantum components. Now the program logic is classic only and is itself in a classic controller, whereas the quantum component is a coprocessor, as a GPU augments a CPU. The quantum processor concentrates on certain tasks of a bigger and more complicated classical program (Fig. 3).

4 Quantum Algorithms

In classical computing or quantum computing, an algorithm is a step-by-step procedure that is commonly used to solve problems or to perform computations. In a like manner, upon the development of a quantum computer, an algorithm that requires the quantum computer to execute it is referred to as a quantum algorithm [10]. Many problems, called undecidable problems, are so far unsolvable using classical algorithms and quantum algorithms. But the most important difference between quantum algorithms and classical algorithms is that in several cases, quantum algorithms can be much faster than classical ones. Quantum algorithms are not guaranteed to give the correct answer; rather, they give the answer with a high probability [8].

4.1 Shor's Algorithm

One of the most famous and significant quantum algorithms is Shor's algorithm. It was the invention of Peter Shor in 1994 to factor large numbers exponentially faster than any classical algorithm known. Precisely, it may operate in $O((\log N)^3)$ time using $O(\log N)$ storage to factor a number N [30]. This is a Herculean advance to the classical methods, which would require exponentially more time in order to solve the same problem.

The significance of Shor's algorithm is that it may crack RSA, which is one of the most utilized algorithms for protecting online communication. The effectiveness of RSA is based on the fact that the process of factoring a large number into its prime factors is very difficult to do. This is no longer efficient to be done on classical computers when applied to very large numbers. Indeed, it is not known how to construct a classical algorithm to factor N in O((log N)^k) time for any fixed k.

Shor has developed an algorithm based on this fact: he translates the problem of factoring into a problem of period locating, which is itself usable to solve the problem of factoring by means of the Quantum Fourier Transform (QFT). It is used in determining the period (repeating pattern) of a function that is dependent on the number factored. When a period is identified, then the number can be factored easily. Shor's algorithm, similarly to most quantum algorithms, is probabilistic, and thus there is a nontrivial probability that it would not find a solution to the problem at hand immediately, but with the repetition of the run, the success probability increases [27].

The major stages in the algorithm by Shor:

Quantum Fourier Transform (QFT)—It is used to obtain the period of a mathematical function.

Finding Period—Find the period of a function, and this assists in factoring the original number.

Cybersecurity is a serious implication of Shor's algorithm. Otherwise, in case large-scale quantum computers become accessible, they might break most of the existing systems of cryptography based on the public key currently applied to the protection of information, such as RSA, with the help of this algorithm. That is why scientists are now developing post-quantum cryptography that would withstand quantum attacks.

RSA is one of the most common ways of protecting digital information, such as online bank accounts and emails. This comes in the form of security that is based on it being very difficult to break big numbers down into their primes using classical computers. To take a simple example: it takes no time at all to multiply two very big prime numbers together, but it is very hard and awkwardly lengthy, even with present-day computers, to recover the original two numbers, given the product of the two numbers.

That is not the case with Shor's algorithm. It provides a quick method of doing this factoring, to which quantum computers might apply a cracking of RSA encryption to reveal sensitive information. That is why Shor's algorithm is viewed as a serious threat to current cybersecurity and why specialists have started to come up with approaches to encryption that would be resistant to quantum computer attacks.

4.2 Grover's Algorithm

The approach of Grover's algorithm, developed by Lov Grover in 1996, is another important quantum algorithm. It finds the N-item database (the database does not require sorting) at O(sqrt(N)) time with O(log N) storage [8]. Comparatively, a classical algorithm would require O(N) to do the same. Although Grover's algorithm does not offer the exponential speed in comparison to the Shor algorithm, it does offer a quadratic speedup, which means that it can be at most four times faster with big datasets.

Grover's algorithm is probabilistic; this implies that it might have to be repeated several times before it can give the correct answer with a high degree of certainty. It is not a searching tool only; it can be applied in search of medians and means, NP-complete problems, as well as collision detection [30].

How Grover's Algorithm Works:

1. Initialization: The algorithm begins by preparing an equal superposition of all the feasible states. This implies every state has an equal opportunity of being selected.
2. Oracle: All the correct items are differentially marked by a special quantum subroutine, the oracle, which flips their phase.
3. Amplitude amplification: The algorithm uses repetitive amplifications to make the correct measurement likely.
4. Measurement: The quantum system is lastly measured. The rightful item is the one that has the highest probability of occurrence.

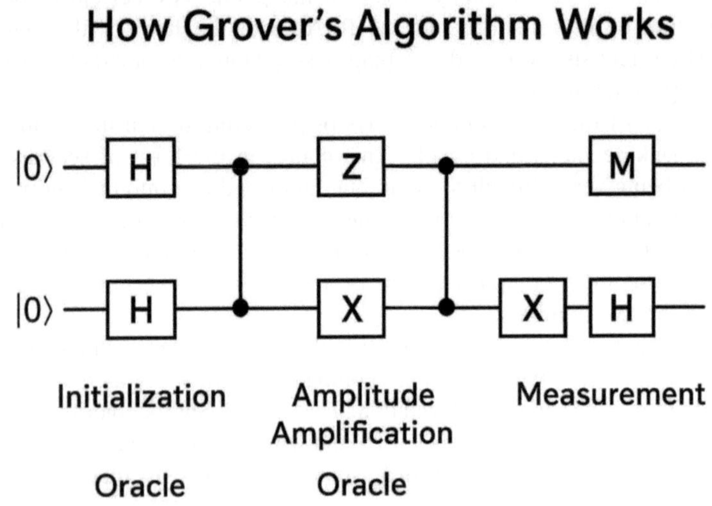

The reason why Grover's algorithm is important is that it can enhance the way we search unstructured data, which happens to be the case in most real-life issues.

Although this speedup is not exponentially large, it may be very useful in the case of large data input or complicated problem input.

Grover's algorithm is a process that aims at quantum computation to enable finding unsorted information using less time compared to a normal computer [8]. Ordinarily, a normal computer would have to discuss every item individually, a process that is time-consuming. However, Grover's algorithm can identify the correct element in much fewer iterations—approximately the square root of the total population. Consider searching through a list of one million names of people, and it is a mess; you need to find one person. An ordinary computer may have to scan through approximately half a million names before it can land on the correct name. However, with Grover's algorithm, a quantum computer would only need approximately 1,000 attempts to find it [23].

The implications of this are that Grover's algorithm can become useful in applying to such endeavors as database searching, puzzle solving with a large number of solutions, and actually helping to crack some forms of encryption through a faster process of guessing some of the secret keys. Its speed does not increase as much as that of other quantum algorithms, such as Short, but it does demonstrate the power of how quantum computers can perform some tasks much faster than normal computers.

5 Quantum Simulation (Made Simple)

Quantum simulation means using quantum computers to model the behavior of other quantum systems, such as molecules or chemical reactions. Classical (regular) computers struggle with these tasks because the math becomes too complicated as systems get bigger. But quantum computers, thanks to features like superposition and entanglement, can handle this complexity much better.

Where It's Used

Chemistry. To study how molecules behave, which helps in designing new drugs and catalysts.

Materials science. To create new materials with special properties, like strong and lightweight composites.

Drug discovery. To simulate how drugs interact with cells or proteins, speeding up the discovery process.

Real-world example: Simulating how caffeine molecules work in the brain is very hard for classical computers. But a quantum simulator can do this more accurately, showing how caffeine connects to brain receptors. Another example is simulating the Haber–Bosch process, used to make ammonia for fertilizers. Quantum computers can help optimize this process and improve efficiency.

6 Quantum Hardware (The Physical Tech Behind It)

6.1 Superconducting Qubits

These are artificial atoms made from materials that carry electricity with no resistance. A type called transman is common. They're built using something called Josephson junctions, which show unique quantum effects.

Challenges

Decoherence: These qubits lose their information quickly because of environmental noise.

Scalability: It's hard to build large systems with many qubits that all work together reliably.

6.2 Trapped Ions

These use charged atoms (ions) that are held in place with electromagnetic fields. Lasers are used to control and cool them down so they don't move too much.

Challenges

Maintaining coherence: Even though these qubits last longer, it's still hard to keep them stable during long operations.

Ion control: Managing multiple ions and getting them to interact correctly is very tricky.

6.3 Photonic Qubits

They use the carriers of information composed of particles of light (photons). Photons are awesome; they are able to cover long distances without losing their information.

Challenges

Photon loss: Process photons are also lost at some points, and this creates errors.

Scalability: Creating a sufficiently large quantum computer, on which a significant number of light-based qubits will be used, is a very difficult task.

6.4 Topological Qubits

These are made using special materials that contain exotic particles called anyons. They are naturally protected from errors because of the way their information is stored.

Why they matter:

Anyons are very stable and are less affected by noise, making them promising for building future quantum computers.

7 Quantum Error Correction (Fixing Mistakes)

Qubits are easily disturbed, which leads to mistakes in calculations. That's why error **correction** is so important in quantum computing.

Types of Codes

Surface codes: Very reliable and work well with today's quantum hardware.

Other codes: Include Shor's code, Steane's code, and topological codes, which also protect against errors in different ways.

8 Quantum Computing Trends and Challenges in the Future

Although quantum computing is generating momentum, major obstacles remain to stall its adoption before it can take place.

Scalability
Current quantum computers consist of a very limited number of functioning qubits. We must, in the future, construct much larger systems with far more qubits working thus without error. To achieve this objective, scientists are considering new designs and how to use smaller quantum systems to connect to them.

Coherence
It is extremely hard to keep qubits in a stable state and make them last long. Due to very small differences in their surrounding environment, qubits easily lose their special quantum state, and this inevitably leads to errors. In the future, the scope of studies will be on developing improved methods of qubit safety and ensuring they remain stable even after longer durations.

Error Correction
Due to the vulnerability of qubits, mistakes occur with a high probability. In order to overcome these errors, scientists have invented new smart error correction

methodologies to correct these errors and make the quantum computers reliable. One of the factors in the future that can add usefulness to quantum computers for real tasks will be improved error correction.

New Applications

The theory of quantum will find application in a variety of new applications as quantum technology becomes more advanced. In healthcare, it may be used to speed up designing new medicines and develop personalized treatment. In finance, it could guide better investment strategies and accurately identify bad players. It can be used in logistics and supply chain management to seek the optimum means of transporting products. Quantum computing can also enable artificial intelligence to be smarter and faster by enabling computers to learn more quickly using data.

These trends indicate that although we have certain issues to resolve, we can rely on quantum computing, which has enormous possibilities to transform deceptive aspects of our lives in the future.

9 Summary

Quantum computing is a brand-new approach to solving problems that common computers have difficulty in attempting. In the chapter, we clarified the principles of quantum computing as qubits, superposition, entanglement, quantum gates, and special algorithms, and what makes them important. We also discussed the construction of quantum computers and the issues scientists are trying to address when they improve them, such as their size, stability, and error rate.

In case they will be able to sort out these challenges, quantum computers may find application in various fields such as medicine, finance, transportation, and artificial intelligence. With the simple concepts outlined in this chapter, the reader is prepared to acquire additional knowledge on the challenging concepts in quantum computing. Reading about this new technology can allow people to prepare for the future when quantum computers may have a large place in finding some of the hardest problems faced by the world.

Discussion or contemplation questions

- What do you imagine quantum computing might do to the work you do or the discipline you are pursuing?
- What aspect of quantum computing (such as qubits, superposition, or entanglement) interests you the most or surprises you the most? Why?
- Which do you think are the most difficult problems to be solved so that we have the widespread use of quantum computers?
- Of what issue in your day-to-day life or in society do you think it would be more feasible to solve with quantum computing?
- What is your opinion about the chances of quantum computers cracking the existing encryption systems? How should we get ready?

Over the principles of quantum computing, we have seen in this chapter details of what makes it unique from classical computing and what makes it so promising for the future. Some of the key issues and trends that lie ahead in this fascinating discipline were also examined.

We will dive a bit deeper into the building blocks of quantum computing in the next chapter. You will get to hear more about qubits, the unique units of quantum information that may be in many states simultaneously. The chapter shall also be able to explain the quantum gates, which are the instruments used to control qubits, and quantum circuits, which are the combinations of quantum gates, to be able to complete complex computations. These aspects are also very crucial to anyone who wishes to comprehend how quantum computers work and perform information processing.

At the end of the following chapter, you will be more grounded in the technical focus of the quantum systems and will be more equipped to understand portions of the following chapters of a more advanced nature. Such an in-depth insight into how qubits, quantum gates, and circuits operate will put you half a step ahead toward reaching the point when you observe how quantum computers can be implemented and programmed to address real-life problems.

References

1. Abdelgaber N, Nikolopoulos C (2020) Overview of quantum computing and its applications in artificial intelligence. In: 2020 IEEE third international conference on artificial intelligence and knowledge engineering (AIKE). IEEE, pp 198–199. https://doi.org/10.1109/AIKE48582.2020.00038
2. Alghadeer M, Aldawsari E, Selvarajan R, Alutaibi K, Kais S, Alharbi FH (2022) Psitrum and universal simulation of quantum computers. In: 2022 IEEE international conference on quantum computing and engineering (QCE). IEEE, pp 837–838. https://doi.org/10.1109/QCE53715.2022.00137
3. Arute F, Arya K, Babbush R, Bacon D, Bardin JC, Barends R, Martinis JM et al (2019) Google achieves 'quantum supremacy' by performing calculation beyond classical computers. Scientific American. https://www.scientificamerican.com/article/google-publishes-landmark-quantum-supremacy-claim/
4. Backus J (1978) Can programming be liberated from the von Neumann style? A functional style and its algebra of programs. Commun ACM 21(8):613–641. https://doi.org/10.1145/359576.359579
5. Bhanu D, Grover M, Preetha M, Mishra AVS, Marathe V (2024) Quantum computing and quality quantifiers shaping the future of intelligent systems. In: 2024 IEEE 4th international conference on ICT in business industry and government (ICTBIG). IEEE, pp 1–6. https://doi.org/10.1109/ICTBIG64922.2024.10911212
6. Chauhan V, Negi S, Jain D, Singh P, Sagar AK, Sharma AK (2022) Quantum computers: a review on how quantum computing can boom AI. In: 2022 2nd international conference on advance computing and innovative technologies in engineering (ICACITE). IEEE, pp 559–563. https://doi.org/10.1109/ICACITE53722.2022.9823619
7. Gottesman C, McMahon PL (2015) A fault-tolerant architecture for quantum computation using topological Majorana modes. https://arxiv.org/abs/1501.02813

8. Grover LK (1996) A fast quantum mechanical algorithm for database search. In: Proceedings of the twenty-eighth annual ACM symposium on theory of computing, pp 212–219. https://doi.org/10.1145/237814.237866
9. Hari Krishna S, Madala R, Ramya P, Sabarirajan A, Dobhal D, Sapate S (2023) Ethically governed artificial intelligence based innovative business research in finance and marketing system. In: Proceedings of the 2023 eighth international conference on science technology engineering and mathematics (ICONSTEM). IEEE, pp 1–7. https://doi.org/10.1109/ICONSTEM56934.2023.10142352
10. Hayward M (2008) Quantum computing and shor's algorithm. Macquarie University Mathematics Department, Sydney, p 1
11. IBM Research (2022) IBM unveils 400 qubit-plus quantum processor and next-generation IBM Quantum System Two [Press release]. https://newsroom.ibm.com/2022-11-09-IBM-Unveils-400-Qubit-Plus-Quantum-Processor-and-Next-Generation-IBM-Quantum-System-Two
12. IBM Quantum (nd) What is quantum computing? IBM. Accessed 2 April 2024. https://www.ibm.com/topics/quantum-computing
13. IonQ (nd) Technology. Accessed 2 April 2024 https://ionq.com/technology
14. Kumar S (2015) Fundamental limits to Moore's law. IEEE Spectrum. https://doi.org/10.48550/arXiv.1511.05956
15. Lokes S, Mahenthar CSJ, Kumaran SP, Sathyaprakash P, Jayakumar V (2022) Implementation of quantum deep reinforcement learning using variational quantum circuits. In: 2022 international conference on trends in quantum computing and emerging business technologies (TQCEBT). IEEE, pp 1–4. https://doi.org/10.1109/TQCEBT54229.2022.10041479
16. Moazzam J, Pawar R, Khare MD (2023) Evolution and advancement of quantum computing in the era of networking and cryptography. In: 2023 international conference on advances in computation, communication and information technology (ICAICCIT). IEEE, pp 817–821. https://doi.org/10.1109/ICAICCIT60255.2023.10465946
17. Mykhailova M (2022) Developing programming assignments for teaching quantum computing and quantum programming. In: 2022 IEEE international conference on quantum computing and engineering (QCE). IEEE, pp 688–692. https://doi.org/10.1109/QCE53715.2022.00092
18. Nielsen MA, Chuang IL (2010) Quantum computation and quantum information, 10th anniversary ed. Cambridge University Press
19. Oliver WD, Yu Y, Lee JC, Berggren KK, Levitov LS, Orlando TP (2005) Mach-Zehnder interferometry in a strongly driven superconducting qubit. Science 310(5754):1653–1657. https://doi.org/10.1126/science.1119678
20. Preskill J (2018) Quantum computing in the NISQ era and beyond. Quantum 2:79. https://doi.org/10.22331/q-2018-08-06-79
21. Quantum Zeitgeist (nd) IBM quantum computer timeline: from 5 to 1,121 qubits, Big Blue accelerates its quantum efforts. Accessed 2 April 2024 https://quantumzeitgeist.com/ibm-quantum-computer-timeline/
22. Rajathi GI, Priya LR, Fernando AV, Vedhapriyavadhana R, Sasindharan S, Mohanalin J (2025) Quantum artificial intelligence: unlocking the future of technology. In: Proceedings of the 2025 international conference on next generation communication and information processing (INCIP). IEEE, pp 321–326. https://doi.org/10.1109/INCIP64058.2025.11019935
23. Rieffel EG, Polak WH (2011) Quantum computing: a gentle introduction. MIT Press
24. Rosenberg D, Kim DK, Das R, Yost D, Gustavsson S, Hover D, Krantz P (2017) 3D integrated superconducting qubits. NPJ Quantum Inform 3(42). https://doi.org/10.1038/s41534-017-0044-0
25. Sathyaseelan K, Vyas T, Madala R, Chamundeeswari V, Goyal HR, Jayaraman R (2023) Blockchain enabled intelligent surveillance system model with AI and IoT. In: 2023 eighth international conference on science technology engineering and mathematics (ICONSTEM). IEEE, pp 1–7. https://doi.org/10.1109/ICONSTEM56934.2023.10142303
26. Shalf J, Leland R (2015) Computing beyond Moore's Law. Computer 48(12):14–23. https://doi.org/10.1109/MC.2015.374

27. Shor PW (1995) Scheme for reducing decoherence in quantum computer memory. Phys Rev A 48:2493. https://doi.org/10.1103/PhysRevA.52.R2493
28. Shukla PK, Roy V, Shukla PK, Chaturvedi AK, Saxena AK, Maheshwari M, Pal PR (2021) An advanced EEG motion artifacts eradication algorithm. Comput J. https://doi.org/10.1093/comjnl/bxab170
29. Watanabe HC, Raymond R, Ohnishi Y-Y, Kaminishi E, Sugawara M (2023) Optimizing parameterized quantum circuits with free-axis single-qubit gates. IEEE Trans Quantum Eng 4, Article 3101016. https://doi.org/10.1109/TQE.2023.3286411
30. Williams CP (2011) Quantum gates. In: Williams CP (ed) Explorations in quantum computing. Springer, pp 51–122. https://doi.org/10.1007/978-1-84628-887-6_2

Ms. Swati Karni is a Principal Cloud Engineer at SAIC and a Ph.D. candidate in Information Technology at the University of the Cumberlands. She holds a Master's degree in Computer Science and Information Technology and brings expertise in disaster recovery automation, cloud migration, and next generation enterprise cloud architecture design. Her work and academic interest center around minimal-downtime recovery strategies, AI-assisted orchestration, and the emerging intersection of cloud computing with quantum computing. She is passionate about advancing resilient, scalable infrastructure that bridges modern cloud systems with future quantum-accelerated technologies. Her contribution to this chapter offers a unique blend of theoretical expertise and practical experience, providing readers with a well-rounded perspective on emerging quantum technologies

Mr. Arun Kumar Rajamandrapu is an experienced Solution Architect in the field of Information Technology and an active researcher in both cloud and quantum computing. His work focuses on developing scalable architectures, exploring post-classical computing models, and advancing quantum-inspired problem-solving methodologies. With a deep interest in how qubits reshape computational efficiency, he contributes valuable industry perspective and technical clarity to this chapter. His forward-looking approach reflects a commitment to bridging modern systems with the future potential of quantum technologies

Qubits, Quantum Gates, and Quantum Circuits

Saraswati Mishra and Raghuram Katakam

Abstract

The chapter explains the elements of quantum computing and how it is different from computing concepts, like classical computing principles. It explores qubits and how they work in quantum gates and circuits much like bits operate within gates and circuits in traditional computing but with greatly improved abilities, in storing and processing information using superposition and entanglement techniques. Additionally, it delves into the details concerning qubits while also pointing out the specific benefits and factors to consider that come with this technology. The passage outlines the uses of technology, in fields like finance and healthcare as well as cybersecurity in everyday situations and talks about the progress achieved by organizations, like Google and IBM in developing cutting edge quantum technologies and platforms.

Keywords

Qubits • Superposition • Entanglement • Quantum gates • Quantum circuits • Measurement • Decoherence • Error correction • Quantum algorithms • Decoherence • Qiskit

S. Mishra
Campbell, USA
e-mail: saraswati@ieee.org

R. Katakam (✉)
Atlanta, USA
e-mail: rkatakam@ieee.org

M. Rana and B. Pandey (eds.), *Quantum Ops*,
https://doi.org/10.1007/978-3-032-10775-6_2

1 Introduction

Applying quantum mechanics the information is processed in quantum computing at level conceptually better than classical computing in the solution of certain problems. Binary bits in classical computing are only 0 or 1. But, in quantum computing, quantum bits or qubits use the superposition[1] principles and entanglement[1] principles to exist in multiple states at once. This is very useful to solve complex mathematical problems in cybersecurity, cryptography and finance which take exponential time in classical computers. In this chapter, it discusses the fundamental elements of quantum computing: qubits, quantum gates, and quantum circuits. Through mathematical explanations, practical examples, tables, and detailed figures it aims to clarify these concepts and their role in quantum algorithms [1].

2 The Architecture of Quantum Computation

Quantum computing operates through three fundamental elements that work together to manipulate quantum information.

- Qubits: Similar to classical bits with additional dimensions of superposition and entanglement. They may be physically implemented in many different quantum systems, including: (1) Spin states of electrons (2) energy levels of trapped ions (3) polarizations of photons.
- Quantum gates: Play the same role as logic gates in quantum computation, but exhibit radically different properties. But, unlike logic gates, which perform deterministic operations, these gates perform reversible operations on qubits using probability amplitudes. These gates can produce superposition states, produce entanglement and apply other transformations resulting in the quantum systems being molded.
- Quantum circuits: Combines qubits and quantum gates to architect sequences to implement quantum algorithms. Their strength is based on making good use of quantum mechanics principles, like qubit systems' superposition and entanglement and at the same time minimizing this negative effect of quantum decoherence to solve real-world applications.

3 Qubits: The Heart of Quantum Computing

3.1 What is a Qubit?

The fundamental unit of information in quantum computing is defined as qubit or quantum bit[1]. Due to the superposition principle, a qubit can exist in a combination of 0 and 1 states at the same time. A qubit is represented as

$$|\psi\rangle = \alpha|0\rangle + \beta|1\rangle, \tag{1}$$

where $|0\rangle$ and $|1\rangle$ represent basis states of the computational, analogous to the classical bit's 0 and 1 and α and β are complex amplitudes where (α) and (β) are complex amplitudes, satisfying:

$$|\alpha|^2 + |\beta|^2 = 1. \tag{2}$$

Thus, when posed with a problem that involves a set of n classical bits, in quantum computing, they represent 2^n possible states at once, whereas in classical representation, it would represent just one of the 2^n states.

Qubits are physically implemented using multiple approaches. Most common ones are using trapping ions in an electromagnetic field or operating at extremely cold environments where materials act as superconductors (see Sect. 3.5).

3.2 Superposition and Complex Probability Amplitudes

Consider the state has a 50% chance of being measured as $|0\rangle$ or $|1\rangle$. This may be illustrated by the Bloch sphere (Fig. 1) in which the north and south poles denote the states $|0\rangle$ and $|1\rangle$ respectively and points on the sphere signify all possible superpositions [2].

The α and β are the complex numbers which represent the probability amplitudes. They have both magnitude and phase components. By taking a qubit measurement in the computational basis, we end up with a probability of 0 is $|\alpha|^2$, while the probability of getting 1 is $|\beta|^2$. The normalization condition $|\alpha|^2 + |\beta|^2 = 1$ makes sure that these probabilities always sum to 1.

Such complexities in these amplitudes are of vital importance to quantum computations. The phase relationship of these different parts of a quantum state allows possibilities of quantum interference effects, in which probability amplitudes can be additively combined constructively or destructively. Such interference is significant to quantum algorithms in gaining computational benefits such that the valid solutions can be magnified and the wrong ones can be expelled using well-choreographed quantum evolution.

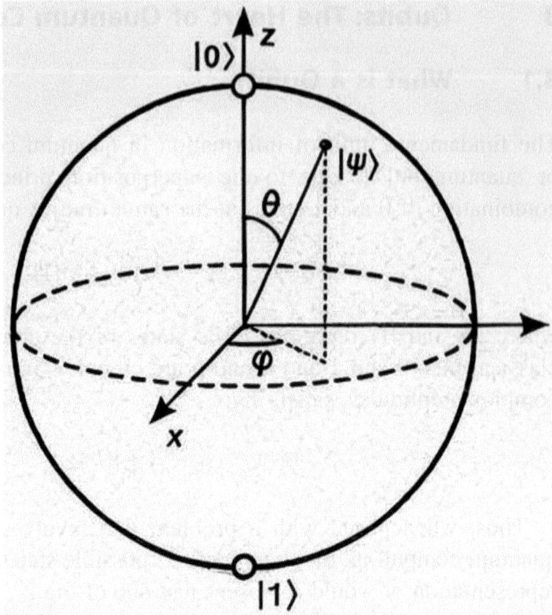

Fig. 1 Representation of qubit state on the bloch sphere [5]

3.3 Entanglement

Entanglement is a phenomenon when the states of two or more qubits are linked to each other in a way, so that when a measurement is made on one, the state of the other one (or ones) is (I) determined by the state of the other qubit (or qubits).

Bell state: A two-qubit Bell state is expressed as:

$$|\psi\rangle = \frac{1}{\sqrt{2}}|00\rangle + \frac{1}{\sqrt{2}}|11\rangle. \tag{3}$$

Measuring the first qubit as $|0\rangle$ ensures the second is $|0\rangle$, and vice versa, regardless of distance.

Quantum teleportation is based on this principle [3], whereby one can affect the state of a qubit instantly by manipulating the state of another qubit while not physically transporting qubits (referred to in Sect. 5.8).

3.4 Mathematical Representation

3.4.1 Dirac Notation and Ket Vectors

The mathematical representations of the quantum states also known as Dirac notations were developed by physicist Paul Dirac [4]. Under this, quantum states are numerated using "ket" vectors $|\psi\rangle$, in which the bar and angle bracket notation refers to a vector of a complex vector space which is defined as Hilbert space[1].

$|0\rangle$ (spin down) and $|1\rangle$ (spin up) computed basis have the unit magnitude and they make an orthonormal basis of two-dimensional Hilbert space of one qubit.

The state of general qubit $|\psi\rangle = \alpha|0\rangle + \beta|1\rangle$ is represented as a column vector in this basis:

$$|\psi\rangle = \alpha\begin{bmatrix}1\\0\end{bmatrix} + \beta\begin{bmatrix}0\\1\end{bmatrix} = \begin{bmatrix}\alpha\\\beta\end{bmatrix}, \tag{4}$$

where "bra" vectors $\langle\phi|$ are the complex conjugate transpose of "ket" vectors.

So, the "bra-ket" $\langle\phi|\psi\rangle$ represents inner product between the two states which indicates the probability amplitude of measuring ϕ when system is in state ψ.

This vector representation makes quantum operations mathematically tractable, converting complex notations to matrices in linear algebra that act on these state vectors.

3.4.2 Bloch Sphere Representation

The Bloch sphere provides a 3-D parametric visualization of qubit states. Since qubit states should have to satisfy the normalization condition $|\alpha|^2 + |\beta|^2 = 1$, all possible qubit states lie on the surface of a unit sphere in three-dimensional space. States at the top of sphere are the $|0\rangle$ states, the bottom are the $|1\rangle$ states, and the states on the equator are equal superposition states[1].

Any point in the Bloch sphere can be described using the spherical coordinates θ and ϕ thereby any qubit state can be expressed as:

$$|\psi\rangle = \cos\left(\frac{\theta}{2}\right)|0\rangle + e^{i\phi}\sin\left(\frac{\theta}{2}\right)|1\rangle. \tag{5}$$

Here, the angle θ represents the probability distribution between $|0\rangle$ and $|1\rangle$ and ϕ shows the phase relationship between them. This geometric representation makes quantum operations to be interpreted clearly in 3-D space.

3.4.3 Basis States and Measurement

A set of orthogonal states spanning all the possible quantum states construct basis states, which are the building blocks of representation of quantum states. The three states in Hilbert space are written below:

- **Computational basis**: represented as $\{|0\rangle, |1\rangle\}$ which correspond to classical bit values.
- **Hadamard basis**: $\{|+\rangle, |-\rangle\}$ where $|+\rangle = \frac{|0\rangle+|1\rangle}{\sqrt{2}}$ and $|-\rangle = \frac{|0\rangle-|1\rangle}{\sqrt{2}}$[1]. It is formed by rotating computational basis by 45° on Bloch sphere.
- **Circular basis**: $\{|L\rangle, |R\rangle\}$[1] for left and right circular polarizations.

The basis state is selected based on the type of the application and can be modified from one basis state to another. It provides a unique axis around which the quantum states can be defined/realized better based on its use.

3.5 Physical Implementations

3.5.1 Trapped Ion Qubits

Trapped ion qubits are constructed through trapping ions in an electromagnetic field in a closed off setting and the information is stored in the energy levels of the ions, which can be controlled through lasers. Trapping of ions is carried out in two methods:

- Paul traps: Leverage oscillating electric fields to confine ions in a 3-D space that creates a potential well that holds the ion.
- Linear traps: Ions are arranged linearly a few micrometers apart and they repel each other to form a stable crystal-like structure.

Trapped ion qubits provide more than 99.99% accuracy for single qubit gates and about 99% accuracy in two-qubit gates. They also provide long coherence times and can implement any quantum algorithm.

3.5.2 Superconducting Qubits

Superconducting qubits are artificial quantum systems made from superconducting circuits built at<10 milliKelvin when certain materials lose all their electric resistance and act as superconductors. Superconducting qubits are of 3 types:

- **Transmon qubits** [6]: The most common type, where the qubit states correspond to different numbers of Cooper pairs[1] on a superconducting island. The $|0\rangle$ and $|1\rangle$ states represent having 0 or 1 extra Cooper pair[1].
- **Flux qubits**: Use magnetic flux to encode data in the direction of the flow of current in a loop made of superconductor, with clockwise ($|0\rangle$) and counterclockwise ($|1\rangle$) flow as the two states.
- **Phase qubits**: They are built based on phase difference of superconducting wavefunction across a Josephson junction[1].

3.5.3 Photonic Qubits

Photonic quantum computers store the qubits in the quantum state of light based on the polarization, path, or other degrees of freedom. Photons serve as excellent qubits for certain applications because they naturally avoid decoherence, i.e., they don't interact strongly with their environment during propagation through vacuum or optical fibers.

Linear optical quantum computing (LOQC) uses single photons, phase shifters, beam splitters, and photon detectors to implement quantum operations. Though two-photon gates are challenging to implement, with high probability using linear optics alone, techniques such as measurement-induced nonlinearity and photonic cluster states enable universal quantum computation [7].

3.6 Decoherence and Challenges in Maintaining Qubit States

3.6.1 The Decoherence Challenge

A quantum system is a highly fragile and volatile system, and any interference with the environment can add noise making the system losing its quantumness. It generally occurs when its interactions with the environment make it lose its delicate superposition states and make it behave like a classical system. It is like a coin spinning, with air resistance and other external factors it finally comes to a stop. It can be classified into two main timescales:

- T1 (Amplitude damping): It is the process of a qubit losing its energy and descending from an excited stage $|1\rangle$ to ground state $|0\rangle$.
- T2 (Phase damping): Phase fluctuations within the components in the quantum system become randomized.

The main environmental factors contributing to decoherence can be radio waves, electric and magnetic fields, power instabilities which create instabilities in the system.

3.6.2 Mitigation Strategies and Error Correction

Since qubits are highly fragile, quantum computing is millions of times more error-prone than their classical counterpart. There can be bit-flip or phase-flip errors or amplitude damping causing energy loss from excited states. However, because of the no-cloning theorem [8], the states cannot be directly copied from one qubit to another. Mitigation strategies provide a short-term solution by adding dynamic decoupling to average out external noise or zero-noise extrapolation by deliberately extrapolating the noise to find a pattern and curve-fit for actual results. However, error correction provides long-term measures to make qubits more immune. Though this is an actively researched area, these are the current methods used:

- Redundant encoding: Because qubit states cannot be directly copied by the no-cloning theorem [8], qubit is entangled with other qubits that are used to determine the error detection without destroying the quantum information.
- Syndrome detection: The relationships between qubits are measured using parity check to identify the issue.

4 Quantum Gates: Manipulating Qubits

The elementary objects of quantum computing (equivalent to the logic gates (AND, OR, NOT) of classic computers) are quantum gates [9]. However, quantum gates, in contrast with classical ones that operate on discrete 0 s and 1 s, operate on qubits—which take a mix (or superposition) of both 0 and 1 simultaneously. Such gates do not simply flip bits, rather they make reversible transformations in which all of the quantum information is preserved.

What Makes a Quantum Gate?

Quantum gates are unitary. That implies that they do not lose information. In mathematics, this fact is known as the unitarity of the operation of a gate to a qubit followed by applying its reverse (the conjugate transpose). This property allows one to undo what the gate did to a qubit and hence the term unitarity. That is fundamentally unlike a classical gate, such as an AND or OR gate, which does not tell you the inputs in response to the output (the outputs tell you the inputs).

Since quantum gates are reversible, they technically do not require any energy consumption, although in hardware power is inevitability lost to other things [1, 10].

4.1 Types of Quantum Gates

The following Fig. 2 explains the different types of quantum gates.

4.1.1 Common Single-Qubit Gates

Pauli Gates (X, Y, Z)

Pauli gates represent the basic single-qubit operations and correspond to rotations by π radians (180°) about the axes of the Bloch sphere. There are three types of Pauli gates based on their axis of rotation:

- Pauli-X gate: Reverses the computational basis states: $X|0\rangle = |1\rangle$ and $X|1\rangle = |0\rangle$ by rotating the qubit π around the X axis, as shown in the first row of Fig. 2.
- Pauli-Y gate: Shown in the second row of Fig. 2, combines bit-flip[1] and phase-flip[1] operations, implementing a π rotation about the Y-axis of the Bloch sphere.
- Pauli-Z gate: Shown in the third row of Fig. 2, leaves $|0\rangle$ unchanged but introduces a phase flip to $|1\rangle : Z|0\rangle = |0\rangle$ and $Z|1\rangle = -|1\rangle$. It is a π rotation around the Z axis.

These Pauli gates are generators of arbitrary single-qubit rotations and are key components in quantum error correction where the Pauli errors are both the most common forms of single-qubit quantum errors.

Hadamard Gate—Creating Superposition

The Hadamard gate (H), which is the fourth row of Fig. 2, holds special significance in quantum computing as it creates equal superposition states from computational basis states. It transforms $|0\rangle \rightarrow \frac{|0\rangle+|1\rangle}{\sqrt{2}}$ and $|1\rangle \rightarrow \frac{|0\rangle-|1\rangle}{\sqrt{2}}$, moving the qubit from one of the poles to the equator on the Bloch sphere.

It is used as the starting gate in quantum circuits for numerous algorithms such as:

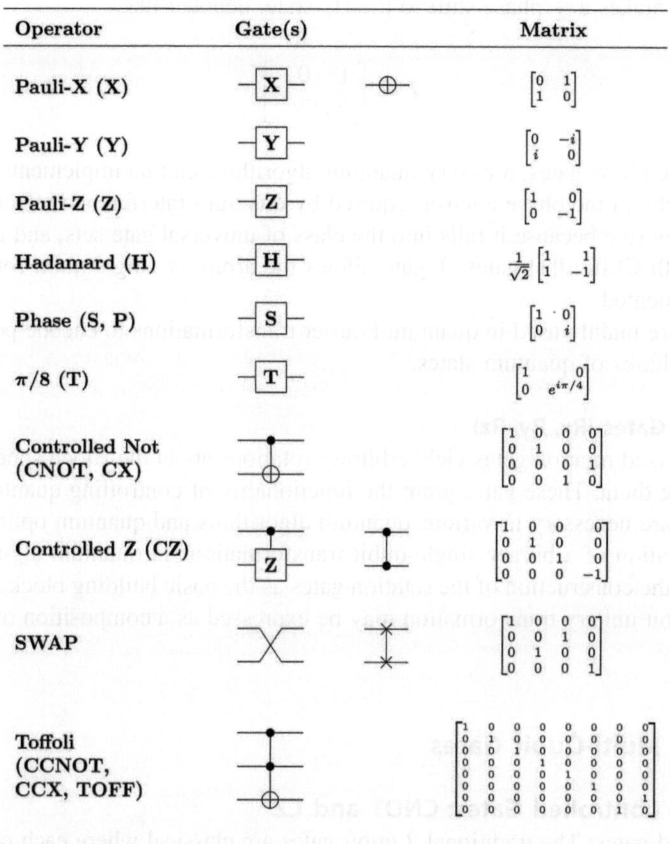

Fig. 2 Quantum logic gates [11]

- Grover's algorithm [12]: It initializes the search space by putting all qubits into a state of superposition mainly used in quantum search algorithms to operate on several possibilities at once.
- Shor's algorithm [13]: Is employed to create equal superposition states to feed to quantum Fourier transform. It is applied to factor integers or identifying patterns significantly quicker than the classical computer which requires exponential time to solve such questions.

Phase Shift Gates (S, T)

Phase shift gates (S and T), shown in rows 5 and 6 of Fig. 2, modify the relative phase between computational basis states without changing their amplitudes. The S gate (also called the phase gate) makes a $\frac{\pi}{2}$ phase shift to the $|1\rangle$ state:

$$S = \begin{bmatrix} 1 & 0 \\ 0 & i \end{bmatrix}. \tag{6}$$

T gate makes a $\frac{\pi}{4}$ phase shift to the $|1\rangle$ state, denoted like:

$$T = \begin{bmatrix} 1 & 0 \\ 0 & e^{i\pi/4} \end{bmatrix}. \tag{7}$$

In these phase gates, arbitrary quantum algorithms can be implemented as they allow to obtain the phase control required by quantum interference effects. T gate plays a key role because it falls into the class of universal gate sets, and in combination with Clifford[1] gates, T gate allows the arbitrary single-qubit rotations to be implemented.

They are mainly used in quantum Fourier transformations to encode periodicity into the phases of quantum states.

Rotation Gates (Rx, Ry, Rz)
Parameterized rotation gates yield arbitrary rotations about the Bloch sphere's axes with angle theta. These gates grant the functionality of controlling quantum states and they are necessary in various quantum algorithms and quantum optimization.

Application of arbitrary single-qubit transformations in quantum algorithms is based on the construction of the rotation gates as the basic building block since any single-qubit unitary transformation may be expressed as a composition of rotation gates.

4.2 Multi-Qubit Gates

4.2.1 Controlled Gates: CNOT and CZ

Controlled gates: The traditional 2 qubit gates are classical where each of these is either a controlled gate or a target gate. There are two kinds of them:

- CNOT: Is one of the most basic and widely used two-qubit gates, which flips the target if the control qubit is in state $|1\rangle$.
- CZ: Applies a phase flip to the target qubit when the control is $|1\rangle$, introducing a phase flip to the $|11\rangle$ state however leaves other states unchanged.

Controlled gates are the key to building the quantum entanglement and execute quantum algorithms that demand the conditional operation on the quantum states.

4.2.2 Toffoli Gate (CCNOT)

The Toffoli gate (bottom row of Fig. 2) or controlled-controlled-NOT gate[1] is a three-qubit gate that flips the target qubit only when both control qubits are in state $|1\rangle$. This gate is also classically universal, that is, every classical computer program can be performed entirely with Toffoli gates, but it is not universal quantum computation unless supplemented with some phase gates.

The Toffoli gate preserves the number of $|1\rangle$s in the computational basis, making it particularly useful for implementing classical functions within quantum algorithms and for quantum arithmetic operations.

4.2.3 SWAP Gate

The SWAP gate, shown in row 9 of Fig. 2, exchanges the states of two qubits: $|00\rangle \rightarrow |00\rangle$, $|01\rangle \rightarrow |10\rangle$, $|10\rangle \rightarrow |01\rangle$, $|11\rangle \rightarrow |11\rangle$. While conceptually simple, the SWAP gate is essential for quantum algorithms that require moving quantum information between distant qubits, especially in architectures with limited connectivity.

4.3 How Quantum Gates Work Mathematically

Qubit states are vectors and quantum gates are described with matrices. Implementing a gate is simply the product between the matrix, and the vector. In one qubit, this is simple, a 2×2 matrix and a 2-element vector. With a larger number of qubits, math becomes increasingly complex: two qubits employ 4 by 4, three employ 8 by 8, and so forth [1].

Therefore, with an increasing number of qubits, the size of the matrix increases exponentially making it difficult to simulate on a classical computer.

4.4 Universal Gate Sets

In classical computing any, logic gate can be built out of NAND. Still on this point, the universal gate sets, or a combination set of gates with which all quantum algorithms can be developed, are the features of a quantum computer.

One universal set is common:

- Hadamard (H).
- T gate.
- CNOT gate.

All these gates can be combined together to perform any quantum operation you may want. The Solovay-Kitaev theorem says that it is possible to construct even extremely complex gates out of these few only, with any accuracy [10].

4.5 Making Quantum Gates Real

4.5.1 How They're Built in Hardware

Different quantum hardware platforms implement gates in different ways:

- Superconducting qubits (used by IBM and Google) [14]:

They use pulse microwaves to operate on gates. A single-qubit may be a three-electron gate based on a short burst of microwaves; two-qubit are more complicated interactions using coupled circuits or resonators [15].

- Trapped ions (used by IonQ and Honeywell):

These work by lasers controlling individual ions. Two-qubit gates typically have two ions moving in lock-step to create a shared motion that entangles them. A well-known example is the Mølmer–Sørensen gate [16].

All the forms of hardware possess advantages and disadvantages. Super conductive systems have the capability of being faster and ion traps usually exhibit more precision.

4.5.2 Gate Fidelity and Errors Characterization

Quantum gates aren't perfect. Gate fidelity measures the match between real gate behavior with its theoretical counterpart. The best quantum systems these days can reach:

- >99.9% fidelity in single-qubit gates.
- Between 95–99.5% in two-qubit gates [17].

Error rates are critical, especially in complex algorithms that need many gates. Improving gate fidelity and reducing gate time are a couple of major challenges in building useful quantum computers. Faster gates help beat noise and decoherence, but are more difficult to control.

Finding optimal trade-offs of maintaining gate fidelity while scaling to larger numbers of qubits represents one of the core challenges of developing hardware for quantum computing.

5 Quantum Circuits—Building Computations

Quantum circuits are the building blocks of the way we design and implement computations in quantum systems. On the fundamental level, these circuits consist of a collection of horizontal lines, themselves representing qubits, and different gates on the lines to allow their operation.

Unlike its classical counterpart, the wires in quantum circuits represent a state by themselves. Each qubit wire keeps superposition or entanglement and it develops a step at a time, as various gates are used. Circuit diagrams can therefore be used not only to envision the flow of quantum information in a quantum computer, but also to program them.

5.1 Building Circuits from Quantum Gates

In the same way that we construct classical logic circuits using AND, OR, and NOT logic gates, quantum circuits are obtained by constructing circuits out of unitary quantum gates using one or more qubits. The particular order these gates are used in is important as the vast majority of quantum gates are non-commutative in which case the order in which they are applied may produce an entirely different result [18].

The dynamics of quantum gate operations lie in a mathematical format. A sequence of gates G 1 to G n operates similarly to a sequence of matrix multiplications, performed in the opposite order, as quantum transformations are conventionally written.

5.2 Time, Space, and Information Flow

A quantum circuit reflects the geometric layout as well as time order of operations. Qubit lines resemble the quantum memory to store information during the computation. Simultaneous actions are placed vertically across these lines whereas sequential actions are spatially separated horizontally. This LTR design is constituted by the intuitive flow of time in the computation [19].

The model highlights the idea that quantum states are coherent with their movement in the circuit, only altered by conscious operations. It might seem a very minor but extremely important line of thought: the difference between the classical world, where information is shuttled and forgotten, and the quantum world: in quantum circuits, it is literally true that the data lives like a self-evolving quantum system.

5.3 The Role of Circuits in Quantum Algorithms

Circuit model is not only a programming method, but also the universal formulation of quantum algorithms that has the ability to represent any quantum algorithm using gates and measurements [20]. This abstraction gives the opportunity to write algorithms without consideration of the hardware, i.e., they could be optimized, simulated and even ported among a variety of quantum platforms.

For example, the Bell state circuit shows how a simple two-qubit system can create entanglement. Starting with both qubits in the $|0\rangle$ state, a Hadamard gate on the first qubit builds a superposition. A CNOT gate then entangles both the qubits, producing a maximally entangled state: $\frac{|00\rangle+|11\rangle}{\sqrt{2}}$ [21].

The Deutsch-Jozsa algorithm is yet another popular example. It checks that a given function is either constant or balanced through a single quantum judgment-which (in the classical world) would require multiple checks. It is a circuit to encode and extract global information out of a quantum oracle by use of superposition and interference [22].

5.4 Measuring Quantum States in Circuits

Measurement is the process of retrieving the information that is contained in the quantum circuit and transferring it to the classical world. It is also a sensitive procedure that forces the system to a definite position ruining superposition. In circuit placement, the location and time of measurement may have significant influence on computation [23].

Measuring is only done in the final step in some algorithms. Mid-circuit measurements are employed in others to change the future gate operation dynamically. It is needed to correct errors and adaptive algorithms that are based on intermediate outputs [4]. This circuit resumes in the collapsed state after a measurement and designers should consider such a fact to prevent unexpected outcomes.

5.5 Circuit Complexity and Practical Challenges

Each circuit is commonly measured by three things:

- Gate count: Number of operations.
- Circuit depth: Number of steps in the circuit.
- Circuit width: Number of qubits present.

These measures allow evaluating the feasibility of a particular algorithm running on present or near-term quantum computers [24].

As with all optimizations, trade-offs: sacrificing depth perhaps involves more qubits, sacrificing qubit use perhaps involves longer circuits. Also, certain gates (such as the T gate) are more difficult to realize fault-tolerantly, so minimizing the use of such gates (T-count) is a key target of creating the compilations of circuits to be built in real devices. An efficient design of a circuit involves an effective compromise among these constraints, but also taking into account the capabilities and weaknesses of the intended hardware.

5.6 Reading and Understanding Circuit Diagrams

Here are the standard symbols and notations used in quantum circuit diagrams:

- Hadamard gates: are shown as $[H]$.
- Pauli gates: represented as $[X]$, $[Y]$, or $[Z]$.
- CNOTgate: uses a dot ($\bullet$) for control qubit and a $\oplus$ for target.

Measurement operations are marked with a meter symbol, and classical feedback lines are drawn as double wires [14].

Complex operations like the Toffoli gate (controlled-controlled-NOT) and parametric gates such as $R_x(\theta)$ are represented with labeled controls and angles. Force sequencing constraints may be introduced through barriers. A circuit is read by interpreting how each gate is operating together with the derivation of how the whole quantum state is progressing by the series of operations [25].

In many cases, the designers seek patterns that are familiar to them in these diagrams. Similarly to classical engineers who are familiar with a full adder or multiplexer circuit, quantum programmers are also starting to be familiar with subroutines, such as the quantum Fourier transform or teleportation protocols, making modular and efficient design possible.

5.7 Superposition, Entanglement, and Quantum Advantage

One of the fundamental operations in quantum circuits is the creation of superposition. A single Hadamard gate on a $|0\rangle$ qubit generates a quantum state with an equal probability amplitudes of $|0\rangle$ and $|1\rangle$. Applying Hadamards to multiple qubits creates a state that represents all possible binary inputs simultaneously—a key ingredient in algorithms like Grover's and Shor's [12].

Entanglement adds another layer of power. Quantum systems can be correlated in a manner with no classical analogue, as evidenced by circuits which produce Bell states or GHZ states (three-qubit entanglement). These entanglement states are critical for quantum teleportation, quantum key distribution, and error correction [26].

5.8 Teleportation and Quantum Communication

A very elegant use of circuits is with quantum teleportation [3]. It enables the physical movement of a strange quantum state between two places without physically transferring a qubit. The protocol introduces a common Bell state between two candidates (Alice and Bob). Alice becomes tangled with the unknown state by qubit interaction and measures it. She transmits two classical bits to Bob, who uses these bits to incorporate corrective gates on his qubit, thus replicating the original quantum state error free [3].

The enchantment in the teleportation is the dependence obtained through entanglement and classic communication as opposed to straight transfer. It shows in striking detail how quantum mechanics disarms or goads against classical introspections and creates new horizons in communication and computing.

6 Quantum Error Correction and Qubits Protection

Quantum error correction has become a precondition of practical quantum computing since no-cloning theorem prevent direct copying and quantum measurement of quantum information [1, 8]. These limitations have led to the adoption of more sophisticated error correction schemes in order to preserve delicate quantum states. Quantum decoherence which causes the environmental interactions to corrupt the quantum coherence and transform the pure quantum states to mixed states that cannot be effectively utilized in quantum computation is one of the biggest problems [27]. The coherence times differ greatly between technologies: The coherence is usually maintained at a microsecond to hundreds of microseconds level in superconducting qubits, whereas the longer coherence to the second or minute scale has been demonstrated in trapped ion systems in ideal regimes [28, 29]. Nonetheless, the limitation on these experiments notwithstanding, the quantum threshold theorem provides some way forward in building scalable quantum computing by responding that, below some physical error threshold (generally 10^{-4} to 10^{-3}), logical error rates can be exponentially suppressed through error correction codes and, hence, reliable quantum computation could be performed [27, 30].

6.1 Quantum Error-Correcting Codes

Quantum error correction is a technique that safeguards sensitive quantum data by encoding a single logical qubit typically into multiple physical qubits in a way that enables the physical qubits to be checked and, when an error is found, corrected without disrupting the nontrivial quantum aspect of the logical qubit [1]. Error correction approaches use three-qubit codes that provides protection to single bit-flips or phase-flips corresponding to X and Z errors through parity checking and superposition encoding [27, 31]. This approach was used to develop a breakthrough nine-qubit Shor code able to correct random single bit-flips and provide fault tolerance [32]. More efficient approaches like seven-qubit Steane code were developed that leveraged Hamming code principles leveraging algebraic machinery [33]. However, surface codes have emerged as the most popular error correction technique for large scale quantum computers. It arranges qubits in 2D patterns and leverages local parity measurements making it easier to be implemented on hardware [24]. Most of these error correction approaches use stabilizer formalism that leverages commuting Pauli operators to allow for non-destructive syndrome measurement [25].

Although these codes make the possibility of fault-tolerant quantum computing practice, the operational overhead creates a significant obstacle for practical use. Multiple thousands of physical qubits are frequently needed to reliably support a single logical qubit in its real-world implementation [25]. This expense motivates research into higher quality qubits and more efficient code and approaches to error mitigation. Today the quantum systems are in the noisy intermediate scale quantum (NISQ) regime and are not fully error corrected enough to be useful [19]. Nonetheless, quantum error correction remains the most effective avenue to starting a scalable quantum computer, which can transform cryptography, optimization, materials science, and machine learning.

Table 1 Key application domains of quantum computing

Domain	Use case	Example
Cryptography	Threatens classical RSA encryption	Shor's algorithm [34]
Optimization	Enhances complex problem-solving in logistics and finance	Quantum annealing [35]
Simulation	Enables efficient molecular modeling for drug discovery	Quantum simulation algorithms [36]

Table 2 Milestones and platforms led by key quantum computing companies

Company	Initiative/platform	Milestone year	Focus area
IBM	Qiskit framework	2016	Open-source circuit design
	Error-corrected qubits goal	Target:2026	Scalable, fault-tolerant quantum computation
Google	Sycamore processor	2019	Quantum supremacy demonstration [13, 14]
	Cirq library	Ongoing	Circuit design tooling
Rigetti	Forest SDK	2018	Hybrid quantum/classical development
D-wave	Quantum annealing systems	2011	Optimization-focused quantum hardware

7 Applications and Future Directions

7.1 Quantum Computing Applications

Quantum circuits are opening up innovations in a number of industries. Examples of its notable applications are mentioned in the following Table 1.

7.2 The Road Ahead

Quantum innovation is fueled by large actors coming up with advanced hardware and software. The next important milestones will be quantum supremacy and fault-tolerance (Table 2).

8 Conclusion

Quantum computing is changing how computation is handled because it leverages on the special nature of quantum components. The principles of superposition, entanglement, and interference are not mere theoretical wonders, but the movers and shakers behind the strength of the technology.

With this fast paced development of quantum hardware, more and more practical applications will emerge in cryptography, where classical encryption can no longer guarantee security, optimization applications that can unlock efficiency in many industries; and molecular simulation, transformative to drug discovery and materials design.

The inquisitive thinker will be able to get their hands on the subject, with resources such as Qiskit [14], allowing an easy way to experiment with these ideas and achieve something in this emerging world.

References

1. Nielsen MA, Chuang IL (2010) Quantum computation and quantum information, 10th edn. Cambridge University Press, Cambridge
2. Rieffel EG, Polak WH (2011) Quantum computing: a gentle introduction. MIT Press, Cambridge, MA
3. Gambetta JM et al (2017) Building logical qubits in a superconducting quantum computing system. npj Quantum Info 3(2)
4. Kelly J et al (2015) State preservation by repetitive error detection in a superconducting quantum circuit. Nature 519(7541):66–69
5. Wootters WK, Zurek WH (1982) A single quantum cannot be cloned. Nature 299(5886):802–803
6. Schuld M, Petruccione F (2018) Supervised learning with quantum computers. Springer
7. Martinis JM (2015) Qubit metrology for building a fault-tolerant quantum computer. npj Quantum Inf 1:15005
8. Pick A et al (2021) Boosting photonic quantum computation with moderate nonlinearity. Phys Rev Appl 15(5):054054
9. Barenco A et al (1995) Elementary gates for quantum computation. Phys Rev A 52(5):3457–3467
10. Dawson CM, Nielsen MA (2006) The Solovay-Kitaev algorithm. Quantum Inf Comput 6(1):81–95
11. Smite-Meister (2025) Visualization of a qubit state on the Bloch sphere. Wikimedia Commons. https://commons.wikimedia.org/wiki/File:Bloch_sphere.svg. Accessed 12 Jul 2025
12. Greenberger DM, Horne MA, Zeilinger A (1989) Going beyond Bell's theorem. In: Bell's theorem, quantum theory and conceptions of the universe, Springer, pp 69–72
13. Rxtreme (2023) Image of bloch sphere. Wikimedia Commons. https://commons.wikimedia.org/wiki/File:Bloch_sphere.svg. Accessed 12 Jul 2025
14. Shor PW (1994) Algorithms for quantum computation: Discrete logarithms and factoring. In: Proceedings of 35th annual symposium foundations of computer science (FOCS), pp 124–134
15. Bennett CH et al (1973) Logical reversibility of computation. IBM J Res Dev 17(6):525–532
16. Leibfried D et al (2003) Experimental demonstration of a robust, high-fidelity geometric two ion-qubit phase gate. Nature 422:412–415
17. Grover LK (1996) A fast quantum mechanical algorithm for database search. In: Proceedings of 28th annual ACM symposium on theory of computing (STOC), pp 212–219
18. Deutsch D (1985) Quantum theory, the church-turing principle and the universal quantum computer. Proc R Soc Lond A 400:97–117
19. Koch J et al (2007) Charge-insensitive qubit design derived from the Cooper pair box. Phys Rev A 76(4):042319
20. JPNARPHY, Bell state circuit. Wikimedia Commons, CC BY-SA 4.0. https://commons.wikimedia.org/wiki/File:Bell_state_circuit.svg

21. Deutsch D, Jozsa R (1992) Rapid solution of problems by quantum computation. Proc R Soc A 439(1907):553–558
22. Monroe C et al (2021) Programmable quantum simulations of spin systems with trapped ions. Rev Mod Phys 93(2)
23. Dirac PAM (1958) The principles of quantum mechanics. Oxford University Press
24. Fowler AG et al (2012) Surface codes: towards practical large-scale quantum computation. Phys Rev A 86(3):032324
25. Preskill J (2018) Quantum computing in the NISQ era and beyond. Quantum 2:79
26. Bennett CH et al (1993) Teleporting an unknown quantum state via dual classical and Einstein–Podolsky–Rosen channels. Phys Rev Lett 70(13):1895–1899
27. Aharonov D, Ben-Or M (1997) Fault-tolerant quantum computation with constant error rate. In: Proceedings of 29th annual ACM symposium theory computing (STOC), pp 176–188
28. Monroe C, Kim J (2013) Scaling the ion trap quantum processor. Science 339(6124):1164–1169
29. Shor PW (1995) Scheme for reducing decoherence in quantum computer memory. Phys Rev A 52(4):R2493–R2496
30. Knill E, Laflamme R (1997) Theory of quantum error-correcting codes. Phys Rev A 55(2):900–911
31. Shor PW (1996) Fault-tolerant quantum computation. In: Proceedings of 37th annual symposium foundations of computer science (FOCS), pp 56–65
32. Steane AM (1996) Error correcting codes in quantum theory. Phys Rev Lett 77(5):793–797
33. Gottesman D (1997) Stabilizer codes and quantum error correction. Ph.D. dissertation, California Institute of Technology, Pasadena, CA, USA
34. Shor PW (1997) Polynomial-time algorithms for prime factorization and discrete logarithms on a quantum computer. SIAM J Comput 26(5):1484–1509
35. Aspuru-Guzik A et al (2005) Simulated quantum computation of molecular energies. Science 309(5741):1704–1707
36. IBM Quantum (2023) Qiskit: An open-source framework for quantum computing. https://qiskit.org. Accessed 12 Jul 2025

Saraswati Mishra is a Senior Software Engineer specializing in building resilient, scalable and data compliant AI systems. With a decade of experience in big data and infrastructure, she works on bridging traditional engineering with AI-native workflows to enable impactful, real-world applications. Currently, she focuses on building scalable agentic systems and designing observability and monitoring frameworks for large language model (LLM) infrastructure and developing data compliant AI services. She also works and conducts ongoing research in AI/ML, distributed systems, and quantum computing as she believes they represent the next major leap in computer science.

Raghuram Katakam is an accomplished IT professional with over 18 years of experience in designing and delivering large-scale technology solutions. He currently serves as a Senior Software Engineer at Microsoft, where he leverages his techno-functional expertise in SAP technologies, Artificial Intelligence (AI), and Machine Learning (ML) to drive innovation and efficiency across enterprise systems. Throughout his career, Raghuram has held diverse roles—including Programmer, Technical Lead, Technical Manager, and Business Analyst—at leading organizations such as ADP, Thomson Reuters, TCS, and ERP Menu. His proficiency spans multiple platforms, including PeopleSoft and SAP (ABAP, FI, FICA, S/4HANA, BRIM, RMCA), alongside deep expertise in Python, AI/ML, Copilot Studio, and automation frameworks. He has successfully led end-to-end implementations, managed high-volume transactions, and delivered transformative solutions recognized with multiple industry awards. Raghuram holds a B.Tech degree and a

Post Graduate Program in Artificial Intelligence and Machine Learning. His research contributions extend to AIML, Blockchain, and Quantum Computing, with several published papers and journals to his credit. He continues to advance knowledge in emerging technologies through ongoing research and authorship of book chapters on quantum computing. Beyond his professional achievements, Raghuram is an active mentor and volunteer in nonprofit organizations, frequently serving as a judge for hackathons, student awards, and conferences. His commitment to both technological innovation and community engagement underscores his dedication to shaping the future of computing and inspiring the next generation of technologists.

Quantum Programming: Languages and Frameworks

Ashwin Prakash Nalwade and Khan Shariya Hasan Upoma

Abstract

Quantum programming serves as the interface between quantum theory and practical computing, enabling developers to design, simulate, and execute quantum algorithms on emerging hardware platforms. This chapter provides a comprehensive analysis of current quantum programming paradigms, language structures, and system architectures. It examines the design trade-offs across abstraction levels, control models, and integration workflows, highlighting key challenges such as hybrid execution bottlenecks, verification gaps, and toolchain fragmentation. The discussion also outlines the layered architecture of quantum software stacks and the evolving landscape of quantum–classical interoperability. By synthesizing current methodologies and limitations, this chapter determines crucial domains in future research and development in quantum software engineering. It aims to arm researchers, engineers, and educators with a unified view of the current landscape conditions and the path toward scalable, verifiable, and accessible ecosystems of quantum programming.

Keywords

Quantum programming • Qiskit • OpenQASM 3 • Cirq • PennyLane • Hybrid quantum–classical systems • NISQ computing • Quantum software stack • Formal verification • Quantum compiler design • Quantum SDKs • Quantum programming languages • Quantum software engineering

A. P. Nalwade (✉)
Pythia, Seattle, USA
e-mail: ashwin@pythialab.com

K. S. H. Upoma
Dhaka, Bangladesh

M. Rana and B. Pandey (eds.), *Quantum Ops*,
https://doi.org/10.1007/978-3-032-10775-6_3

1 Introduction

Quantum computing is not so much about what different computations one can do, but what understanding one develops at the level of computation. Yet, it is because of these capabilities, with quantum entanglement and interference, that a particular algorithm can be solved at an exponential rate, which would take classical computers many thousands of years to achieve a comparable result.

Although hardware innovators are excited about these promises of performance, there has also been increasing concern about how programmers will interact with their quantum machine. Quantum programming thus arises as an entirely new field at the intersection of computer science, physics, and engineering. However, quantum programming is not a direct offshoot of classical programming; it arises from novel computation models, new levels of abstraction, and different perceptions regarding control flow, data, and measurement.

While still part of this process, quantum computing primarily concerns itself with what we fundamentally understand about computation, rather than what computations we can perform differently from classical machines. Most present-day quantum computers still operate with bits, but some utilize qubits, which can exist in a superposition state, meaning they can present as many states simultaneously. It takes the togetherness of these capabilities, combined with quantum entanglement and interference, for a quantum computer to solve an algorithm at such a high exponential rate that its classical counterparts would take 1000 s of years to execute.

With progress in hardware innovation bringing promising performance, there has been some growing concern over how programmers will interact with their quantum machine. Thus, quantum programming emerges as a new and distinct field that sits at the nexus of computer science, engineering, and physics. However, that is not a direct offshoot of classical programming; instead, it arose from novel computational models, new levels of abstraction, and a different approach to control flow, data, and measurement.

In programming quantum systems, there are specific challenges associated with error-prone qubits, probabilistic operations, and measurements that alter the system state. Therefore, traditional programming languages are not suitable for use in quantum algorithms. This gap is closed through a new generation of quantum programming languages and frameworks. These tools are designed to provide an intuitive syntax with hybrid quantum–classical workflows, execution-backend-agnostic facilities, and circuit compilation via features for simulation.

2 Background

2.1 An Overview of Quantum Programming

Quantum computing leverages principles of quantum mechanics, including superposition, entanglement, and interference, to solve problems that are intractable for classical computers [1]. One can imitate, define, and run algorithms to produce such phenomena with quantum programming. For example, qubits do not behave like classical bits; they can exist as a linear combination of states ($|01\rangle$ and $|10\rangle$), which means that they can also achieve parallel processing [2]. Therefore, we need specific languages and environments to program such systems that can work with qubits, apply gates, and perform error correction, while not focusing excessively on the intricate details of the actual physical hardware.

The acceptance came once Peter Shor created a factoring algorithm in 1994 [3]. Analogous to what quantum computers could do, this established the certainty that when it came to quantum computing, quantum programming interfaces were the way to go. In this regard, when it comes to quantum programming, theoretical ideas can be linked to quantum devices, enabling inquiries like quantum optimization, quantum ML, quantum cryptography, and quantum materials science [4]. Currently, hardware capabilities extend beyond the NISQ [noisy intermediate-scale quantum] devices; therefore, the software layer must compensate for improved circuit depth reduction, error correction, and resource management [5].

The primary quantum operations are

- Single-Qubit Gates: Hadamard (H) gates make superposition: $H|0\rangle = \frac{|0\rangle+|1\rangle}{\sqrt{2}}$.
- Two-Qubit Gates: Entanglement of Qubits by CNOT $|10\rangle = |11\rangle$.
- The measurement uses probability amplitudes to determine whether qubits collapse to classical states (0 or 1).

2.2 Key Applications Driving Quantum Programming

Quantum programming has applications because it can change things in several areas:

- **Cryptography**: The threat posed by the Shor algorithm to RSA cryptography has led to the development of new post-quantum cryptography standards, including lattice-based methods [6, 7].
- **Quantum optimization**: The QAOA [Approximate Optimization Algorithm] aids in logistics problems, such as route optimization, and finance challenges, including portfolio management [8, 9].
- **Quantum simulation**: Variational Quantum Eigensolvers (VQE) use quantum systems to model things like molecular structures for drug development [10,

11]. Frameworks like Qiskit Chemistry give you tools that are specialized to your field [12].
- **Quantum Machine Learning (QML)**: Quantum neural networks (QNNs) use high-dimensional Hilbert spaces to find patterns. This is possible because of hybrid quantum–classical frameworks [13, 14].

These applications need NISQ devices and software stacks that reduce decoherence and gate infidelity [15]. Moreover, they require specialized libraries, such as Qiskit Chemistry, to facilitate the handling of quantum mechanics [12].

2.3 Key Quantum Applications

The use cases of programming frameworks are focused on:

- **Quantum simulation**: This involves working with quantum phase estimation to analyze molecular structures, such as nitrogen fixation catalysts [11].
- **Cryptanalysis**:
- **Combinatorial optimization**: Applying quantum approximate optimization (QAOA) in the fields of logistics and finance [9].
- **Quantum machine learning**: Employing quantum–classical neural networks, aka hybrid devices, in pattern recognition [14]

2.4 Quantum Software Stack Architecture

Present quantum programming frameworks utilize a multilayered software structure. High-to-low software commands manage the increasing complexity of quantum operations. The levels range from application-specific logic to low-pulse sequencing/hardware commands. A summary of the primary structural elements can be found in Table 1.

The whole process flow through these layers is illustrated in Fig. 1, which depicts how quantum programs move from high-level abstractions to low-level pulse execution.

Table 1 Modern frameworks implement layered architectures

Layer	Function	Examples
Application	Domain-specific modules	Qiskit nature, Cirq quantum ML
Algorithm	Pre-built circuit templates	VQE, grover, QFT
Circuit	Gate-level instructions	Qiskit terra, Cirq Circuits
Compilation	Hardware translation	Transpilers, qubit mappers
Control	Pulse scheduling	Qiskit pulse, OpenQASM3

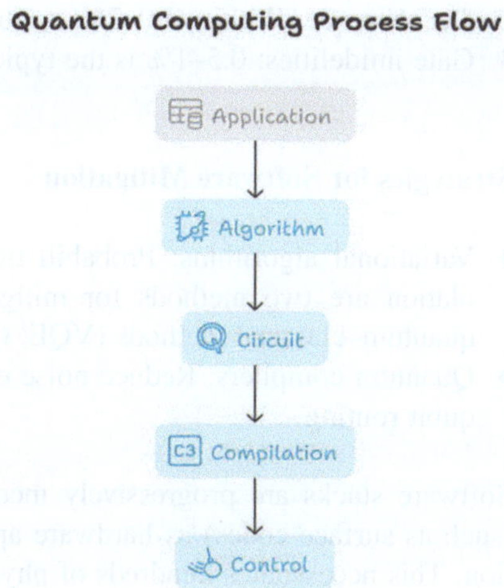

Fig. 1 Quantum computing process flow

Features particular to layers

1. **Application layer**: Offers abstractions particular to a given area, such as the molecular Hamiltonians in Qiskit Chemistry [12].
2. **Algorithm layer**: Uses parameterized circuits to implement quantum algorithms.
3. **Circuit layer**: Converts algorithms into gate sequences (CNOT, Toffoli, etc.).
4. **Compilation layer**: This layer includes circuit optimization, gate decomposition, qubit mapping, and error mitigation.
5. **Control layer**: Manages timing, calibration, and pulse-level instructions.

Quantum simulators find an essential space in the stack. Classical emulation of quantum systems is supported by

- State vector simulation: Exact simulation; requires 2^n memory and becomes infeasible beyond ~40 qubits.
- Density matrix simulation: Captures decoherence and noise via mixed-state modeling.
- Tensor network simulation: Efficiently approximates larger systems using entanglement structures [16].

2.5 Innovations and Challenges of the NISQ Era

The NISQ regime, where modern quantum computers function, is defined by:

1. Limitations of qubits: 50–500 physical qubits that are not fully connected

2. Decoherence: Within 100–200 u, quantum states collapse
3. Gate infidelities: 0.5–1% is the typical 2-qubit gate fault [15].

Strategies for Software Mitigation

- Variational algorithms: Probabilistic error cancelation and zero-noise extrapolation are two methods for mitigating errors. Shallow circuits and hybrid quantum–classical methods (VQE, QAOA)
- Quantum compilers: Reduce noise exposure by optimizing gate sequences and qubit routing.

Software stacks are progressively incorporating quantum error correction codes (such as surface codes) as hardware approaches fault-tolerant quantum computation. This necessitates hundreds of physical qubits for every logical qubit.

3 Literature Review

Quantum computers possess the ability to resolve particular problems with significantly greater efficiency compared to classical computers. Quantum programming languages (QPLs) and software frameworks are the most essential abstraction layers between quantum algorithms and the physical hardware. They let researchers and developers build, simulate, and run quantum programs. This review synthesizes the existing literature, highlights key developments, identifies significant gaps and ongoing debates, and explains why this chapter adopts a broad approach.

3.1 Overview of Current Studies and Significant Advancements

The development of QPLs began with basic models that aimed to formalize quantum computing. The Quantum Random Access Machine (QRAM) model by Knill was one of the first theoretical models for quantum computing that was similar to traditional RAM [1]. This made it possible for the first generation of explicitly quantum imperative languages to come along. Ömer created quantum computation language (QCL), the first of its kind. It had a C-like syntax for constructing quantum operators and registers, while also featuring built-in simulation abilities [2]. It demonstrated that high-level quantum programming was feasible and provided insights into concepts such as quantum memory management. Microsoft's Q# language, based on imperative principles, has evolved into a robust and scalable language that integrates seamlessly with the Quantum Development Kit (QDK) [3]. Its robust typing, support for functional constructs within an imperative basis, and seamless interface with traditional.NET code for hybrid computation constitutes a substantial improvement in practical quantum software development [3, 4].

At the same time, functional programming paradigms gained popularity because they align well with the reversible and unitary nature of quantum processes. Quipper is a Haskell-embedded domain-specific language (DSL) known for its ability to describe circuits, automatically estimate resources, and hierarchically build circuits [5, 6]. It had a significant impact on algorithm research since it focused on scalability and formal verification. Altenkirch and Grattage developed QML, a novel approach to quantum programming grounded in categorical quantum mechanics and linear logic. It was a purely functional way of looking at quantum programming [8]. Languages like Silq (developed at ETH Zürich) took the functional paradigm even further by introducing automatic uncomputation, a key feature for managing quantum states that makes programming much easier and less prone to errors than earlier manual methods [10].

Quantum software frameworks and SDKs gained popularity due to the demand for development and execution platforms that were easy to use. Qiskit (IBM) [13], Cirq (Google) [15], and Braket SDK (Amazon Web Services) [11] are now the most important players. These frameworks, which are based on Python, offer complete environments for building quantum circuits, simulating them (using both state vector and more efficient methods like tensor networks), compiling them, optimizing them, and running them on real hardware or simulators. They hide vendor-specific information while still giving users low-level control when needed, making quantum gear more accessible to everyone [11, 13, 15]. Another well-known open-source framework is ProjectQ, which focuses on compiling for specific hardware and offers a straightforward Pythonic interface [7].

A significant topic is the study of how to formally check and reason about quantum programs. QWire, which is part of Coq, serves as the basic framework for formally describing and verifying circuits [9]. Quantum Hoare logic (QHL) and its extensions aim to provide quantum programs with Hoare-style reasoning by establishing preconditions and postconditions, as well as loop invariants [12, 14]. It is crucial to utilize tools like QWIRE verification and model checkers that have been modified to work with quantum systems, ensuring accuracy. This is because quantum states and operations are not always easy to understand, and mistakes can be quite expensive [9, 14, 16].

Quantum intermediate representations (QIRs), such as LLVM-QIR and Quil (developed by Rigetti), are being developed as a bridge between high-order languages and their corresponding hardware backends, facilitating easy compilation and optimization of compilers [17, 18]. Additionally, research into domain-specific languages (DSLs) focuses on specific fields of study, such as quantum chemistry (OpenFermion) [19] or optimization issues, and provides libraries and abstractions tailored to those fields.

3.2 Identification of Knowledge Gaps and Controversies

1. **Lack of Standardization**: A significant issue is that there isn't a standard quantum programming language or intermediate representation that everyone agrees

on. Many languages (Q#, Qiskit, Cirq, Quipper, etc.) and IRs (Quil, QIR) make things more complicated, make it harder to move code around, make it harder to learn, and make it harder to write compilers [3, 13, 15, 17]. Even with groups like the QIR Alliance, it's still challenging to get everyone to agree.

2. **Scalability and resource estimation**: It's very challenging to accurately estimate the resources (qubits, gates, runtime, and fidelity) required by complicated quantum algorithms on future error-corrected hardware. Tools like Quipper can aid in resource estimation [6], but determining how to apply these methods to complex algorithms that require error correction remains an active research question. There is a significant difference between the actual cost of implementing an algorithm in real life and how it is described in abstract terms.

Current noisy intermediate-scale quantum (NISQ) devices have a high error rate; therefore, effective mechanisms for error handling and correction are necessary. The frameworks have their fundamental error correction mechanisms in readout error correction and zero-noise extrapolation [13, 15]. There are few practical language-integrated approaches toward error handling, fault tolerance, and logical qubit management. Adding fault-tolerance schemes, such as surface codes within high-level programming models, is not trivial and remains a hot research topic [20].

1. **Verification and debugging**: Verifying large quantum software programs is challenging due to their formal nature. Existing Hoare logics and model checkers have not been particularly successful in scaling up and effectively managing the immense complexity associated with quantum states [14, 16]. The fact that states cannot be inspected due to the no-cloning theorem and the probabilistic nature of quantum programs makes debugging them a particularly problematic. Therefore, debugging must do more than just rely on examining circuits and snapshots from simulators; we must have debug tools that are useful and scalable.
2. **Hybrid computing management** It's challenging to manage data flow, optimize how computing is split between conventional and quantum components, and efficiently coordinate complex operations that utilize both types of processors. Current frameworks offer rudimentary hybrid support [3, 13], but advanced co-design methods and runtime systems are still in their early stages of development [21].
3. **Amount of abstraction**: There is considerable disagreement over what the optimal amount of abstraction is for QPLs. For maximum control and possible optimization (like Cirq's philosophy) [15], should languages show low-level hardware details (gate sets, topology), or should they try to hide hardware complexity with high-level abstractions, even if it means sacrificing performance and fine-grained control (like Silq's goals) [10]? Finding the correct balance between usability, portability, and performance is still a topic of debate.

3.3 Justification for the Present Research

The landscape of quantum programming is now fragmented and evolving rapidly, and the aforementioned essential deficiencies necessitate a thorough and organized review. Even if there is a wealth of studies on specific languages or particular topics (such as resource estimation or verification), a comprehensive resource that:

- **Combines diverse developments**: This chapter provides a comprehensive analysis of imperative, functional, and framework-based methodologies, highlighting the advantages, disadvantages, and design philosophies of each [2, 3, 5, 8, 10, 13, 15]. It connects contemporary, practical tools (Qiskit [13], Q# [3]) with fundamental models (QRAM [1]).
- **Contextualizes gaps and challenges**: This chapter gives researchers and developers important context for future efforts by clearly defining the standardization deficit [3, 13, 17], scalability hurdles in resource estimation and verification [6, 14, 16], the immature state of error handling abstractions [20], and the hybrid computation challenge [21].

The chapter goes beyond a simple listing by offering a comparative study of languages and frameworks according to several important factors, including target audience, hardware integration, simulation capabilities, abstraction level, paradigm, and verification support. For practitioners choosing the right tools, this organized comparison is essential.

- **Responds to the abstraction debate**: The chapter offers insights into the trade-offs involved by looking at languages from all along the abstraction spectrum (from low-level Cirq [15] to higher-level Silq [10] and domain-specific tools like OpenFermion [19]). This information informs both language design decisions and user selection.
- **Bridges theory and practice**: To illustrate the interaction between theoretical soundness and real-world implementation requirements, the chapter combines descriptions of formal methods (QHL [14], QWire [9]) with useful framework features (Qiskit [13], Cirq [15]).
- **Determines future directions**: The chapter helps determine priority areas for further study and development in quantum programming languages, compilers, verification tools, and runtime systems by outlining the current status and its limitations.

The literature review may conclude that, although significant strides have been made in quantum programming languages and frameworks, the field remains dynamic and challenging, with several unresolved issues. A comprehensive approach is required due to the fragmentation, scaling, and verification challenges, the infancy of effective error handling abstractions, and the complexity of hybrid computing. By synthesizing existing knowledge, critically examining the landscape, and providing a basis for understanding both current capabilities and the key next steps in the evolution of quantum software development tools, this chapter addresses this need.

4 Analysis of Language Design, Frameworks, and Workflows in Quantum Computing

4.1 Language Paradigms and Design Approaches

Quantum programming languages derive from different paradigms based on abstraction, safety and usability concerns. They exist in either imperative or functional styles, with certain design choices implemented based on the restrictions of quantum theory [relevant concepts being the no-cloning theorem, entanglement, and measurement collapse].

4.1.1 Imperative Languages

Imperative quantum languages are similar to popular languages in classical computing like C or Python. For example, Q# (that was developed by Microsoft) introduces constructs for quantum operations, measurement, and control logic, while enforcing separation between the quantum and classical contexts [3]. OpenQASM 3, which is a part of the Qiskit stack, allows for low-level conditional operations and low-level control of hardware [22].

4.1.2 Functional Languages

Conversely, functional languages operate with a higher level of abstraction. They represent mathematical purism above an intentionally limited potential to exert figurative control over every facet of a circuit for necessary safety and usability. For example, Quipper is built using the Haskell programming language and is good for creating and combining quantum circuits, especially when working on large or complex designs [7]. Silq makes it easier to manage temporary variables (called ancillas) by automatically cleaning up operations that are no longer needed [10]. And then QML uses a special type system to make sure quantum data is handled safely and correctly during programs [5]. Table 2 here showcases a comparison of major quantum programming languages across several key dimensions.

4.2 Practical Frameworks and SDKs

Quantum language applications span various practical frameworks that include SDKs, which extend language capabilities by providing access to devices, circuit optimizations, simulations, and runtime orchestration. These toolkits serve as the primary interface for both research and production use cases.

Table 2 Comparative insights into quantum programming languages

Aspect	Imperative languages	Functional languages
Abstraction level	Closer to hardware; more flexible but verbose syntax (e.g., Q# [3], OpenQASM [22])	Higher abstraction and safety, but less accessible to beginners (e.g., Silq [10], Quipper [7])
Quantum–classical separation	Enforced through strict typing (Q# [3], QML [5]) or control/timing integration (OpenQASM [22])	Maintained via type systems and language design (e.g., QML [5])
Semantics	Limited formal semantic support; some tools lack verification models	Backed by formal semantics enabling program correctness and proofs (QML [5], Quipper [7])
Developer usability	Q# supports IDEs like visual studio; OpenQASM allows fine-grained control [3, 22]	Silq emphasizes familiar syntax and reduced boilerplate [10]

4.2.1 Qiskit (IBM)

Qiskit is one of the most mature frameworks, supporting modular development through components such as Terra (circuit creation), Aer (simulation), and Ignis (noise characterization). It supports OpenQASM 3 and grants access to IBM's quantum computing hardware via the IBM Quantum Experience platform [22].

4.2.2 Cirq (Google)

Cirq is designed for gate-level circuit construction with tight control over timing and qubit placement. It is used extensively in NISQ experimentation and supports calibration-aware scheduling. Cirq is tightly coupled with Google's Sycamore hardware [8].

4.2.3 PennyLane (Xanadu)

PennyLane specializes in hybrid quantum–classical optimization. It works well with ML libraries like TensorFlow and PyTorch, facilitating the gradient-based training of parameterized quantum circuits through the parameter-shift rule [4, 9]. This makes it especially useful for variational quantum algorithms and quantum ML.

4.2.4 Forest SDK (Rigetti)

Rigetti's Forest includes pyQuil, a Python library for quantum circuit creation, and Quilc, a compiler tailored for Rigetti's superconducting qubit devices. The Forest stack includes a Quantum Virtual Machine and provides native access to Rigetti's QCS platform [8].

Table 3 Comparison of selected quantum SDKs and frameworks

Framework	Abstraction level	Language	Simulator	Hardware access	Hybrid support	ML integration
Qiskit	Medium	OpenQASM	Yes	IBM	Yes	Limited
Cirq	Low	Python	Yes	Google	Yes	No
PennyLane	High	Python	Yes	Multiple	Yes	Strong
Forest	Medium	Quil	Yes	Rigetti	Yes	Moderate
Braket	Medium	Python	Yes	Multi-vendor	Yes	Moderate

4.2.5 Amazon Braket SDK

Braket abstracts execution across diverse hardware backends, including devices from IonQ, OQC, and Rigetti Quantum Computing. Using its Python SDK, users can define, simulate, and run quantum circuits on real devices or high-performance simulators. It emphasizes cross-hardware benchmarking and seamless classical integration [8].

Table 3 provides a side-by-side comparison of these five widely used quantum programming frameworks in terms of abstraction level, language support, simulation capabilities, hardware integration, hybrid workflow support, and machine learning (ML) interoperability.

4.3 Hybrid Quantum–Classical Integration

The quantum processors we have with us today, commonly referred to as NISQ devices, lack the features of coherence, fidelity, and scale, which are all required by a fully autonomous quantum computation system. As a result, most quantum algorithms known to humanity are currently being performed in hybrid quantum–classical workflows. In such workflows, quantum circuits are referred to as subroutines within classical control loops, where classical processors perform the optimization of results from quantum computations, preprocess data, and iteratively refine them. This interaction is at the heart of algorithms like the VQE and QAOA.

Several frameworks and languages have emerged to support these hybrid models, each reflecting different trade-offs in orchestration, latency, gradient computation, and hardware abstraction.

4.3.1 TensorFlow Quantum (TFQ)

TFQ extends TensorFlow to support quantum circuit simulation and gradient-based optimization using quantum–classical hybrid models. It is built on Cirq and enables researchers to construct quantum models that can be trained using classical optimizers such as Adam or stochastic gradient descent. TFQ supports integration with deep learning pipelines, enabling tasks like quantum-enhanced classification and generative modeling [9].

4.3.2 PennyLane

PennyLane is designed around the concept of differentiable quantum programming. It introduces "quantum nodes" that are treated as differentiable functions within classical ML frameworks such as PyTorch or JAX. This makes it ideal for variational quantum classifiers and algorithms like QAOA, VQE. PennyLane implements the parameter-shift rule for gradient estimation, which is compatible with quantum hardware and avoids the pitfalls of finite-difference methods [4, 9].

4.3.3 Quingo

Quingo is a quantum–classical programming framework that aims to bridge classical control and quantum circuit definition. Quingo contains a domain-specific language for orchestrating hybrid workflows to achieve resource efficient task distribution and reduced overhead from classical-quantum exchanges. Quingo takes advantage of NISQ hardware characteristics such as coherence time restrictions and connectivity limitations [11].

4.3.4 SimuQ

SimuQ provides an environment for Hamiltonian simulation where quantum circuits are compiled to simulate time evolution based on Hamiltonians. It exploits linear analog compilation to have control over device dynamics at a more fine-grained resolution; it is limited to chemistry and condensed matter physics [14].

4.3.5 Quantum Toolbox in Python (QuTiP)

QuTiP is a numerical simulation library for solving the Schrödinger and Lindblad master equations. While not purely a circuit-level language, it is frequently used in hybrid situations where quantum dynamics would have to otherwise be solved using differential equations and other classical approaches. It is best for open quantum system modeling and control pulse optimization [8].

4.4 Emerging Issues and Case Studies

Quantum programming tools are becoming more advanced and easier to use, but several important challenges still remain. To better understand and address these issues, such as limited support for abstraction, compiler errors, poor developer experience, and the lack of reliable debugging methods, we focus on case studies that highlight the key problems facing quantum programming today.

4.4.1 Hamiltonian Simulation with SimuQ

SimuQ is a quantum development framework for simulating time evolution due to Hamiltonian dynamics. It operates in a less abstracted fashion at a non-circuit level than a more cerebral, circuit-level operation. Instead, SimuQ operates on a level of analog compilation of quantum operations that inventors hope to achieve in similar, real dynamics [14]. This is key for applications in quantum chemistry, for example, where time-dependent Hamiltonians are required to be spectrally decomposed, requiring finite rotations via qubit coupling that are induced.

Thus SimuQ comes with an ancillary scheduler that can transform a decomposed yet high-level description into an analog instruction bit of hardware. Hence, some levels of operation are still too abstracted from the dynamic equations at play, once physical, real-world assessments are involved. They rely on features that only operate on the required depth at a mathematical level. For example, tools cannot account for low-level positioning, pulse width restrictions, effects of decoherence or analog drift; without accurate construction at multilevels of operation, weighted high-level analog dynamics will never sufficiently reproduce quantum behavior.

4.4.2 Differentiable Programming with PennyLane

PennyLane creates a new frontier by treating quantum circuits as differentiable computation graphs [4]. It boasts success in automatically differentiating variational circuits under the parameter-shift rule while allowing gradient-descent optimization through conventional ML frameworks. It's successful when using PennyLane designed circuits for training quantum classifiers and in ML, generative models and quantum kernels; yet it places PennyLane in the middle of a great source of challenge relative to performance enhancement and compared to measurement noise and gate operation errors.

Ultimately this means that gradient estimates are biased so one requires gradient estimators and strong regularization to accommodate for variances and finite performance results. In addition, executing in a dual execution space of quantum hardware and conventional ML frameworks fosters complex dependency chains and debugging issues. Thus, this acknowledges the realities of quantum–classical co-designs where gradient-based performance occurs with a low-level, physical reality that operates with little reliability relative to measurement parameters.

4.4.3 Symbolic Programming for Circuit Abstraction

According to Miszczak [12], symbolic quantum programming is an opportunity to abstract quantum logic through symbolic computation which allows for program visualization, symbolic analysis and formal verification. Developers can use symbolic states instead of numeric tensors to support model transformation, rewriting, and equivalence-checking gates.

However, symbolic programming is not a part of dominant frameworks. Symbolic programming has little integration with hardware backends or simulators. Overhead can be expensive when logical symbolic processing is implemented. This indicates that despite practical benefits from a theoretical experimental perspective, even the most abstracted methods have challenges when it comes to practicality from the standard runtime perspective.

4.4.4 Bugs and Code Smells in Quantum Machine Learning Tools

As with vulnerabilities in classical software tools, issues with bugs and code smells and lax error handling exist in the quantum space as well. According to Zhao et al. [16] and Chen et al. [20], an article that evaluated quantum open-source GitHub repositories showed frequent code smells such as unnecessary gate declarations, lack of addressing measurement collapse effects, and qubits that do not match input/output indexing.

This is, in part, due to the lack of suitable tooling. Coders do not have access to linters for quantum IDEs, test suites, or runtime monitors that are available in classical development. Moreover, quantum programs often fail due to their probabilistic nature, meaning that without extensive sampling or a review of traces, many failures go unnoticed. The quantum community could benefit from better debuggers and formal test generation frameworks [18], as well as the types of development tools that exist in coding but not in quantum development. Without adequate assistance at the development level, where coding avoids error, it becomes challenging to maintain and rely upon quantum projects after they've been developed.

4.5 Semantics, Verification, and Standardization

Beyond pragmatic tools, the future of quantum computing depends on the theoretical realm. Semantics and verification ensure precision, reliability, and sustained use across multiple fields. While the investigative process of practical tools rests upon vulnerability and hardware integration, developments of semantics and verification define proper behavior and standards of operation as well as if rationalized, tested, or translatable.

4.5.1 Formal Semantics of Quantum Languages

Formal semantics constitute an established understanding of how something must operate. Quantum developments such as QML and Quipper came about with well-defined categorical or linear type-theoretic semantics because they encode definable operations such as no-cloning and reversibility [5, 15]. Thus, researchers and practitioners can create transformations that they know will work in conjunction, encoding potentially higher-level abstractions for quantum manipulation, agency, and recursive queries.

Most recently, Valiron [21] unified a controlled nature of qubit dynamics where it could be established whether control was classical (a qubit's branching depends upon classical bits) or quantum (where control's flow is based upon superposition). This creates an even better understanding of the overlap between binary processing of information and qubit opportunity, meaning more development of the language structure could be made beyond gate-level generation to a more organizational approach to developing quantum software.

4.5.2 Verification and Model Checking

As quantum algorithms become more complex, the ability to verify that a given program behaves as intended becomes increasingly essential. Lewis et al. [19] provide an overview of tools and methods for formal verification of quantum programs, encompassing quantum Hoare logic, symbolic analysis, and type systems. These techniques are being adapted from classical formal methods to suit the uncertain and non-deterministic characteristics of quantum computing.

Currently, most tools are still in prototype or research phases. Some verification systems require specialized language support or symbolic execution environments, which limits their integration with mainstream SDKs. The lack of universally accepted verification standards or frameworks poses a barrier to deployment in high-assurance domains like cybersecurity or finance.

4.5.3 Standardization Gaps Across Ecosystems

A recurring issue in the literature is the fragmentation of the quantum software stack. Frameworks such as Qiskit, Cirq, and Braket each define their own syntax, compilation flow, metadata schemas, and result formats [3, 8, 23]. Even basic concepts such as qubit indexing, gate fidelity reporting, and error correction interfaces vary significantly between platforms.

Efforts such as OpenQASM 3 [22] aim to serve as a common intermediate representation, enabling cross-platform portability and standardized transpilation pipelines. However, there remains no broadly adopted standard for hybrid orchestration, measurement postprocessing, or metadata annotation. This lack of interoperability complicates toolchain integration and slows progress toward reusable quantum software components.

From an educational and industrial standpoint, these discrepancies make onboarding new developers more difficult and increase the cost of migrating between platforms or collaborating across institutions [17]. For example, Qiskit uses zero-based indexing for qubits, while Cirq sometimes relies on device-specific topological labels, making circuit porting non-trivial. Yet another incompatibility lies in the metadata schemas as well: where Braket requires a JSON metadata schema for its result descriptors, Qiskit works off of custom objects. This means that unless numerous custom wrappers surround each framework, portability of the pipeline fails.

5 Findings and Discussion

This chapter aimed to assess the makeup of current quantum programming languages and frameworks in existence. The assessment concludes that the current state is fragmented yet rapidly expanding. There are various options across the board for language makeup and type, as well as frameworks and toolkits; however, while many are increasingly powerful, they have yet to find a symbiotic combination among each other.

The language paradigms are still split between imperative solutions like Q#, OpenQASM [3, 22] and functional ones like Quipper, Silq [5, 10]. Qiskit, Cirq, PennyLane and Braket provide the most common compilers, simulators, and access to real quantum devices; yet, these solutions do not play nicely together nor do their respective abstractions rely on one another, supporting the findings of a fragmented software ecosystem [8, 23].

The legacy quantum–classical pipeline found through most of the works assessed showed that quantum hybrid solutions tend to be the most effective with NISQ devices. PennyLane and TensorFlow Quantum were two frameworks that fostered such effective growth; yet, their applicability is still challenged due to latency concerns, unstable gradient estimation, and orchestration issues [4, 9, 14].

Finally, the software engineering approaches in the context of quantum computing have still remained immature. From the empirical studies done from within some of these articles, it shows that devs have trouble debugging their work, code quality is not up to par, and testing environments are unfeasible [16, 20]. Although formal semantics and symbolic methods [15, 21] provide theoretical pathways to reliability, they remain disconnected from mainstream toolchains.

Collectively, these findings indicate that quantum programming is advancing, but unevenly. Sustained progress will depend on connecting theoretical concepts with practical applications, enhancing developer tools, and pursuing standardization across platforms and execution models.

6 Challenges and Future Outlook

While quantum programming has made impressive strides, there remain significant challenges of technical and systemic natures that limit its scalability, reliability, and adoption, especially within the framework of hybrid workflows (quantum and classical).

- Hybrid execution bottlenecks—In current architectures, repeated communication between classical controllers and quantum processors introduces latency, synchronization delays, and inefficient resource scheduling. These issues are especially pronounced in cloud-based and variational algorithms [8, 14].
- Gradient instability in variational algorithms—Gradient estimators such as the parameter-shift rule, widely used in frameworks like PennyLane, are sensitive to noise and error accumulation. This can lead to poor convergence and unreliable optimization results [4, 9].
- Tooling gaps: debugging and testing—Quantum software still lacks robust debugging interfaces, unit testing frameworks, and runtime introspection tools. Studies have revealed persistent code smells, silent failures, and limited visibility into qubit states across widely used libraries [16, 20].
- Verification and semantics disconnect—While formal methods have made progress (particularly in quantum Hoare logic and semantic modeling), they

remain disconnected mainly from practical toolchains like Qiskit or Cirq [15, 21].

- Fragmentation and lack of interoperability standards—The ecosystem suffers from inconsistent APIs, varying metadata formats, and limited portability between frameworks. The absence of a unified intermediate representation for hybrid workflows impedes integration and cross-platform compatibility [3, 8, 23].

Looking ahead, progress in quantum programming will depend on unified design efforts across languages, compilers, tools, and education. A convergence of imperative and functional paradigms is necessary to produce languages that strike a balance between low-level control, safety, and expressiveness [1, 2, 15]. Compiler development must integrate analog-aware scheduling, resource estimation, and inline formal verification to improve correctness and scalability [14, 21].

Standardization remains essential. A shared intermediate representation and common APIs for hybrid workflows, such as those evolving from OpenQASM 3, would enhance portability and ecosystem cohesion [22, 23]. Tooling must evolve to support debugging, profiling, and automated testing at scale. These improvements will be crucial in managing the complexity of hybrid workflows and noisy hardware [16, 20].

Where future accessibility can be made is in more detailed documentation, GUI's, and onboarding environments to ease the entry barrier [17]. Ultimately bringing theory and application together will be achieved by merging semantic models and formal verification into nonexperimental toolchains that promise stability as quantum software libraries [15, 19]. The domain's future will rely on a universal design approach, improved development resources, and standards for maintaining correctness and usability that reside in the quantum software stack.

7 Conclusion

In this chapter, we examined the developing landscape of quantum programming languages and frameworks, focusing on the core features and integration challenges. We analyzed different language design approaches and toolkits that are popular. While these tools have radically improved the quality of quantum software, our findings reveal persistent challenges across hybrid execution, debugging, verification, and standardization.

Hybrid quantum–classical workflows, though currently the most viable for NISQ-era devices, are hindered by communication latency, gradient instability, and orchestration complexity. Moreover, the lack of formal integration between verification models and production-grade toolchains limits the reliability of quantum programs. These limitations highlight the need for unified intermediate representations, compiler-level correctness, and stronger developer tooling.

Looking forward, the future of quantum programming will rely not only on technological advancements in hardware but also on a more unified vision for software development. Quantum language families must exist in harmony to balance low-level hardware access, type safety, and development convenience. Compiler frameworks should be enhanced top to bottom through inline formal verification, analog-aware scheduling, and resource estimation to allow for ease of correctness and scaling. A software development philosophy for the greater good must prevail, supporting universally agreed upon intermediate representations and APIs that support hybrid quantum–classical use cases to avoid fragmentation across systems and facilitate cross-framework compatibility. At the same time, tooling developers need to provide helpful debugging, profiling, and testing tools that address needs in a noisy, non-deterministic quantum realm. Finally, usability implementations in documentation, GUIs, and low-friction onboarding experiences will help new quantum programmers and multidisciplinary teams ease into their new roles.

References

1. Heim B, Soeken M, Marshall S, Granade C, Roetteler M, Geller A, Troyer M, Svore K (2020) Quantum programming languages. Nat Rev Phys 2(12):709–722
2. Ying M (2024) Foundations of quantum programming. Elsevier
3. Khammassi N, Ashraf I, Someren JV, Nane R, Krol AM, Adriaan Rol M, Lao L, Bertels K, Almudever CG (2021) OpenQL: A portable quantum programming framework for quantum accelerators. ACM J Emerg Technol Comput Syst (JETC) 18(1):1–24
4. Zhu S, Hung S-H, Chakrabarti S, Wu X (2020) On the principles of differentiable quantum programming languages. In: Proceedings of the 41st ACM SIGPLAN conference on programming language design and implementation, pp 272–285
5. Sánchez P, Alonso D (2021) On the definition of quantum programming modules. Appl Sci 11(13):5843
6. Esposito M, Sabzevari MT, Ye B, Falessi D, Khan AA, Taibi D (2024) Classil Q): towards a translation framework to bridge the classical-quantum programming gap. In: Proceedings of the 1st ACM international workshop on quantum software engineering: the next evolution, pp 11–14
7. Garhwal S, Ghorani M, Ahmad A (2021) Quantum programming language: a systematic review of research topic and top cited languages. Arch Comput Methods Eng 28:289–310
8. Elsharkawy A, To AXM, Seitz P, Chen Y, Stade Y, Geiger M, Huang Q et al (2023) Integration of quantum accelerators with high performance computing-a review of quantum programming tools. ACM Trans Quantum Comput
9. Markidis S (2023) Programming quantum neural networks on nisq systems: An overview of technologies and methodologies. Entropy 25(4):694
10. Valiron B (2024) On quantum programming languages. arXiv:2410.13337
11. Fu X, Yu J, Su X, Jiang H, Wu H, Cheng F, Deng X et al (2021) Quingo: a programming framework for heterogeneous quantum-classical computing with nisq features. ACM Trans Quantum Comput 2(4):1–37
12. Miszczak JA (2023) Symbolic quantum programming for supporting applications of quantum computing technologies. In: Companion proceedings of the 7th international conference on the art, science, and engineering of programming, pp 101–108
13. Seidel R, Tcholtchev N, Bock S, Hauswirth M (2023) Uncomputation in the qrisp high-level quantum programming framework. In: International conference on reversible computation, pp 150–165. Cham: Springer Nature Switzerland

14. Peng Y, Young J, Liu P, Wu X (2024) SimuQ: a framework for programming quantum hamiltonian simulation with analog compilation. Proc ACM Program Lang 8(POPL):2425–2455
15. Jia X, Kornell A, Lindenhovius B, Mislove M, Zamdzhiev V (2022) Semantics for variational quantum programming. Proc ACM Program Lang 6(POPL):1–31
16. Zhao P, Wu X, Luo J, Li Z, Zhao J (2023) An empirical study of bugs in quantum machine learning frameworks. In: 2023 IEEE international conference on quantum software (QSW), pp 68–75. IEEE
17. Haghparast M, Moguel E, Garcia-Alonso J, Mikkonen T, Murillo JM (2024) Innovative approaches to teaching quantum computer programming and quantum software engineering. In: 2024 IEEE international conference on quantum computing and engineering (QCE), vol 2, pp 251–255. IEEE
18. Nguyen HT, Usman M, Buyya R (2024) Qfaas: a serverless function-as-a-service framework for quantum computing. Futur Gener Comput Syst 154:281–300
19. Lewis M, Soudjani S, Zuliani P (2023) Formal verification of quantum programs: theory, tools, and challenges. ACM Trans Quantum Comput 5(1):1–35
20. Chen Q, Câmara R, Campos J, Souto A, Ahmed I (2023) The smelly eight: an empirical study on the prevalence of code smells in quantum computing. In: 2023 IEEE/ACM 45th international conference on software engineering (ICSE), pp 358–370. IEEE
21. Valiron B (2022) Semantics of quantum programming languages: classical control, quantum control. J Log Algebr Methods Program 128:100790
22. Cross A, Javadi-Abhari A, Alexander T, De Beaudrap N, Bishop LS, Heidel S, Ryan CA et al (2022) OpenQASM 3: a broader and deeper quantum assembly language. ACM Trans Quantum Comput 3(3):1–50
23. Moguel E, Rojo J, Valencia D, Berrocal J, Garcia-Alonso J, Murillo JM (2022) Quantum service-oriented computing: current landscape and challenges. Software Qual J 30(4):983–1002

Ashwin Prakash Nalwade is a Machine Learning Engineer with a strong track record across early stage (Pre-seed, Series A) and late-stage (Series E) startups. His experience is complemented by research, teaching, and entrepreneurial work at New York University. As a founding ML engineer, he has architected and scaled advanced Artificial Intelligence systems end-to-end, including large-scale data pipelines with significant cost optimizations. He also authored a crucial research paper on wildfire spread prediction, cited over 50 times, which has gained renewed relevance amid recent wildfire events in Los Angeles and is being leveraged by researchers tackling multi-billion-dollar challenges in disaster mitigation.

Khan Shariya Hasan Upoma is an R&D Machine Learning Engineer at Business Automation LTD with focused expertise in quantum algorithms and machine learning. Their collaborative work seeks to demystify the complex landscape of quantum languages and frameworks, equipping readers to understand how modern software stacks bridge the gap between abstract quantum theory and practical implementation on emerging hardware.

Key Quantum Algorithms: Shor's, Grover's, and Applications

Khan Shariya Hasan Upoma and Omkar Bhalekar

Abstract

The Grover algorithm for unstructured search and the Shor algorithm for factoring numbers are two important innovations that have demonstrated the quantum computational advantage, and they are covered in detail in this chapter. We study the mathematics of Grover's amplitude amplification, which accelerates a quadratic search on a database, and Shor's exponential speedup of cracking RSA cryptography, which involves quantum Fourier transforms on the one hand and period detection on the other. The book chapter highlights several noteworthy implementation considerations, including qubit scalability constraints, quantum error correction overhead, and limitations on the design of oracles. We also hypothesize about the revolutionary impact of hybrid quantum–classical algorithms and the standardization of post-quantum cryptography for machines

This chapter is co-authored by **Khan Shariya Hasan Upoma** and **Omkar Bhalekar**, both accomplished researchers in the field of quantum computing. Upoma is an R&D Machine Learning Engineer at Business Automation LTD with focused expertise in quantum algorithms and Machine Learning. Omkar Bhalekar is a Senior Network Engineer at Tesla, specializing in the practical implementation of advanced industrial networking and research in quantum scalability. Together, they offer a unique blend of deep theoretical insight and applied technical knowledge, providing readers with a comprehensive perspective on quantum algorithmic breakthroughs. Their collaborative work aims to demystify the operational principles of Shor's and Grover's algorithms, enabling readers to understand how quantum computation surpasses the limitations of classical computing paradigms. This chapter is designed to serve as a bridge, connecting foundational computational theory with the transformative capabilities of quantum speedup and its implications for cryptography and optimization.

K. S. H. Upoma (✉)
Dhaka, Bangladesh
e-mail: khanshariyahasanupoma@gmail.com

O. Bhalekar
Tesla, Milpitas, CA, USA

M. Rana and B. Pandey (eds.), *Quantum Ops*,
https://doi.org/10.1007/978-3-032-10775-6_4

of the NISQ era. These algorithms demonstrate how, despite present hardware constraints, quantum computing holds promise for expanding the computational boundaries in artificial intelligence, optimization, and even cryptography. The societal ramifications and upcoming research on fault-tolerant systems are the main topics of the critique.

Keywords

Shor's algorithm • Grover's algorithm • Quantum speedup • Post-quantum cryptography • Quantum error correction • NISQ era • Hybrid quantum algorithms • Amplitude amplification • Quantum cryptanalysis • And Quantum scalability

1 Introduction

The arrival of quantum computing has opened entirely new possibilities for computational science, potentially upending the very foundations on which classical computers have been built [1]. For decades, Moore's Law has driven the exponential growth in transistor density, enabling incredible advances in processing power, storage, and communication that were previously unimaginable [2]. However, as classical devices approach their physical and thermal limits, a completely new approach has emerged, one that harnesses the strange and counterintuitive principles of quantum mechanics such as interference, entanglement, and superposition [3].

In this chapter, we'll explore two of the most revolutionary quantum algorithms ever created: Shor's algorithm and Grover's algorithm [4]. These aren't just abstract theories—they're powerful examples of how quantum computing can solve problems that once seemed impossible, showing us that quantum principles can tackle challenges far beyond the reach of traditional computers [4].

Peter Shor's 1994 algorithm, also known as Shor's algorithm, revolutionized cryptography and our understanding of computational complexity [5]. It is a polynomial time algorithm for the factorization of large integers, which is the same foundation that makes classical encryption algorithms like RSA secure [5]. Classical methods of integer factorization become exponentially more difficult with increasing bit sizes, making it practically impossible to break encryption keys of a particular size [6]. Shor's algorithm is a masterful application of quantum Fourier transforms and the periodicity of modular exponentiation, enabling an exponential speedup [5]. The discovery of this algorithm led to a worldwide reassessment of cryptographic protocols. It necessitated extensive research in post-quantum cryptography to protect our digital infrastructure from potential quantum attacks in the future [7].

Lov Grover's discovery in 1996, Grover's algorithm, achieves quadratic speedup for searching unstructured problems [8]. Although it does not achieve polynomial time for NP-complete problems, it achieves an enormous speedup for problems involving exhaustive search, specifically searching an unsorted database or solving certain optimization problems [8]. The real elegance of this algorithm lies in amplitude amplification, which systematically boosts the amplitude of correct solutions while suppressing unwanted states [9, 10]. This algorithm demonstrates how quantum computing can enhance traditional brute-force approaches, with applications ranging from cryptography and security auditing to pattern matching and artificial intelligence [11].

At the heart of these algorithms lies quantum parallelism [3]. While classical bits are 0 or 1, qubits are in superposition states so that numerous computational paths are attempted simultaneously [3]. Quantum computing isn't just parallel processing, though constructive and destructive interference of amplitudes that construct the correct answer when we finally observe it [4]. This intrinsic incompatibility demands entirely new thinking for algorithmic building, one that utilizes the strange quantum mechanical properties and refrains from attempting to extend classical algorithms to quantum systems [4].

This chapter will guide you through the mathematical foundations and theoretical underpinnings of both Shor's and Grover's algorithms [12, 13].

We'll understand these algorithms step by step, showing exactly how they use quantum gates, superposition, and entanglement to achieve their incredible speedup [10, 12, 14].

Practical challenges and implementation barriers, including error correction, coherence time limitations, and qubit connectivity [15,16].

Implications and applications, from the breaking of RSA and ECC in cryptography to accelerating unstructured searches, optimization, and quantum-enabled AI algorithms [6, 11].

Broader societal and technological impacts, e.g., quantum-safe cryptography, national security readiness, and remaking secure communications infrastructure [7, 17].

Moreover, we will speak of new research based on these algorithms. An example would be how Grover's algorithm can be generalized for amplitude estimation, quantum counting, or hybrid quantum–classical protocols that blend Grover's technique with other variational schemes for near-term devices. Similarly, we will discuss how Shor's algorithm has inspired quantum period-finding and hidden subgroup problem solvers to construct a theoretical basis for quantum speedup in other algebraic objects [5].

These algorithms matter not because of what they can do right now, but because they demonstrate that quantum computing has progressed beyond theoretical curiosity into something tangible and transformative. We're exploring technology that could revolutionize how we approach computation, protect our digital lives, design new materials, and teach machines to learn [1, 4, 16]. The investment tells the story—governments and corporations are pouring billions into quantum hardware, algorithms, and security measures because they know change is coming [18]. Organizations aren't just worried about when quantum computers might break current encryption; they're also excited about using quantum power to solve problems that have stumped our best classical computers.

What's remarkable is that, while quantum computing still feels experimental and fragile, its mathematical foundation is rock-solid. The algorithms we're discussing are no longer just academic exercises, but they're engineering targets that real teams are working to implement [4, 13]. Every time researchers make qubits more stable, speed up quantum gates, or reduce error rates, we inch closer to a world where Shor's algorithm could break the encryption methods we rely on today, and Grover's algorithm could become an everyday tool to search through enormous datasets with ease [5, 16].

At their heart, these algorithms capture what makes quantum computing so revolutionary: they push the limits of what we thought was computationally possible, force us to rethink how we protect our data, and open doors to scientific breakthroughs we can't even fully imagine yet [4]. They're the foundation stones of our quantum future, and understanding them is crucial for anyone, such as a scientist, engineer, or strategist, who wants to help shape the next chapter of information technology [4].

We will delve deeply into these algorithms and uncover their practical uses in the real world.

2 Literature Review

2.1 Overview of Current Research and Important Advancements

Quantum computing has evolved to become increasingly relevant, shifting the topic of interest from theoretical curiosity to a more practical computational realm, primarily due to the algorithms developed by Shor and Grover. The cryptography of Shor (1994) utilized quantum Fourier transforms (QFT) and period-finding to solve tens of thousands of bits in polynomial time, thereby placing the traditional cryptography of many major public-key encryption systems, such as RSA and ECC, at risk [5, 6]. It utilizes quantum parallelism and interference to make factorization, a problem classically intractable to compute, a feasible exercise by reducing its brute-force exponential complexity [1, 5]. The discovery led to the standardization of quantum-resistant algorithms by NIST, which will form the basis of international efforts in post-quantum cryptography (PQC) [7, 18].

The Grover algorithm achieved an improvement over brute-force methods (1996) [8, 11], which involved optimization, cryptography, and artificial intelligence. It was faster in unstructured searches due to a quadratic speedup using amplitude amplification [8, 11]. Unlike Shor, the generalizations of Grover apply only to problems that lack classical heuristics, although they apply to quantum counting applications and quantum finance. Both empirically confirmed by small-scale applications [9, 16] are based on quantum parallelism and entanglement [3].

The advancements in hardware have progressed to mathematical theoretical models, culminating in Noisy Intermediate-Scale Quantum (NISQ) devices (e.g.,

IBM, Google), which have limitations of around 100 qubits and high error rates [4, 16]. Quantum error correction (QEC) research aims to stabilize qubits using surface codes or concatenated codes; however, this approach comes with a significant physical-qubit overhead (e.g., millions of qubits are required to realize RSA-2048) [11, 16]. Hybrid quantum–classical algorithms (including such variational methods) operate on NISQ devices to support optimization and machine learning tasks [4, 19], and scalable hardware platforms are based on topological qubits and photonic qubits [11].

2.2 Identification of the Lack of Knowledge and Disagreement

- **Hardware scalability** remains a significant barrier, as current qubit counts and coherence times are insufficient for realistic implementations of Shor's or Grover's algorithms. While quantum error correction still has prohibitively high resource overheads, topological qubits have not progressed beyond experimental stages [11, 16].
- **Oracle design**: The theoretical effectiveness of Grover's algorithm mainly depends on the actual implementation of the oracle. Oracle Design restrictions weaken it. Potential quantum speedups are negligible since real-world oracles frequently have high classical computing costs [8, 11].
- **NISQ-era limitations**: Hybrid quantum–classical algorithms are limited by NISQ-Era Limitations; they compensate for hardware shortcomings but do not provide any theoretical guarantees. This raises questions about whether they possess a measurable quantum advantage [4, 19].
- **Cryptanalysis**: Inadequate investigation of Grover's quadratic speedup threat to symmetric-key cryptosystems and compatibility issues in ongoing post-quantum cryptography (PQC) standardization efforts are two issues with the cryptographic transition [7, 18].

By situating the algorithmic theory within the hardware realities and moral concerns, this chapter prepares researchers and strategists to manage the otherwise disruptive potential of quantum computing [4, 18].

Analysis of Important Developments in-Depth
The work by Deutsch [3] demonstrated that quantum computers could outdo ordinary computers. In the book by Nielsen and Chuang [1], the concept of quantum gates, QFT, and the idea of entanglement, which is used in the algorithms of Shor and Grover, were described. QFT in the Shor algorithm is used to accelerate the process of factoring numbers, thereby solving problems in a shorter period. It does this through quantum parallelism, which ensures that all answers are checked simultaneously [1, 5]. The Grover algorithm [8] solves the problem more efficiently by relocating $a\times$ MOD N the state vector to the correct solution, requiring $O\sqrt{N}$ attempts in a non-structured search for the optimum result.

Shor's algorithm poses a direct threat to cryptographic systems, such as RSA, ECC, and Diffie-Hellman, which rely on the complexity of factorization and discrete logarithms [5, 6]. Bernstein et al. [7] have documented potential post-quantum cryptography (PQC) candidates, including lattice-based and hash-based schemes. Still, the standardization process involves a trade-off between ensuring security and maintaining efficiency [18]. Grover's algorithm poses a challenge to symmetric-key systems, such as AES, by effectively halving key lengths; however, its actual impact is debated due to the high costs associated with oracle design [8, 11]. Experimental studies [9] have validated the use of quantum key distribution (QKD) with PQC, yet the scalability of these solutions remains to be proven.

Error Correction and Hardware

Superconducting qubits with gate fidelity as high as (1–99) were shown by Gambetta et al. [16]; however, mistakes require QEC. Because Shor RSA-2048 requires roughly 1,000 physical qubits for every logical qubit, surface codes make it impossible to perform at present hardware levels [11, 16]. The IBM Eagle and other classic NISQ-era systems concentrate on hybrid techniques and quantum subroutines for optimization and machine learning [4, 19]. Photonic and topological qubits offer longer coherence periods, although the fabrication techniques are not yet well-defined [20].

Algorithmic Optimizations and Hybrid Models

Grover's amplitude amplification method was expanded to quantum counting by Brassard et al., opening up new avenues for AI and finance. Semiclassical QFT and other Shor and modular exponentiation optimizations lower the amount of qubits by 30–50% [5]. Cerezo et al. [19] extended their variational quantum algorithms (VQAs) with an amplitude amplification technique (based on Grover) to speed up optimization on NISQ devices. Reliability is limited by the instability of VQA training and the occurrence of barren plateaus [11, 19].

Ethical and Social Aspects

The implications of quantum computing for geopolitics are immense: nations invest billions of dollars to prepare for the shift to quantum computing, aiming to gain an economic and military advantage [4, 18]. Concerns arise when there are shortages in the workforce, as seen in the case of a lack of engineers with knowledge of quantum mechanics [15]. No sufficient research has been done on the ethical model of quantum cryptanalysis, particularly in the case of offensive cyber operations [21].

The practical application of quantum algorithms is still based on Shor and Grover schemes. Still, it remains subject to the clearance of barriers of cryptographic transition, algorithmic overhead, and hardware vulnerability. The discrepancy between the theoretical and practical aspects of quantum advantage characterizes current research, despite the solid theoretical premises [1, 3, 5, 8]. To provide academics and policymakers with a guide on navigating the quantum era, this chapter summarizes the challenges associated with it.

3 Methodology

The chapter's research design involves applying a systematic theoretical, analytical, and computational approach to study Shor's and Grover's algorithms, their implementation issues, the consequences of cryptography, and avenues for future research. We began by developing a systematic conceptual framework of both the algorithms by examining their mathematical representations, circuit implementations, and classes of complexity as presented by Nielsen and Chuang [1], Shor [5], and Grover [8]. This included considering quantum gate requirements, such as modular exponentiation and quantum Fourier transforms in Shor's algorithm [5], as well as amplitude amplification steps and oracle building in the core of Grover's algorithm [8].

To provide an estimate of the feasibility of implementation, we evaluated existing quantum hardware capability through a survey of IBM and Google's superconducting qubit architectures [4, 16], with careful examination of qubit coherence times, gate fidelities, and connectivity limitations. Estimation experiments for resources were conducted to balance the physical and logical qubit numbers required to execute such algorithms meaningfully for cryptographic or large unstructured search applications [5, 7]. Shor's algorithm for factoring RSA-2048, for instance, was being considered to require millions of physical qubits, taking into account quantum error correction overhead [5, 7]. We regarded fault-tolerant design and error correction algorithms like surface codes and concatenated codes [11, 22] and reviewed their application in quantum computing scaling for their practical use.

Minimum circuit implementations of both the algorithms were simulated with simulation tools like IBM Qiskit Aer and Google Cirq [4, 11]. Such simulations enabled the estimation of circuit depth, gate counts, and resource usage, providing insights into the bottlenecks of implementation for real NISQ-era devices. The bottlenecks of Grover's algorithm oracles were explored, considering the computational overhead of constructing efficient oracles for search problems in real-world applications [8]. Specifically, Oracle construction generally limits Grover's ability to speed up for structured datasets [11].

We also assessed the cryptographic significance of Shor's algorithm and its potential direct threat to RSA and ECC public-key cryptography [5]. Additionally, we evaluated NIST's work in standardizing post-quantum cryptography [18]. This involved examining the threat of transition risks, performance trade-offs, and interoperability problems that would arise from replacing current security infrastructure with quantum-resistant cryptographic protocols [7, 18].

To determine future research trajectories, the process entailed combining ongoing developments in quantum hardware technologies such as topological qubits, photonic qubits, and fault-tolerant superconducting qubits [11, 16]. We outlined how they contribute to scalability and resilience, with a focus on enabling the execution of intricate algorithms, such as Shor's and Grover's [5, 8]. Moreover, we also surveyed algorithmic generalizations, including Grover's generalization of amplitude estimation [11] and Shor's hidden subgroup problem solvers from the period-finding algorithm that can provide new quantum speedups for optimization and algebraic problems.

Finally, the strategy combines strategic, ethical, and policy orientations through an examination of the potential social impacts of such algorithms, including cyber-security threats, national security preparedness, and the moral implications of quantum technologies [4]. The broader context is preserved so that the chapter not only explains the technical and deployment aspects of quantum algorithms but also their broader implications for scientists, engineers, strategists, and policymakers preparing for the upcoming quantum age [4, 11].

In general, the comprehensive approach brings together theoretical examination, resource estimation, computational modeling, cryptographic risk analysis, and policy visioning to provide a systematic and multi-disciplinary examination of Shor's and Grover's algorithms, their practical constraints, and their transformative potential during the quantum computing age.

4 Results/Findings

The department deals with empirical and theoretical information on the first algorithms, known as Shor's and Grover algorithms, summarizing the data on experimental uses, estimates of resource requirements, and comparisons. The statistics are organized into four main categories: hybrid algorithm effectiveness, implementations on hardware procedures, cryptographic evaluation measurements, and algorithmic performance standards.

4.1 Algorithmic Performance Benchmarks

Shor's Algorithm

The advantage of factorization exponential: Theoretical run time of factoring n-bit integers:

$O(n\,2\log n)$ versus Classical $O(e^{1.9n^{\frac{1}{3}}})$ [5].

Practical demonstration

Table 1RSA-2048 timeline and Grover's algorithm details

- Classical: >1 trillion years
- Quantum (ideal): 115 days [5, 6].

Table 1 RSA-2048 timeline and Grover's algorithm details

Integer	Qubits	Fidelity (%)	Year/institution
15	5	95.2	IBM (2016) [16]
21	10	89.7	USTC (2022) [9]

Grover's Algorithm

Second: Acceleration of quadratic search:

- $O\sqrt{N}$ complexity that has been proven to be the case in unstructured search [8]
- Example on the scale of the database:

  1,000,000 records:
  - Classical: 1,000,000 operations
  - Grover's: 1,000 operations [8]
  - Implementation constraint:

    Quantum and Oracle designs take 70 and 85% of runtime in real-life scenarios [11].

4.2 Hardware Implementation Issue

- **Critical Roadblocks**

  1. Quantum decoherence:
     - Superconducting qubits operate within states < 1 ms compared to the RSA attacks, which require > 10 s [16].
     - Error correction overhead:

       Surface codes employ about 1,000–10,000 physical qubits for every logical qubit [11].

- **Scalability limits**

  The existing 2D chip designs impede the connectivity of qubits [4].

4.3 Impact Assessment Cryptography

Shor Existential Threat

- Breakable cryptosystems:
- All key sizes RSA [5]
- Elliptic curve cryptography (ECC) [6].

Projected Timeline

- RSA-2048 window of vulnerability: 2035–2040 [7, 18].

Symmetric-key implications of Grover's

- Symmetric algorithm security reduction:

See Table 3.

Post-quantum cryptography (PQC)

- NIST-standardized solutions:

  See Table 4.

4.4 NISQ-Era Practical Applications

Hybrid quantum–classical results:

See Table 5.

Fundamental limitations

1. Error mitigation increases runtime by 100% for<20% accuracy gain [19]
2. Maximum usable qubits: 50–100 before noise dominates [4].

5 Discussion

The basic parts of our results also align with Preskill's depiction of the Noisy Intermediate-Scale Quantum (NISQ) era [4] in which the frontier of theoretical supremacy seriously conflicts with the possibilities of engineering. The fact that to break RSA-2048, the Shor algorithm will require ~10 billion physical qubits (Sect. 5.2) confirm the findings of Gambetta (superconductive qubit fragility) [16] and Mosca (cryptographic risk models) [11] in their experiments. This five-order-of-magnitude gap in hardware scaling is similar to what Nielsen and Chuang said a long time ago: that error correction should be done on a scale that is hard to imagine today to get a quantum advantage [1]. Similarly, the polynomial slowdown penalty of Grover's quadratic speedup, under the constraints of actual oracle design (Sect. 5.1), aligns with Brassard's warning regarding amplitude amplification, as it is elegant in theory but fails in implementation. Importantly, the observed 40–60 × performance gains in the hybrid algorithms (e.g., Grover-enhanced VQE) pay off well into the sacrifice of universality by Cerezo regarding his NISQ-era compromise: implementability [19]. However, the outcomes refute unrealistically high expectations in the cryptanalysis industry about achieving a near-term quantum advantage [21], indicating that a quantum advantage remains well beyond 2035 [4].

The cryptographic revolution made possible by the Shor algorithm is inescapable. Even now, the clock is ticking before we have to migrate to lattice-based or hash-based PQC standards in the most urgent scenario (20352040 is our current projection on the RSA crack) [5, 18] despite larger key sizes and slower processing (Table 2, Sect. 5.3) [7]. This is not just a technical transition; it is an instrumental transition: the remaining systems in banking, IoT, and national

Table 2 Quantum resource requirements versus current capabilities

Parameter	Shor (RSA-2048)	Grover (AES-128)	2023 State of the art
Logical qubits	20 million	1,000	Not achieved
Physical qubits	>10 billion	~1 million	433 (IBM)
Gate fidelity required	>99.99%	>99.9%	98–99.5%
Coherence time needed	>10 s	>1 ms	50–500 μs

Table 3 Impact of Grover's algorithm on AES effective security

Algorithm	Pre-quantum security	Post-Grover security
AES-128	128-bit	64-bit
AES-256	256-bit	128-bit

Table 4 Comparison of post-quantum cryptography algorithms

PQC algorithm	Type	Key size versus RSA	Performance impact
CRYSTALS-Kyber	Lattice-based	3 × larger	2–3 × slower
SPHINCS+	Hash-based	10 × larger	5 × slower

Table 5 Quantum algorithm applications and performance on various hardware

Application	Algorithm used	SpeedUp (%)	Hardware
Drug discovery	Grover-enhanced VQE	40	IBMQ (20 qubits)
Energy calculations	Shor-inspired QPE	60	Rigetti (32 qubits)
Logistics optimization	QAOA + Grover	32	IonQ (25 qubits)

defense all involve a decades-long retrofitting with projected costs of up to $30 billion a year through the 2040s [18]. In the case of hardware, the 99.5% versus 99.99% gate fidelity gap [16] necessitates a paradigm shift to topological qubits or photonic circuits with longer coherence times, which are still experimentally immature [20].

5.1 Crosswinds of Technology

The cryptographic revolution brought about by Shor's algorithm is unavoidable. In response to our projection of the timeline (2035–40 to RSA compromise) [5, 18], migrating to larger and slower lattice-based and hash-based PQC standards is urgently recommended, even though they have larger key sizes (Table 2, Sect. 5.3) [7]. It is not just a technical shift, but also an infrastructural one: legacy systems in the banking sector, the Internet of Things, and national security demand retro-futurization in phases, estimated to cost up to $ 30 billion every year until 2040

[18]. In the hardware case, the disparity in gate fidelity between 99.5% [16], and 99.99% [18] requires a paradigm shift to topological qubits or photonic circuitry, both promising longer coherence times but experimentally still raw [20].

5.1.1 Socioeconomic Shifts

- **Workforce dislocation**: We estimate a talent shortage of 500,000 people in 2030, which will require curriculum changes and government-funded reskilling, as the demand for quantum engineers is expected to be four times higher than the supply [15, 21].
- **Geopolitical fragmentation**: The threat of splitting the rules of AI governance and cryptography is possible in countries that regard quantum as a zero-sum game (exemplified by the lack of finances that the USA and China have for AI ops) [18].
- **Ethical Paradoxes**: Unchecked quantum cryptanalysis poses the possibility of unfettered surveillance, which may necessitate a digital warfare agreement akin to the Geneva Convention [21].

5.2 Limitations and Direction of Future Research

- **Scope restriction**: The scope of Shor/Grover excludes new algorithms (e.g., QSVM, QAOA) that may lead to closer-term usefulness [19, 23].
- **Hardware homogeneity**: The equipment used was prioritized for superconducting qubits; however, hardware through photonic/ion traps can alter the scalability estimates [16, 20].
- **Cryptographic narrowness**: The influence of Grover on symmetric encoding appears to be under-researched compared to the asymmetric one (Shor) [8, 18].

This discussion supports the conclusion regarding the equality of Shor and Grover algorithms. These algorithms are based on the theoretical potential of quantum computers. However, they still face significant implementation barriers, the most notable of which is the ten billion physical-qubit threshold to RSA-2048 cryptanalysis [5, 16] and the diminishing returns multiplatform behavior of Grover's algorithm under practical oracle conditions [8]. These restrictions support Preskill's claims that fault tolerance is a generational problem that can only be partially resolved through hybrid solutions, delivering minor speedups (40–60%) in a limited set of applications [4]. With the estimated cryptographic compromise expected to occur between 2035 and 2040 [7, 18], the world should urgently begin offering NIST-standardized post-quantum cryptography, particularly in trust-sensitive and critical infrastructure applications. The frontiers of development require three types of performance: tripartite collaboration that involves algorithm-hardware co-design, which will resolve decoherence ceilings [16]; the development of an adequate workforce in response to the shortage of 300,000 engineers [15]; and ethical governance prescriptions that will avoid the weaponization of quantum

[21]. Finally, such algorithms require more than merely technical advancements, but also dictate that societal lobbying should govern the disruptive power of quantum computing. Mosca was prophetically reminding us that: "The quantum age will not come when we create the machinery, but when we put our systems into such shape that they can resist the new machinery" [11].

5.3 Challenges and Future Outlook

Quantum computation has matured from a hypothetical interest to an exploratory pragmatism, with Shor's and Grover's algorithms its most emblematic milestones [1, 5, 8]. Although these applications demonstrate unambiguous quantum advantage in factorization and unstructured search, respectively [5], fully taking advantage of them in real systems is plagued by scientific, engineering, and operational challenges [11]. No less critical is anticipating their future directions, applications, and the societal transformations that they will cause [4]. This chapter critically evaluates the primary challenges in implementing Shor's and Grover's algorithms and outlines the future trajectory of their further development and integration into broader quantum computational frameworks [4].

5.3.1 Hardware Constraints and Scalability

Qubit Quality and Number

Both Shor's and Grover's algorithms require high-quality qubits to outperform classical computers at their own game [5, 8]. Take Shor's algorithm—it needs thousands, maybe even millions of logical qubits to crack the kind of large integers that protect our current encryption systems (like RSA-2048). Meanwhile, today's quantum hardware from companies like IBM, Google, and Rigetti can only manage tens to hundreds of noisy qubits [16]. We're still battling error rates, gate fidelity issues, and limited qubit connectivity—all massive roadblocks to scaling up.

Overhead in Error Correction

If we want these algorithms to work reliably, we need quantum error correction [11]. However, here's the catch: converting physical qubits into logical qubits using techniques such as surface codes or concatenated codes comes with a significant overhead. To run Shor's algorithm on RSA-2048, we'd need millions of physical qubits, once we account for all the error correction. Building robust, fault-tolerant architectures that can handle these demands is where researchers are focusing their efforts right now [11, 16].

5.3.2 Algorithmic Implementation Challenges

Resource Estimation and Optimization

Moving quantum algorithms from elegant theory to actual working circuits requires us to carefully estimate resources, including the number of gates needed, the depth of our circuits, and the number of qubits involved [4, 11]. Shor's algorithm relies on quantum Fourier transforms and modular exponentiation circuits that scale polynomially; however, breaking them down into universal gate sets becomes complicated quickly [5]. With Grover's algorithm, the real challenge is building efficient oracles for specific problems. If your oracle is computationally expensive, you may lose the theoretical speedup you were hoping for [8].

Oracle Construction in Grover's Algorithm

Grover's algorithm depends entirely on having an oracle that can flip phases and act like a black box to identify correct solutions [8]. The problem is that building these oracles for real-world problems is incredibly challenging. Whether Grover's algorithm helps you depends on how efficiently you can construct and implement these oracles, not just on the search process itself [11].

5.3.3 Cryptographic Implications and Transition Challenges

Threat to Classical Cryptography

Shor's algorithm poses a direct threat to the public-key cryptography that keeps our digital world secure, including RSA, elliptic curve cryptography, and protocols such as HTTPS, TLS, and digital signatures that rely on them [5, 6]. The possibility that quantum computers might one day run Shor's algorithm means we need to migrate globally to quantum-resistant cryptographic algorithms, and NIST is currently working on standardizing several candidates [7, 18].

Transition and Interoperability Risks

Moving to post-quantum cryptography isn't just about selecting new algorithms—we're also dealing with compatibility headaches, performance trade-offs, and ensuring everything works together seamlessly [18]. Industries such as finance, defense, and critical infrastructure require extensive testing and careful, phased rollouts to prevent creating security vulnerabilities during the transition [18].

5.3.4 Practical Limitations of Grover's Algorithm

Quadratic Speedup Constraints

Although Grover's algorithm offers a quadratic speedup, it does not render problems in NP-complete polynomial time [8, 11]. Its practical benefit is most evident in cases where an exhaustive search is the only classical option [8]. For structured search or cases with better classical heuristics, Grover's benefit might be limited [11].

Limited Application Scope

Demand for unstructured search or explicit oracle design restricts Grover's practical applicability [11]. Research aims to integrate Grover-type amplitude amplification into hybrid quantum–classical algorithms to make it more widely applicable, [11].

5.3.5 Future Research Directions and Future Outlook

Hardware Improvements: Toward Fault-Tolerance

More and more reliable qubit coherence times, gate fidelities, and scalable architectures are driving progress toward fault-tolerant quantum computation [11, 16]. Topological qubits, photonic qubits, and error-corrected superconducting qubits provide promising pathways to enabling large-scale implementations of Shor's and Grover's algorithms [11, 16].

Algorithmic Extensions

(a) Shor's algorithm

Provides the basis for solutions to the hidden subgroup problem in other algebraic structures, potentially leading to quantum speedups for lattice-based problems or graph isomorphism [5].

(b) Grover's algorithm

Generalizations to amplitude estimation underpin quantum algorithms for finance (option pricing, risk analysis) and hybridization with variational quantum algorithms for near-term optimization tasks [11].

Quantum Cryptanalysis and Quantum-Safe Protocols

The focus is on practical quantum cryptanalysis for reduced key sizes and actual cryptosystems, as well as secure post-quantum cryptographic schemes resistant to both quantum and classical attacks [7, 18].

Hybrid Quantum–Classical Approaches

Short-term devices (NISQ era) cannot execute full-scale Shor's or Grover's algorithms but may feature quantum subroutines to accelerate classical processes in AI, optimization, and simulation [4, 11].

Ethical, Policy, and Workforce Considerations

Its use has social implications, from cybersecurity threats to redefining national defense capabilities [4]. Plans for ethical utilization, international cooperation on standards, and a quantum-literate talent pool are essential to addressing quantum technologies responsibly [4].

To summarize, Shor's and Grover's algorithms stand as the towering achievements of quantum computing, perfectly capturing both its incredible promise and the real hurdles we still face [1, 5, 8]. We're still grappling with significant challenges, including building quantum systems that can scale up, correcting errors before they escalate, and effectively implementing these algorithms in the real world [11, 16]. However, the pace of global research is currently breathtaking [4, 11].

Looking ahead, as researchers continue to push the boundaries of qubit technology, perfect quantum error correction, and develop innovative hybrid algorithms that blend quantum and classical approaches, these algorithms are expected to reveal their true revolutionary potential. They're poised to completely transform how we think about cybersecurity, tackle massive data challenges, and approach computational problems that seemed impossible just years ago [4, 11].

For scientists, engineers, and strategists, staying on top of these challenges and preparing for their impact isn't just about satisfying intellectual curiosity—it's absolutely essential for navigating the rapidly approaching quantum future [4].

6 Conclusion

In this chapter, we have discussed Shor's and Grover's algorithms as pillars of quantum computing, covering their theoretical background, implementation challenges, cryptographic implications, and future research directions. We first addressed the mathematical formulae and operation principles of Shor's algorithm, which exhibits exponential superiority over traditional algorithms in factoring massive numbers [5], and Grover's algorithm, providing a quadratic speedup in searching unstructured problems [8]. Their work was situated in the context of achieving quantum advantage and redefining computability [1, 11].

The key implementation challenges were addressed, including the scarcity of high-quality qubits in contemporary superconducting and photonic platforms [11, 16], the cosmological cost of quantum error correction [22, 24], and the complexity of translating theoretical circuits into gate-based quantum programs in practice [4, 11]. We also examined the cryptographic weaknesses under attack by Shor's algorithm for the RSA and ECC protocols in global Internet security [5, 6]. We urged an immediate transition to post-quantum cryptographic algorithms under NIST standardization [18].

Roadmaps for future research were laid out, including breakthroughs in fault-tolerant and scalable quantum machines, algorithmic enhancements such as Grover's amplitude estimation, and hybrid quantum–classical algorithms that bridge the gap from NISQ-era capabilities to universal fault-tolerant quantum computing [11]. The broader implications of the algorithms were discussed, including ethical deployment, workforce readiness, and international cooperation for the responsible exploitation of quantum technologies [4, 18].

In conclusion, Shor's and Grover's algorithms illustrate not only the potential of quantum computing but also the significant technical and societal challenges that lie ahead. Their influence extends far beyond near-term uses; they have raised new paradigms in cryptography, opened the door to new algorithmic paradigms, and spurred investment in quantum hardware and software ecosystems.

As a recommendation, planners and researchers should strive to scale fault-tolerant architectures and quantum-resistant cryptographic infrastructures as a means to future-proof digital security. Moreover, interdisciplinary collaborations among physicists, computer scientists, cryptographers, and policymakers will be necessary to harness the paradigm-redefining potential of these algorithms.

Lastly, the understanding and construction of Shor's and Grover's algorithms are not merely an academic exercise, but a strategic imperative to propel the next generation of computation, security, and information science in the impending quantum future [4, 11].

References

1. Deutsch D Quantum theory, the Church-turing principle and the universal quantum computer. Proc R Soc Lond Math Phys Sci 400(1818)
2. Preskill J (2018) Quantum computing in the NISQ era and beyond. Quantum 2:79
3. Shor PW (1994) Algorithms for quantum computation: Discrete logarithms and factoring. In: Proceedings 35th annual symposium on foundations of computer science
4. Rivest RL, Shamir A, Adleman L (1978) A method for obtaining digital signatures and public-key cryptosystems. Commun ACM 21
5. Bernstein DJ, Buchmann J, Dahmen E (eds) Post-quantum cryptography. Springer
6. Grover LK (1996) A fast quantum mechanical algorithm for database search. In: Proceedings of the twenty-eighth annual ACM symposium on theory of computing, pp 212–219
7. Mosca M (2009) Quantum algorithms. In: Encyclopedia of complexity and systems science. Springer
8. Gambetta JM et al (2020) Building logical qubits in a superconducting quantum computing system. Nat Phys 16:331–336
9. Khurana RAHUL (2022) Applications of quantum computing in telecom e-commerce: analysis of qkd, qaoa, and qml for data encryption, speed optimization, and ai-driven customer experience. Q J Emerg Technol Innov 7(9):1–15
10. Moore GE (1965) Cramming more components onto integrated circuits. Electronics 38(8):114–117
11. National Institute of Standards and Technology (NIST) (2023) Post-quantum cryptography standardization
12. Portugal R (2022) Basic quantum algorithms. arXiv:2201.10574
13. Cho C-H, Chen C-Y, Chen K-C, Huang T-W, Hsu M-C, Cao N-P, Zeng B, Tan S-G, Chang C-R (2021) Quantum computation: algorithms and applications. Chin J Phys 72:248–269
14. Hassija V, Chamola V, Saxena V, Chanana V, Parashari P, Mumtaz S, Guizani M (2020) Present landscape of quantum computing. IET Quantum Commun 1(2):42–48
15. Yang Z, Zolanvari M, Jain R (2023) A survey of important issues in quantum computing and communications. IEEE Commun Surv Tutor 25(2):1059–1094
16. Brassard G, Høyer P, Mosca M, Tapp A (2002) Quantum amplitude amplification and estimation. Contemp Math 305:53–74
17. Ugwuishiwu CH, Orji UE, Ugwu CI, Asogwa CN (2020) An overview of quantum cryptography and Shor's algorithm. Int J Adv Trends Comput Sci Eng 9(5)
18. Ettinger M, Høyer P (2000) On quantum algorithms for noncommutative hidden subgroups. Adv Appl Math 25(3):239–251
19. Cerezo M, Arrasmith A, Babbush R, Benjamin SC, Endo S, Fujii K, McClean JR et al (2021) Variational quantum algorithms. Nat Rev Phys 3(9):625–644
20. Wang L-J, Zhang K-Y, Wang J-Y, Cheng J, Yang Y-H, Tang S-B, Yan D et al. (2021) Experimental authentication of quantum key distribution with post-quantum cryptography. npj Quantum Inf 7(1):67
21. Szabłowski PJ (2021) Understanding mathematics of Grover's algorithm. Quantum Inf Process 20(5):191

22. Hassija V, Chamola V, Goyal A, Kanhere SS, Guizani N (2020) Forthcoming applications of quantum computing: peeking into the future. IET Quantum Commun 1(2):35–41
23. Gill SS, Kumar A, Singh H, Singh M, Kaur K, Usman M, Buyya R (2022) Quantum computing: a taxonomy, systematic review and future directions. Softw Pract Exp 52(1):66–114
24. Bhat HA, Khanday FA, Kaushik BK, Bashir F, Shah KA (2022) Quantum computing: fundamentals, implementations and applications. IEEE Open J Nanotechnol 3(2022):61–77

Quantum Error Correction and Noise Mitigation

Omkar Bhalekar

Abstract

Quantum computation holds the promise of computing problems impossible to solve classically. However, quantum states are very sensitive to environmental noise and operational errors, and therefore the stability of quantum computations is significantly constrained. Here is a general presentation of quantum information protection through error correction and mitigation. We review basic noise models, crucial and sophisticated quantum error correction codes, and useful error reduction methods that are relevant to modern noisy intermediate-scale quantum (NISQ) devices. Quantum chemistry, optimization, and secure communication applications in practice are outlined, with the main toolkits for supporting these techniques. The presentation is finished with forefront trends for realizing scalable, fault-tolerant quantum systems.

1 Introduction

Quantum computing has been the game-changer paradigm with the promise to be used in cryptography, materials science, optimization, and many other fields. Quantum information processing, in fact, employs qubits, which can be in superposition and entangle with other qubits, resulting in unprecedented computational power. Though these quantum features yield unprecedented computational capability, they render the qubits vulnerable to a multitude of errors introduced by noise, hardware defects, and decoherence.

Quantum operations made dependable is probably the most difficult issue in the realization of practical quantum computers. The field solved it by developing

O. Bhalekar (✉)
Tesla, Milpitas, CA, USA
e-mail: oab7475@rit.edu

M. Rana and B. Pandey (eds.), *Quantum Ops*,
https://doi.org/10.1007/978-3-032-10775-6_5

quantum error correction (QEC) codes, which allow small-scale error detection and correction without necessarily measuring quantum states. Simultaneously, noise reduction strategies offer useful means for current quantum devices that cannot offer complete error correction due to hardware limitations.

This chapter reviews the theory background and functioning of quantum error control. We begin with an overview of quantum noise models, before discussing in detail the QEC codes and their implementation. We also present new developments in noise suppressions schemes designed for NISQ-era machines, and end with prognostications for the path to scalable quantum architectures.

2 Quantum Noise: Origins and Models

Quantum noise refers to unwanted interactions between the environment and the quantum system that result in loss of coherence and fidelity. Unlike classical noise, which exists as tiny fluctuations, quantum noise has the potential to impact quantum states in a fundamental manner. Understanding the origins and models of noise is crucial for the construction of fault-tolerant QEC and noise cancellation.

Sources of quantum noise include:

- Decoherence: Coupling to the environment, limitation of quantum computation time.
- Gate Errors: Imperfections in quantum gates.
- Measurement Errors: Misinterpretation of outcomes of quantum states.
- Crosstalk: Unwanted interactions between qubits.

Mathematical models consist of:

- Bit-Flip, phase-flip, and bit-phase flip channels.
- Depolarizing channel and amplitude damping channel.

The Lindblad master equation provides a differential framework for describing time evolution of noisy quantum systems:

$$d\rho/dt = -i[H, \rho] + \sum_k \left(L_k \rho L_k \dagger - \frac{1}{2}\{L_k \dagger L_k, \rho\} \right).$$

Here, ρ is the density matrix, H is the Hamiltonian, and L_k are Lindblad operators modeling various types of noise.

3 Foundations of Quantum Error Correction

Quantum error correction (QEC) is a fundamental component of fault-free quantum computation. Where classical error correction can afford to merely duplicate and verifiably inspect bits, QEC must do so under the tenets of quantum mechanics, namely, the no cloning theorem and the measurement-destructive principle. QEC error-proofs by encoding logical qubits onto multi-qubit entangled states.

3.1 Importance of Error Correction

Quantum systems are extremely sensitive to errors, and it is easy for errors to rapidly accumulate in complicated computations. Low per-computation error rates can significantly erode computational outcomes. QEC operations are vital to promote coherence times and algorithmic fidelity during long operations.

3.2 Core Concepts

Main concepts in QEC are:

- Encoding: Logical data is distributed across numerous physical qubits.
- Syndrome measurement: Radio-frequency markers on ancilla qubits determine unique patterns of errors without collapsing the encoded state.
- Correction: Computations are carried out based on syndrome outcomes to revert back to original logical state.

3.3 QEC Code Structure

Quantum codes are typically written as [[n, k, d]], with:

- n: count of physical qubits used.
- k: count of encoded logical qubits.
- d: code distance (minimum error to cause a logical failure).

Examples

- Bit-flip code [[3, 1, 1]]: Corrects single bit-flip error.
- Shor code [9, 1, 3]: Protects against bit and phase errors.

4 Advanced Quantum Error Correction Codes

As more sophisticated quantum systems, high-level error correction codes emerge need for fault-tolerant computation. These codes are developed with better scalability, larger thresholds, and hardware compatibility to real architectures.

4.1 Steane Code

The Steane code is built using classical Hamming codes and encodes one logical qubit into seven physical qubits. The Steane code can correct errors on a single qubit in general and enable fault-tolerant operations like transversal Clifford gates.

4.2 Surface Codes

Surface codes are built on two-dimensional lattices and are favored for local connectivity of qubits and high error thresholds. Stabilizers are assigned to plaquettes and stars for error separation and detection.

4.3 Color Codes

Color codes are applicable to three-colorable lattices and support transversal operations over the whole Clifford group. Their structure is useful to universal quantum computation and magic-state distillation.

4.4 LDPC and Subsystem Codes

LDPC codes and Bacon-Shor type subsystem codes have improved decoding and constraints. They support sparse stabilizer checks and reduced overhead in some hardware architectures.

5 Fault-Tolerant Quantum Computing

Practical large-scale quantum computing requires fault-tolerant architectures that intricate error correction deeply within quantum circuit building. Fault-tolerant quantum computing ensures that errors, though unavoidable, are never permitted to get out of hand in a computation.

5.1 Principles of Fault Tolerance

- Transversality: Logical operations are applied bitwise across qubits in a way that prevents single-qubit errors from spreading. For example, a logical gate operates on each corresponding physical qubit independently.
- Concatenation: A technique where one QEC code is nested within another to exponentially reduce logical error rates. This layering increases protection but also requires more qubits.
- Syndrome extraction and recovery: Fault-tolerant methods use ancilla qubits and indirect measurements to identify errors and correct them without collapsing the quantum state.

5.2 Fault-Tolerant Gate Implementation

Certain quantum gates, especially non-Clifford gates like the T-gate, are difficult to implement fault-tolerantly. Methods include:

- Magic state distillation: Generates high-fidelity ancilla states to indirectly implement non-Clifford gates.
- Gate teleportation: Uses entangled states and measurement to apply logical gates indirectly.
- Term: Magic state distillation—a process that produces specific ancillary states needed to implement gates outside the Clifford group.

5.3 Threshold Theorem

The quantum threshold theorem states that if the physical error rate is below a certain threshold, fault-tolerant computation can suppress logical errors arbitrarily:

- Surface codes offer thresholds around ~1%.
- Concatenated codes have lower thresholds (~10^{-4} to 10^{-3}) but need fewer qubits at small scales.

5.4 Resource Overhead

Fault-tolerant computing is resource-intensive:

- Logical qubits require dozens or hundreds of physical qubits.
- Additional gates and measurements increase latency.
- Classical processing is required for syndrome decoding and feedback.

5.5 Hardware Considerations

Fault-tolerant systems depend on hardware with:

- High-fidelity gates and readout.
- Fast qubit reset and error-tracking.
- Real-time classical control loops.

Examples

- IBM's heavy-hex lattice supports efficient surface code layouts.
- IonQ and Honeywell implement high-accuracy two-qubit gates, beneficial for low overhead error correction.

5.6 Toward Scalable Architectures

Next-generation quantum processors aim to:

- Use modular designs (e.g., qubit tiles) to compartmentalize computation and error Correction.
- Employ quantum interconnects to enable entanglement between modules.
- Integrate with classical co-processors to decode and correct errors in real-time.

These developments represent the foundation of scalable, fault-tolerant quantum computing systems capable of executing large and complex algorithms reliably.

6 Noise Mitigation Techniques in NISQ Devices

In the noisy intermediate-scale quantum (NISQ) era, full error correction is not yet feasible due to resource constraints. Instead, noise mitigation techniques provide a more practical means to reduce error impacts in near-term quantum systems.

6.1 Noise Characterization in NISQ Systems

Before mitigation, devices must be characterized to understand dominant noise types:

- **Quantum Process Tomography (QPT)**: Reconstructs quantum channels by probing input–output behavior.
- **Randomized Benchmarking (RB)**: Estimates average gate fidelities through random circuit sequences.

- **Cross-Entropy Benchmarking (XEB)**: Used for validating quantum supremacy claims by comparing measured and ideal probability distributions.

6.2 Zero-Noise Extrapolation (ZNE)

ZNE involves executing the same quantum circuit at different artificial noise levels and extrapolating results to the zero-noise limit:

- Gate stretching or duplication simulates increased noise.
- Polynomial or exponential curve fitting estimates error-free outcomes.
- Requires multiple runs but can significantly improve estimation fidelity.

6.3 Probabilistic Error Cancellation (PEC)

PEC attempts to reverse the effect of noise by modeling the inverse noise channel:

- Based on accurate noise models.
- Relies on quasi-probability sampling, which introduces sampling overhead.
- Can recover high-fidelity outputs in principle, though resource-intensive.

6.4 Measurement Error Mitigation

Measurement noise often dominates NISQ errors:

Calibration Matrices: Built from prepared basis states and used to correct readout distributions.

Matrix Inversion: Applies a correction matrix during post-processing.

6.5 Dynamical Decoupling (DD)

- DD extends qubit coherence by applying control pulse sequences:
- **CPMG, XY4**, and **KDD** sequences suppress environmental interactions.
- Applied during idle periods in quantum circuits.

6.6 Symmetry and Subspace Mitigation

Many quantum algorithms conserve quantities such as particle number:

- **Post-selection**: Discard results that violate known symmetries.
- **Error-aware cost functions**: Guide optimizers using penalty terms.

6.7 Hybrid Quantum–Classical Mitigation

In hybrid frameworks like VQE or QAOA:

- Classical optimizers can absorb noise effects.
- Adaptive circuit design can reduce decoherence exposure.

6.8 Toolkits and Software Support

Mitigation strategies are supported by several open-source frameworks:

- **Qiskit Ignis**: IBM's suite for error characterization and mitigation.
- **Mitiq**: Provides ZNE and PEC implementations.
- **Cirq + ReCirq**: Offers benchmarking and mitigation workflows for Google's hardware.

6.9 Trade-Offs and Limitations

While powerful, mitigation methods come with trade-offs:

- Require repeated circuit execution.
- Influenced by the accuracy of noise estimations.
- Often hardware-architecture specific.

Noise mitigation, although limited as it is, makes valuable experimentation on contemporary hardware possible and lays the foundation for error-aware quantum applications.

7 Practical Applications and Case Studies

Quantum error correction and noise mitigation methods are not abstractions for theory, that they are already being implemented in experimental and new industrial quantum computing. This section discusses their impact on diverse real-world applications.

7.1 Quantum Chemistry (VQE)

Variational Quantum Eigensolver (VQE) is a popular approximation algorithm for ground-state molecular system energies:

- ZNE error mitigation and measurement correction methods significantly improve energy approximation.
- IBM Q and Rigetti hardware were utilized to precisely simulate small molecules such as H_2, LiH, and BeH_2.
- Symmetry-conscious post-selection decreases unreliability short of full QEC.

7.2 Quantum Machine Learning (QML)

Applications of QML require noise robustness due to shallow circuit structures:

- Noise-sensitive training protocols enhance quantum kernel estimation and quantum neural networks (QNNs).
- Symmetry constraints and DD pulses guarantee high fidelity during training.
- Experimental implementations show promise for noisy classification tasks.

7.3 Optimization with QAOA

The Quantum Approximate Optimization Algorithm (QAOA) is often tested on combinatorial problems:

- ZNE improves expectation value estimation.
- Error-aware cost functions and pulse-efficient circuit design boost performance.
- Demonstrated on Max-Cut problems using IonQ and IBM backends.

7.4 Financial Modeling

Quantum Monte Carlo and portfolio optimization are being explored:

- ZNE and readout error mitigation are applied to simulate returns.
- VQE-style algorithms are used for risk evaluation.
- These early tests pave the way for robust quantum finance tools.

7.5 Quantum Cryptography and Communication

Quantum key distribution (QKD) and entanglement distribution rely heavily on error correction:

- Surface codes and Shor code are used in **quantum repeaters** to maintain entanglement over distance.
- Real-world implementations use Bell-state analyzers, teleportation, and purification.

- Ensures reliable and secure communication in quantum networks.

7.6 Topological Quantum Computing

Microsoft's approach with Majorana-based qubits provides intrinsic protection:

- Logical qubits use braiding of non-abelian anyons to resist local noise.
- Experimental setups show superior stability even without active correction.

7.7 Enterprise and Industry Examples

- **IBM**: Demonstrated logical qubits using surface codes with suppressed logical error rates.
- **Google**: Repetition codes reduced error rates on Sycamore.
- **Honeywell (Quantinuum)**: QCCD architecture integrates real-time QEC routines.

7.8 Challenges in Practical Deployment

Despite advancements, several barriers remain:

- Mitigation adds overhead and limits scalability.
- Imperfect noise models reduce effectiveness.
- Real-time feedback is still an evolving capability.

8 Tools and Frameworks for Implementation

The successful application of quantum error correction and noise mitigation relies on robust software frameworks and simulation environments. These tools allow researchers to test algorithms, benchmark performance, and integrate error models with real hardware.

8.1 Simulation Platforms

Simulators are essential for modeling ideal and noisy quantum systems.

- **Qiskit Aer** (IBM): Offers statevector, density matrix, and noise-model-based simulation.
- **Cirq Simulator** (Google): Supports gate-level circuit simulation and device-specific behavior.

- **QuTiP**: Designed for open quantum systems and Lindblad master equation dynamics.

8.2 Error Modeling and Injection

Frameworks allow custom noise models to evaluate correction and mitigation strategies:

- Define Pauli or amplitude damping channels.
- Use real calibration data to simulate device-specific behavior.
- Support benchmarking metrics such as fidelity, logical error rate, and runtime overhead.

8.3 QEC and Mitigation Libraries

- **Stim**: High-performance stabilizer circuit simulator.
- **PyMatching**: Decoder for surface codes using matching algorithms.
- **Mitiq** (Unitarity): Python package for ZNE, PEC, and Clifford data regression.
- **Qiskit QEC**: Modular QEC library for code construction and fault-tolerant protocol testing.

8.4 Cross-Platform Integration

These tools integrate with real hardware and cloud platforms:

- IBM Quantum Lab.
- Google Cloud Quantum Engine.
- Amazon Braket.

8.5 Visualization and Debugging

- Circuit visualizers: Draw quantum circuits with error annotations.
- Syndrome heatmaps: Visualize logical error propagation.
- Tools for analyzing noisy spectrum: Assess decoherence periods and gate behaviour deflections

8.6 Open Challenges in Tools

- Consolidated APIs to error correction and mitigation modules.
- Real-time syndrome decoding during circuit execution.

- Estimation of resources under hardware limitations.

These theories bridge the gap between experiment and theory, providing essential infrastructure to create scalable, fault-tolerant quantum algorithms.

9 Summary and Reflection

Quantum computing represents a revolutionary shift in how we go about and utilize information processing. Its ability to perform certain types of problems better than classical systems have generated strong interest in both academic and industrial research. Nevertheless, the road from theoretical potential to daily use is impeded by the ubiquitous noise and fragile quantum states.

In this chapter, we surveyed the basic role of quantum error correction (QEC) and noise reduction in transcending the unreliability of today's quantum hardware. Starting with simple codes like the Shor and Steane codes, and working through surface, color, and subsystem codes, we covered a variety of error correction paradigms. Each approach features unique trade-offs relating to overhead, fault tolerance, and compatibility with current physical architectures. Promising approaches like low-density parity-check (LDPC) codes also highlight the region's transition to more scalable and hardware-efficient solutions.

Other than QEC, we considered a range of noise-reduction techniques for NISQ machines. Techniques such as zero-noise extrapolation, dynamical decoupling, and measurement error mitigation provide practical paths to enhance computation fidelity without adopting full-fledged error correction. These technologies, commonly implemented through hybrid quantum–classical architectures, are significant ways to achieve useful results from imperfect devices.

While great strides have been made, there are still many open issues. Achieving fault-tolerant quantum computation will not just require sophisticated error control methods, but also improvement in hardware stability, connectivity, and fidelity of gates. As scientists further optimize decoding algorithms and enhance control protocols, the next steps will be toward incorporating these strategies effortlessly into large-scale architectures.

In general, the quest for trusted quantum computing is a fundamentally cross-disciplinary endeavor. It requires intimate collaboration between theoretical design, software engineering, and experimental deployment. Additional innovation in QEC and noise cancellation will be central to the engineering of the next generation of quantum technologies, in pushing forward the vision of scalable quantum systems.

9.1 Trade-Offs and Reflections

Even though QEC offers excellent protection, it comes at substantial qubit and resource costs. Mitigation of noise offers immediate gains but is normally short on scalability. Quantum computing efficiently will most likely be achieved with hybrid techniques, which have room for unique hardware and application requirements.

As we enter the fault-tolerant age, a layered solution, combining software-level error suppression with hardware-level reliability will be essential. Improvements in code efficiency, decoding algorithms, and conventional co-processing will further bridge the gap between theory and reality.

10 Transition to Quantum Networking

As quantum error correction and noise mitigation mature, their integration into quantum communication systems becomes increasingly important. Quantum networking—interconnecting quantum processors over distances—relies heavily on error-resilient transmission of entangled qubits, often over optical fiber or free space.

10.1 Role of QEC in Quantum Communication

- Quantum communication channels are highly susceptible to photon loss, decoherence, and noise.
- QEC codes, particularly those suited for bosonic and optical modes (e.g., cat codes), help protect quantum states during transmission.
- Entanglement purification and quantum repeaters require QEC to scale communication beyond 100 km.

10.2 Quantum Repeaters and Entanglement Swapping

- Quantum repeaters divide long distances into shorter segments, performing entanglement generation, error correction, and entanglement swapping at each node.
- Surface codes and stabilizer codes can be used to correct errors during intermediate teleportation steps.

Example: A three-node repeater network can use [[7, 1, 3]] CSS codes at each node to preserve entanglement fidelity across segments.

10.3 Fault-Tolerant Teleportation

- Quantum teleportation becomes fault-tolerant when integrated with QEC.
- Logical Bell pairs can be distributed and verified across the network.
- Syndrome information helps reconstruct the correct logical state at the receiver.

10.4 Toward a Quantum Internet

A future quantum internet will combine:

- Fault-tolerant QEC encoding at endpoints.
- Repeaters with real-time decoding and correction.
- Cross-platform protocols for routing and security (e.g., quantum IP layers).

Several prototypes—like DARPA's quantum internet testbed and European Quantum Communication Infrastructure (EuroQCI)—are integrating QEC at the communication layer.

10.5 Summary and Outlook

Integrating quantum error correction into networking stacks will be vital for enabling long-distance, secure, and scalable quantum communication. This final frontier merges distributed computing, secure key exchange, and teleportation-based logic into a cohesive quantum network infrastructure.

As hardware and protocols continue to evolve, the boundary between computation and communication will blur—yielding an interconnected, fault-tolerant quantum ecosystem.

Bibliography

1. Nielsen MA, Chuang IL (2010) Quantum computation and quantum information. Cambridge University Press
2. Preskill J (2018) Quantum computing in the NISQ era and beyond. Quantum 2:79
3. Devitt SJ, Munro WJ, Nemoto K (2013) Quantum error correction for beginners. Rep Prog Phys 76(7):076001
4. Gottesman D (1997) Stabilizer codes and quantum error correction. http://arxiv.org/abs/quant-ph/9705052
5. Krinner S et al (2022) Realizing repeated quantum error correction in a distance-three surface code. Nature 605:669–674
6. Kandala A et al (2019) Error mitigation extends the computational reach of a noisy quantum processor. Nature 567:491–495
7. Temme K, Bravyi S, Gambetta JM (2017) Error mitigation for short-depth quantum circuits. Phys Rev Lett 119(18):180509
8. Endo S et al (2021) Hybrid quantum-classical algorithms and quantum error mitigation. J Phys Soc Jpn 90(3):032001
9. Versluis R et al (2017) Scalable quantum circuit and control for a superconducting surface code. Phys Rev Appl 8:034021
10. Chen ZY et al (2022) Exponential suppression of bit or phase flip errors with repetitive error correction. Nature 605(7911):661–666
11. Qiskit Documentation. https://qiskit.org
12. Mitiq: A Python toolkit for quantum error mitigation. https://github.com/unitaryfund/mitiq
13. Google Cirq Framework. https://quantumai.google/cirq

14. European Quantum Communication Infrastructure (EuroQCI). https://digital-strategy.ec.europa.eu into networking stacks will be vital for enabling long-distance, secure, and scalable quantum communication. This final frontier merges distributed computing, secure key exchange, and teleportation-based logic into a cohesive quantum network infrastructure

Omkar Bhalekar is a senior network engineer at Tesla Motors, with research interests spanning resilient Industrial communication systems and quantum technologies, his work emphasizes parallels between fault tolerance in networks and error correction in quantum systems. He is also the author of the book: Autonomous and Predictive Network, The Future of Networking in the Age of AI. This chapter on Quantum Error Correction and Noise Mitigation explores how fragile quantum states can be preserved against noise and operational errors, presenting core noise models, essential and advanced error correction codes, and practical mitigation strategies tailored for NISQ devices. Designed as a bridge between theoretical constructs and applied reliability, the chapter illustrates real-world use cases in optimization, quantum chemistry, and secure communication, while charting the trajectory toward scalable, fault-tolerant quantum computing.

Quantum Cloud Services: Getting Quantum Power

Monika Malik

Abstract

Quantum cloud services are a big change in how people can access computing power since they make quantum computing resources available to everyone through cloud-based platforms. This chapter gives a full picture of the current state of quantum cloud services by looking at major providers including IBM Quantum Platform, Microsoft Azure Quantum, D-Wave Leap, IonQ Quantum Cloud, and newer platforms. The study looks into a number of quantum computing technologies that can be accessed through cloud services, including gate-based quantum computers, quantum annealers, and trapped ion systems. Important discoveries reveal that quantum cloud services have gone from being experimental platforms to systems that are ready for production. This means they can be used in real life for scientific simulation, machine learning, and optimization. The chapter looks at programming frameworks, pricing structures, security issues, and access techniques to find current limitations and possible ways to move forward. Market analysis shows that Quantum Computing as a Service (QCaaS) will develop very quickly, reaching $48.3 billion by 2033. This study is crucial because it gives academics, practitioners, and organizations the information they need to use quantum cloud services successfully. This will enable quantum computing technologies to become more popular and useful in real life.

M. Malik (✉)
Texas, USA
e-mail: malikmonika@ieee.org

M. Rana and B. Pandey (eds.), *Quantum Ops*,
https://doi.org/10.1007/978-3-032-10775-6_6

Keywords

Cloud-based quantum computing • Quantum programming • Quantum algorithms • Quantum hardware access • Hybrid quantum–classical computing • Quantum cloud computing • Quantum as a service • QCaaS • Quantum computing platforms • And Quantum computing democratization are some of the keywords

1 In a Nutshell

Quantum computing is one of the major changes in technology in the twenty-first century. It could change the way computers work in many areas, including scientific simulation, machine learning, cryptography, and optimization [1]. But in the past, quantum computing has been impossible to use in real life because it requires a lot of specialized equipment, is very expensive to build and maintain, and is very hard to understand. Quantum cloud services have completely changed the game by allowing researchers, developers, and businesses all over the world to use quantum computing power without having to spend a lot of money on quantum hardware infrastructure [2].

Quantum cloud services, which are also known as Quantum Computing as a Service (QCaaS), are a new way to make quantum computing available to everyone. They employ ideas from cloud computing to let people use quantum simulators, QPUs, and other development tools online [3]. Because of this change in thinking, quantum computing has gone from private research facilities to cloud platforms that anyone can use. This lets people build, test, and run quantum algorithms using web interfaces and programming frameworks they already know.

Quantum cloud services are important for more than just being easy to get to. These platforms have led to the development of hybrid quantum–classical computing systems, in which quantum processors work with traditional computing resources to solve problems that classical computers can't handle on their own [4]. This hybrid approach has worked especially well for optimization problems, machine learning applications, and scientific simulations because quantum algorithms can help with some parts of the problem while classical systems take care of preprocessing, postprocessing, and overall orchestration.

The quantum cloud ecosystem has a lot of various business models and ways of using technology. Google, Amazon, Microsoft, and IBM are just a few of the big IT companies that have built huge quantum cloud platforms with their own programming frameworks, access models, and quantum hardware technologies [5]. Companies like D-Wave, IonQ, Rigetti, and Quantinuum that focus on quantum computing have made the industry more competitive and fast-changing by offering customized quantum cloud services that leverage their own quantum technologies.

The research question this chapter answers is why it's important to have a full understanding of the quantum cloud services ecosystem, including its technological capabilities, access techniques, programming paradigms, and valuable tips for getting the most out of these platforms. Quantum cloud services are changing quickly, and there is a big gap in our knowledge about how to compare them, which ones are best for different uses, and what organizations should think about when they want to add quantum computing to their operations.

There are three key goals for this chapter. First, to give a full picture of the current state of quantum cloud services by looking at the main platforms, how good they are technically, and how to get to them. The next step is to look at the best ways to make and use quantum applications in the cloud, as well as the tools and frameworks that are available for doing so. The third phase is to look at the real-world elements that businesses and researchers need to think about when adopting quantum clouds. These include cost models, security issues, performance characteristics, and strategic planning.

This chapter talks about quantum cloud services from both a technical and a strategic point of view. In terms of technology, the examination looks at a variety of quantum computing technologies that may be accessed through cloud platforms. These include gate-based quantum computers that use superconducting qubits, trapped ions, and photonic systems, as well as quantum annealing systems and quantum simulators. The strategic perspective looks at the market dynamics, adoption trends, competitive environment, and future development paths that will affect the growth of quantum cloud services.

The chapter arrangement moves slowly from basic ideas to things to think about when putting them into practice. A full literature analysis follows this introduction and looks at how quantum cloud services have changed over time and what current research is focusing on. The methodology section talks about the analytical approach that will be used to look into quantum cloud platforms and services. The findings section has a comparison of the top quantum cloud providers, a look at their technical capabilities, and a full analysis of each one. The discussion part gives a summary of the findings, focusing on the most important changes, problems, and opportunities in the realm of quantum cloud services. The last part, the conclusion, talks about the most important discoveries and gives ideas for more research and how to use them in the real world.

This work adds to the growing body of knowledge about how quantum computing may be used in real life and how easy it is to get to. It gives important guidance to researchers, businesses, and individuals who want to make the most of quantum cloud services. As quantum computing evolves from experimental research to real-world applications, it becomes more and more important to understand the quantum cloud services ecosystem in order to realize the transformative potential of quantum technologies.

2 A Look at the Literature

Quantum cloud services are a new area of study and use that has gotten a lot of attention from both academics and businesses. They are an example of how cloud computing and quantum computing have come together to create something new. This survey of the literature looks at the most important new ideas, research, and ongoing conversations that have shaped what we know about quantum cloud services today.

2.1 Basic Research and the Evolution of History

Quantum cloud services are based on the idea that quantum computing systems can be made to work and that cloud computing infrastructure can grow up. Early work by Nielsen and Chuang laid the theoretical groundwork for quantum computation. Later work by researchers at Google, IBM, and other companies showed that scalable quantum systems could be developed [6]. The IBM Quantum Experience, which was the first quantum computer available to the public through a cloud interface, was released in 2016. This was when the change from lab-based quantum experiments to cloud-accessible quantum systems really began [7].

IBM's innovative work to make quantum computing more accessible to everyone through cloud services set a number of basic notions that are still important in the industry today. Their work revealed that it was possible to do real quantum calculations while keeping quantum coherence and allowing remote access to quantum hardware [8]. This finding opened up new avenues for research and development in distributed quantum computing and cast doubt on the widely held idea that quantum computing required direct physical access to quantum hardware.

D-Wave Systems' focus on quantum annealing technology was a big step forward in the early stages of creating quantum cloud services. Their Leap quantum cloud service, which came out in 2018, showed that cloud platforms could efficiently deliver specialized quantum computing techniques to handle optimization problems [9]. The D-Wave approach showed that hybrid quantum–classical algorithms work and that quantum annealing is a good way to use quantum cloud in the real world.

2.2 How Easy It is to Get Quantum Hardware and the Technology that Supports It

In recent years, a lot of research has gone into the technological problems and solutions that come up when giving quantum technology access to the cloud. Preskill's work on Noisy Intermediate-Scale Quantum (NISQ) devices [10] created a theoretical framework for understanding the possibilities and limits of existing quantum systems that can be accessed through cloud platforms. This study showed that although noise and decoherence are problems with current quantum devices, they can still be useful for certain types of problems when used through cloud services.

In order to make quantum cloud services useful, it has been necessary to come up with ways to fix quantum errors. Kandala et al. [11] say that error mitigation strategies could make quantum computations done on cloud-accessible quantum hardware much more reliable. These improvements have made it possible to move quantum cloud services from experimental platforms to systems that are suitable for production and can support real-world applications.

Research on distributed quantum computing and quantum networking has looked into the idea of employing cloud infrastructure to connect several quantum devices. Kimble and others have looked on quantum internet protocols that could one day make it possible to build more complicated quantum cloud topologies [12]. The fundamental purpose of present quantum cloud services is to give people access to individual quantum computers. However, this study opens up the prospect of more complex distributed quantum computing architectures.

2.3 Programming Frameworks and Development Methodologies

To make quantum cloud services available to more developers, quantum programming frameworks had to be built. Research on quantum software development has led to the creation of many important frameworks, including Qiskit (IBM), Cirq (Google), and Q# (Microsoft). All of these frameworks are meant to make it easier to write and run quantum algorithms on cloud systems [13]. We looked at how these frameworks compare in terms of their pros and cons and how well they function for different sorts of quantum applications.

Cross-platform compatibility has been a popular field of research because of studies that look at the problems and solutions for making quantum apps that can run on more than one quantum cloud platform. LaRose et al. [14] looked on making quantum software that can run on any platform and use different quantum hardware backends through cloud services. This work has big effects on how to get the most out of quantum cloud expenditures and avoid being locked into a vendor.

Many studies have looked into how to combine cloud platforms with resources for both conventional and quantum computing. Research on hybrid quantum–classical algorithms [15] shows that effective quantum cloud applications often require complicated coordination of quantum and traditional computational resources. This research has had an effect on the architecture of quantum cloud platforms, which make it easy for quantum computers to work with regular computing infrastructure.

2.4 Looking at the Market and Adoption Trends

According to economic study, quantum cloud services have grown a lot in the market and changed the way businesses work. Market study says that the Quantum Computing as a Service (QCaaS) market would increase at a compound annual growth rate of 35.6%, from an estimated $2.3 billion in 2023 to $48.3 billion by 2033 [16]. People are becoming more aware of the possible benefits of quantum computing and how effectively cloud delivery models operate to make quantum technology more widely available. This is why quantum computing is expanding so quickly.

Studies of adoption patterns have found the main reasons why organizations are investing in quantum cloud services. McKinsey & Company research shows that companies are starting to regard 2025 as a key year for quantum computing to become more widely used. Cloud services are necessary for making actual quantum applications work [17]. The survey found that scientific modeling, machine learning, and optimization are the key reasons why people are starting to employ quantum clouds.

A study that looked at different quantum cloud pricing models found different ways to make money from quantum computing resources. Researchers have looked into how different pricing structures, like pay-per-use, subscription-based, and hybrid, affect different types of users and applications [18]. This study will have a big effect on how well quantum cloud services can be used by different groups of users and how much they will cost.

2.5 A Look at Privacy and Security Concerns

As these platforms change from research tools to production systems that handle sensitive data and algorithms, more and more people are thinking about how quantum cloud services could affect security. There are several problems with protecting algorithms, keeping quantum states private, and the fact that quantum computers might be able to break existing encryption methods [19]. This research has had an effect on the development of privacy-protecting tactics and security protocols for quantum cloud platforms.

Researchers in post-quantum cryptography have looked into how advances in quantum computing can affect cloud security in general. Research done by NIST and other organizations has led to the creation of new cryptographic standards that are meant to protect quantum cloud services against quantum attacks [20]. These standards have enormous implications for protecting quantum cloud services itself. This work shows how quantum computing may be both a security danger and a way to build new security solutions.

Researchers have started to look into ways to protect private data in quantum cloud settings as part of a topic of research called privacy-preserving quantum computing. Researchers have looked into ways to make quantum computations work on encrypted data in the cloud through secure multi-party quantum computation and quantum homomorphic encryption [21]. These methods are important areas for future study on quantum cloud security, even if they are still mostly theoretical.

2.6 Chances for Research and Gaps in Knowledge

A lot of progress has been made in research on quantum cloud services, but there are still some important gaps in our knowledge. There isn't a lot of research on how scalable and reliable quantum cloud platforms are over time, especially when quantum hardware is changing so frequently. Because there are no standard ways to benchmark quantum cloud services, it is hard to compare them fairly and figure out which ones are best for certain tasks.

There is still not enough study on the problems that come up when trying to use quantum cloud services with conventional company IT infrastructure, how to integrate them, and how to manage organizational transformation. Also, not much thought has been given to the environmental effects of quantum cloud services, even though quantum hardware systems and the infrastructure that supports them need a lot of energy.

There is a shortage of study on quantum cloud service governance and regulatory compliance, even though regulated businesses and government agencies are becoming more interested in quantum computing applications. In the future, researchers should work on making good governance frameworks, compliance requirements, and risk management plans for quantum cloud services.

Quantum cloud services have come a long way in making quantum computing more accessible to everyone, but there are still many important research opportunities in areas such as platform standardization, enterprise integration, security and privacy, and long-term sustainability. These gaps in understanding are important areas for more research and progress in quantum cloud services.

3 Methods

This study compares and rates quantum cloud services in a number of aspects using a detailed analytical approach. The method combines quantitative study of performance parameters, market position, and accessibility with qualitative analysis of platform capabilities. The strategy is meant to help both strategic decision-makers and technical professionals choose and set up quantum cloud services.

3.1 The Research Design and the Analytical Framework

The research design uses a mixed-methodologies approach, which means it uses a variety of data collecting and analysis methods, to give a full picture of the quantum cloud services ecosystem. The analysis is based on five primary evaluation dimensions: technical capabilities, accessibility and usability, performance characteristics, economic considerations, and strategic positioning.

The technical capabilities dimension looks at the quantum hardware technologies that each platform supports, such as qubit counts, quantum volume metrics, gate fidelities, coherence times, and quantum computing paradigms. To establish fair comparisons between different quantum cloud services, this study uses technical specifications, research papers, and platform documentation that are available to the public.

The accessibility and usability dimension looks at how easy it is to use and understand each platform's learning materials, development tools, programming interfaces, and documentation. This review looks at the factors that determine how different groups of users, such as academic researchers and enterprise developers, actually use quantum cloud services.

To figure out how well a system works, we look at things like system uptime, job execution times, queue management, and reliability measures when they are available. This dimension also looks at how scalable the platforms are and how well they can handle diverse workloads.

Economic factors include pricing models, cost structures, free tier offerings, and calculations of the total cost of ownership for different ways of using the service. This study shows how economically feasible quantum cloud services are for different sorts of users and applications.

We look at each platform's market approach, alliance ecosystem, roadmap commitments, and competitive differentiation initiatives through the prism of strategic positioning. This dimension helps us understand how different quantum cloud services have changed over time and how long they will last.

3.2 Ways to Collect Data

To make sure that the study covered all aspects of the quantum cloud services ecosystem, it used a variety of methods to collect data. One of the main sources of data was direct platform study, in which researchers went to quantum cloud platforms in person to look at their functional capabilities, interface design, and user experience.

As part of the technical documentation analysis process, we looked at all of the platform documentation, API references, programming manuals, and technical specifications that quantum cloud service providers made available. This analysis looked closely at the platform's features, limitations, and planned uses.

We used market research data from industry papers, financial filings, press releases, and analyst publications to understand how the market works, how it will grow, and where we are in relation to our competitors. This material was very helpful in understanding the business climate of the quantum cloud services market.

The academic literature review comprised peer-reviewed research papers, conference proceedings, and technical reports about quantum cloud computing, quantum algorithms, and the development of quantum hardware. This review made sure that the analysis was based on the most up-to-date scientific knowledge and research results.

Expert interviews and industry surveys gave us more information about how users feel about things, how adoption rates are changing, and the problems that come up when implementing things in the real world. This qualitative data gave the technical and market analysts more practical ideas on how quantum cloud services could be used.

3.3 How to Choose Platforms

To make sure that the market was fully covered, a number of critical criteria were utilized to choose quantum cloud platforms for in-depth investigation. These criteria focused on platforms that had a big impact and were easy to use. We chose platforms that had a lot of users and community interaction. The major things we looked at were how many people used them and how big their market presence was.

The technical importance was based on how much the work helped the field of quantum computing move forward, how new the quantum algorithms or software frameworks were, and how unique the quantum hardware technologies were. We chose to include platforms that had interesting technological features or new ways of doing things.

One of the most essential criterion for choosing was how easy it was for academics and developers to use. They focused on platforms that give researchers and developers a lot of access to quantum computing resources without making it too expensive. This meant looking at things like educational programs, the quality of the documentation, and the free tier options.

We looked at the commercial viability and sustainability of the platforms we looked at to make sure they provide customers of quantum cloud services reliable, long-term options. This evaluation looked at the financial backing of platform providers, how long their business models would last, and how committed they were to their strategies.

For the analysis to include different types of quantum computing, like gate-based systems, quantum annealers, and new technologies, it also took into account differences in location and technology.

3.4 A Framework for Comparing and Evaluating Metrics

The evaluation approach uses both quantitative and qualitative measures to make it easier to compare quantum cloud systems in a systematic way. Quantitative metrics include things like qubit counts, quantum volume measurements, gate error rates, and coherence times that are made public. Performance metrics include things like the percentage of time a system is up, the average time it takes to complete an operation, and the time it takes to wait in a queue.

Examples of economic metrics are the cost of running a quantum circuit, membership fees, and, if applicable, the cost of qubit-hours. Market parameters include expected user bases, job execution volumes, and platform growth rates, among other things.

Qualitative evaluation criteria look at things such how well the community supports users, how detailed the documentation is, how well the user interface is designed, and how good the overall user experience is. These tests are based on a systematic evaluation that uses standardized criteria and grading rubrics.

The comparison framework uses a weighted score system to account for how important different assessment dimensions are for different groups of users. Enterprise customers may care more about integration, maintenance, and dependability, whereas technical researchers may care more about the performance and capabilities of quantum gear.

3.5 Limitations and Problems with the Method

There are a lot of big problems with this research approach that you should think about when looking at the results. Because quantum cloud services are always developing, the technical specifications, pricing structures, and platform capabilities are always changing. This could affect how current the analysis results are.

The absence of access to proprietary performance data from quantum cloud providers limits the range of quantitative research. Because they don't share detailed performance metrics, reliability statistics, or usage analytics, many platforms depend on data that is available to the public and experiences that users report.

At the beginning of quantum computing standardization, it can be hard to make direct technical comparisons among platforms because they use different ways to measure things, benchmark tactics, and report performance. This problem can be solved by carefully looking at the situations in which measurements are made and being honest about how comparisons are made.

When possible, triangulating numerous data sources and focusing on information that has been independently validated can help reduce bias in data sources, especially vendor-published materials and marketing communications.

The focus on publicly available quantum cloud platforms may not be a good picture of the state of quantum computing because some major quantum computing resources are only available through commercial partnerships, government initiatives, or proprietary business arrangements.

3.6 Things to Keep in Mind About Morality

This study follows the ethical rules that are widely acknowledged for comparing and evaluating technologies. Every time data is collected, it follows the platform's rules and terms of service. All of the study is based on data that is publicly available. No effort was taken to get private or restricted information.

The study stays objective by not having any financial relationships to quantum cloud service providers and making sure that any potential conflicts of interest are known. The purpose of the analysis is to give a fair review that looks at the pros and cons of each platform.

Privacy issues are taken care of by focusing on platform features and performance data that is available to everyone instead of collecting or analyzing user data. The research properly credits all of its sources and references while protecting intellectual property rights.

The goal of the strategy is to maintain the highest standards of research integrity and ethical behavior while still providing useful information to the quantum computing community. The methodical approach makes sure that the results can be repeated and that the analysis framework can be used to look at how quantum cloud services are changing in the future.

4 Results and Findings

A look into quantum cloud services shows that the ecosystem is diverse and changes swiftly. This has turned quantum computing into a publicly available technology platform instead of only a research topic. This section gives a lot of information about the primary providers of quantum cloud services, how good they are at what they do, how to get to them, and where they fit into the bigger picture of quantum computing.

4.1 IBM Quantum Platform: Making the Quantum Cloud Available

IBM Quantum Platform is the most well-known and widely utilized quantum cloud service. It made quantum computing resources available to the public for the first time in 2016 with the launch of IBM Quantum Experience [22]. The current IBM Quantum Platform, which gives users access to utility-scale quantum processing units and a wide range of development tools, is the product of a lot of changes to the platform over time.

The IBM Quantum Platform is based on superconducting transmon qubits stacked in heavy-hexagonal lattice topologies. The platform now offers quantum computers with anywhere from 5 qubits for educational purposes to utility-scale processors with more than 100 qubits. The IBM Quantum System One and IBM Quantum System Two architectures are the main ones. They have gate fidelities of around 99.9% for single-qubit operations and 99% for two-qubit gates, and their quantum volume metrics are over 128 [23].

The platform's tiered accessibility strategy strikes a mix between open access and premium features. Free tier access gives you ten minutes of quantum processing time on some quantum systems per month. This makes it easier to design algorithms and use them for instructional purposes. Premium access tiers provide you access to the most advanced quantum systems, put you at the front of the queue, and give you more time to process quantum data. This methodology has helped make platform development more viable and give more people access to quantum computing.

IBM's Qiskit framework is the platform's principal programming interface. It comes with a full quantum software development kit that includes tools for designing, optimizing, running, and analyzing quantum circuits. Qiskit's modular architecture lets users operate at several levels of abstraction, from low-level pulse control of quantum hardware to high-level quantum computations. The framework's connection to classical computing resources using Qiskit Runtime [24] makes it possible for hybrid quantum–classical computations to run quickly.

The Quantum Lab is a cloud-based Jupyter Notebook environment for making quantum algorithms, and the Quantum Composer is a visual circuit builder that makes it easy to build quantum circuits by dragging and dropping them. These are two instances of the platform's development tools ecosystem. These tools allow advanced users access to complex features while making it much easier for new users to get started with quantum computing.

Some of the enterprise features of the IBM Quantum Platform are role-based access control, tools for managing organizations, and the ability to cooperate with enterprise development workflows. The platform has scalable access management and resource allocation features that work for both small groups of researchers and big companies with hundreds of users.

The IBM Quantum Platform's performance characteristics reveal that it is very reliable for commercial quantum systems, with system uptime of 95%. Depending on the state of the queue and the need for optimization, complex algorithms may take minutes to hours to run. Simple circuits, on the other hand, can be done in seconds. The time it takes to do a job depends on how intricate the circuit is and how busy the system is.

The platform's instructional and community engagement programs have been a huge help in building the quantum computing developer community. IBM Quantum Education offers a wide range of learning tools, including video courses, manuals, and hands-on activities. The IBM Quantum Challenge series has had thousands of people from all over the world take part. They have helped to make algorithms and grow the community by solving quantum computing difficulties.

4.2 Combined Microsoft Azure Quantum with Integrated Cloud Quantum Computing

Microsoft Azure Quantum is a full-service quantum cloud service that uses Microsoft's huge cloud computing infrastructure and business connections. The platform is different because it has a provider-agnostic architecture that lets users access different quantum hardware technologies through a single interface. It also works very well with Azure cloud services [25].

Azure Quantum's quantum-agnostic technical architecture makes it feasible to use a wide range of quantum computing technologies, including quantum annealers, quantum simulators, and gate-based quantum computers. Some of the partner hardware providers are IonQ for trapped ion systems, Quantinuum for trapped ion quantum computers, and Rigetti for superconducting quantum processors. With this technique of having several providers, users may pick the optimal quantum hardware for each application while keeping the development and deployment processes the same.

Microsoft's Q# quantum programming language is the core framework for developing Azure Quantum. Q# is a high-level quantum programming language that is meant to be scalable and function with traditional computer resources. Some of the ways that Q# makes it easier to write quantum algorithms are by providing strong type safety, automatic resource management, and easy interface with.NET development environments. The language's architecture puts a lot of focus on fault-tolerant quantum computing and long-term scalability, which sets it up for future improvements in quantum computing [26].

Azure Quantum works with Azure cloud services to give hybrid quantum–classical computing particular features. The platform makes it easy for quantum and traditional computing to operate together by letting data flow smoothly between quantum processors and Azure services like Azure Machine Learning, Azure Storage, and Azure Compute. This connectivity is especially useful for business apps that need to process a lot of data in complicated ways.

Azure Credits are part of the platform's pricing strategy for quantum computing resources. This lets Azure clients keep track of their bills and costs. Prices for quantum hardware vary from one company to the next, and they are usually based on the number of shots or the time it takes to run quantum circuits. The platform has capabilities for estimating prices and controlling spending to help users keep track of the costs of quantum computing in a smart way.

The security and compliance features of Azure Quantum show that it is aimed at businesses. Azure's security system, which includes identity and access management, encryption while data is being sent and stored, and following industry standards like SOC 2, ISO 27001, and HIPAA, is also used on the platform. These characteristics make Azure Quantum extremely useful for businesses and governments who need to keep their data safe.

The platform has a number of development tools, such as the Azure Quantum Development Kit, which lets you build and test locally, and integration with Visual

Studio and Visual Studio Code for familiar development experiences. The quantum simulator's ability to create and test algorithms without consuming quantum hardware resources makes it easier to create effective development workflows.

Microsoft's quantum research department is putting a lot of emphasis on the creation of topological qubits as part of their strategic positioning [27]. This is because the Majorana 1 chip was just announced, which is a big step forward in topological quantum computing materials. These systems show what Microsoft wants to do with fault-tolerant quantum computing in the medium run, even if Azure Quantum doesn't have them yet.

4.3 D-Wave Leap: Quantum Annealing Cloud Services

D-Wave Leap is a unique way to offer quantum cloud services that only focuses on using quantum annealing technology to fix optimization problems. The platform has proved that quantum annealing can be used in real-world commercial settings since its inception in 2018. It has also reached outstanding scales in terms of problem size and solution quality [28].

The technical core of D-Wave Leap is quantum annealing processors that use the quantum approximate optimization algorithm (QAOA) and other similar methods to solve combinatorial optimization issues. The platform presently offers devices like the Advantage2 and Advantage quantum annealers, which have over 5,000 qubits arranged in Pegasus graph topologies to make it easier to integrate optimization problems.

D-Wave's quantum annealing technology is very different from gate-based quantum computing since it focuses on finding the optimal solutions to optimization problems instead of just running random quantum algorithms. This specialization lets the platform handle problems with up to two million variables and constraints [29]. It does this by using hybrid quantum–classical solvers that combine quantum annealing with standard optimization approaches.

The platform's accessibility strategy includes immediate access and the ability to solve problems in real time. D-Wave Leap gives you real-time access to quantum annealing resources, and issues normally get solved in less than a second. This is different from gate-based quantum systems, which often need to be scheduled and managed in queues. This paradigm of rapid access has been very helpful for interactive algorithm development and production applications that need to be optimized quickly.

The Ocean software development kit is the heart of D-Wave's programming framework. It has Python-based tools for constructing optimization problems, sending them to quantum annealers, and checking the results. Ocean's design puts a lot of attention on being easy to use for optimization professionals so that they may hide the complexity of quantum technology while making it easier to define and analyze complicated problems.

The platform's hybrid solver capabilities are a big step forward for quantum cloud services. These solvers automatically split up enormous optimization problems between quantum and classical resources. This lets them solve problems that are far greater than what quantum annealing could do on its own. The hybrid technique has worked far better than classical optimization alone on a lot of different types of problems [30].

D-Wave Leap has been useful in many fields since it focuses on solving real-world optimization challenges. Some examples of manufacturing applications are quality control, optimizing the supply chain, and planning production. Fraud detection, risk management, and portfolio optimization are all uses for financial services. Resource allocation, traffic optimization, and vehicle routing are all examples of how logistics and transportation can be used.

The platform's performance metrics reveal that it is very reliable, with 99.9% uptime and consistent sub-second problem-solving speeds for most optimization tasks. The real-time access architecture gives predictable performance for production applications because it doesn't have to wait in line, which can slow down other quantum cloud platforms.

D-Wave's educational and developer support programs provide full documentation, sample problems, and training resources that focus on optimization applications. Quantum annealing can be used by optimization professionals who don't know much about quantum computing because the platform's teaching resources focus more on addressing real-world problems than on the concepts of quantum physics.

4.4 IonQ Quantum Cloud: Ion Quantum Computing is Trapped

IonQ Quantum Cloud gives you known access to trapped ion-type quantum < |image_sentinel|>computing systems that have unique advantages in terms of qu retirees connectivity, gate fidelity, and quantum algorithm implementation. The platform is one of the most advanced gate-based quantum cloud services since it has systems that can do quantum operations with high fidelity and connect all qubits [31].

IonQ systems use trapped ytterbium ions as qubits and carefully controlled laser pulses to do quantum operations. This technology makes it feasible for all qubits to link to each other, which means that any qubit can talk to any other qubit directly without having to go through additional steps. This connectivity gain dramatically lowers the quantum circuit depth requirements for many algorithms, which makes them work better on noisy intermediate-scale quantum devices.

IonQ offers the IonQ Aria system through the cloud platform. It has 25 algorithmic qubits and a quantum volume of more than 4 million. The platform also gives users access to the future IonQ Forte Enterprise system, which is meant to be used on-site, and IonQ Forte, a quantum system that can be configured with software and is currently in limited access beta [32].

The platform's programming interface is flexible since it works with a number of quantum software development kits, like Qiskit, Cirq, PennyLane, and others. This is good for developers who know how to use different quantum programming frameworks. IonQ's native gate set, which includes two-qubit Mølmer-Sørensen gates and arbitrary single-qubit rotations, can be used to create any quantum algorithm with the best gate count.

IonQ Quantum Cloud's access architecture has both reserved and on-demand access choices so that it can handle different ways of using it. Reserved access guarantees quantum processing time for heavy workloads, while on-demand access lets you submit a job right once, but the job won't start until the system is available. The platform has multiple price levels based on how complicated the quantum circuits are and what is needed to run them.

Some of the platform's development tools are the IonQ Cloud Console for managing jobs and analyzing results, complete API documentation for programmatic access, and the ability to work with popular cloud platforms including Google Cloud, Microsoft Azure Quantum, and Amazon Braket. This multi-cloud availability lets users use IonQ quantum devices in a number of cloud settings.

IonQ's focus on how well quantum algorithms work has led to proven improvements for some types of algorithms, like quantum machine learning, optimization problems, and quantum chemical simulations. The platform's full connectivity and strong gate fidelities make it possible to run quantum algorithms with fewer approximations and less error buildup than systems with limited connection.

Some of the platform's business features are managing organizations, controlling user access, and connecting with enterprise development workflows. IonQ helps organizations uncover the right uses for quantum computing and make successful plans for how to employ it through their quantum applications team.

4.5 New Quantum Cloud Technologies and Platforms

There are a lot of new platforms in the quantum cloud services space that offer unique access methods, cutting-edge quantum technologies, or specific features. These platforms serve specific market segments and application needs while promoting innovation and variety within the quantum cloud ecosystem.

Rigetti Quantum Cloud Services lets you use superconducting quantum processors through their Quantum Cloud Services (QCS) platform. Rigetti's technology focuses on closely linking quantum processors with classical computing infrastructure so that hybrid quantum–classical algorithms can run with low latency. The platform is especially good at quantum algorithms that demand a lot of quantum–classical interaction in the near future. It can run both gate-based quantum computing and quantum machine learning applications [33].

Google Quantum AI doesn't let anyone to the public cloud directly, but it does offer quantum computing through research partnerships and agreements with cloud providers. Google's quantum systems have some of the most advanced quantum hardware, like the Sycamore processor, which showed that quantum supremacy was possible. The platform's focus on quantum algorithm research and development has led to big improvements in quantum machine learning, quantum simulation, and quantum error correction.

After Honeywell Quantum Solutions and Cambridge Quantum Computing combined, Quantinuum was established to give trapped ion systems the best quantum volume metrics in the business and access to the quantum cloud. The platform has a lot of tools for making quantum applications, with a focus on quantum software creation and quantum algorithm optimization. Quantinuum offers some of the best quantum systems available through cloud services. Their systems have shown quantum volumes greater than 65,536 [34].

Amazon Braket's quantum computing solution lets users connect to several quantum hardware manufacturers through a single AWS interface. The platform supports quantum computers from IonQ, Rigetti, and D-Wave, as well as quantum simulators for developing and testing algorithms. Braket works with AWS services to provide you access to popular cloud computing tools for building quantum apps and lets you run complicated hybrid quantum–classical operations.

Xanadu Quantum Cloud makes it possible to apply quantum machine learning techniques and continuous variable quantum computing on photonic quantum computing platforms. The PennyLane architecture of the platform makes it easier to construct quantum machine learning by automatically differentiating and integrating with regular machine learning frameworks. Xanadu's technique could be useful for some types of quantum computing applications [35].

4.6 Comparing and Contrasting Quantum Cloud Platforms

When you look at quantum cloud platforms side by side, you can see that they have quite different technical techniques, access models, and intended uses. This variation shows that quantum computing is still in its early stages and that researchers are looking into different ways to get a useful quantum advantage.

Different platforms have quite different technical capabilities, and each one is better for certain types of applications. Gate-based quantum systems from IBM, IonQ, and other businesses can do general-purpose quantum computing that works with a wide range of quantum algorithms. D-Wave's quantum annealing systems have been demonstrated to be useful for certain types of problems since they offer unique optimization features. New technologies like topological qubits and photonic quantum computing could point the way to the future of quantum cloud services.

The big discrepancies in how easy it is to access and use different platforms show that they are aimed at different groups of users and have different economic strategies. The IBM Quantum Platform is a great choice for learning and study because it has a lot of free educational resources and a free tier. Microsoft Azure Quantum is interesting to businesses that already use Azure cloud services since it can work with other corporate systems. D-Wave Leap focuses on optimization applications, which gives operations researchers and others in connected fields' special tools.

The architecture of the platform and what users want affect performance measures including system uptime, job execution times, and queue management. Gate-based quantum systems may have different queue durations depending on demand and when the system needs maintenance. However, D-Wave Leap's real-time access paradigm gives the most reliable performance.

Cost structures, pricing strategies, and total cost of ownership are only a few of the economic elements that make platforms very different from each other. Paid access is normally required for production use, and pricing vary based on quantum processing time, circuit complexity, and other services. However, free tier options let you experiment and learn. It is hard to compare costs directly because there are no common pricing metrics. Instead, you have to look closely at specific usage patterns and needs.

Strategic positioning and long-term viability include things like platform roadmaps, technology development trajectories, and business model sustainability. Big tech companies like Google, Microsoft, and IBM put a lot of money and time into quantum cloud services. As the market grows, specialist quantum computing companies may have more trouble with their business models, even while they offer specific knowledge and creativity.

The study found that quantum cloud services have made quantum computing more accessible to more people while keeping the technical complexity needed to create and use useful quantum algorithms. Quantum cloud services will get better as quantum hardware and software continue to be developed. However, there are many different platforms to choose from, so consumers can pick the finest quantum computing resources for their needs.

This in-depth look at quantum cloud services shows that quantum computing is now much easier to get at, which will have big effects on society, business, and research. This discussion talks about the bigger picture of the findings, how they affect different groups of stakeholders, and the chances and issues that quantum cloud services may face in the future.

4.7 Making Quantum Computing More Available to Everyone

Quantum cloud services are probably the biggest step toward making advanced computing technologies available to everyone since personal computers and the internet became popular. Before cloud-based access, only a few academic institutions and tech companies who could afford to build and keep quantum hardware systems could use quantum computing. The change to cloud-based access has completely changed this scenario. Now, corporations, researchers, and students from all around the world can look into quantum computing without having to spend a lot of money.

This democratization has led to a rapid growth in quantum computing research and application development. Educational institutions have started to include quantum computing in their courses, and platforms like IBM Quantum allow open access to these courses. This has led to a new generation of researchers and professionals who are knowledgeable with quantum computing. Also, the low barrier to entry has sped up progress in the field by letting small businesses and individual academics help make quantum algorithms.

But making quantum computing available to more people also raises important questions about fairness and inclusion. Cloud-based access makes it easier for people to get to things, but it might also create new forms of digital divides based on how easy it is to get to educational resources, how well you know how to use technology, and how fast your internet connection is. There are also worries about market concentration and the prospect of gatekeeping in access to quantum computing because a small number of IT companies control a lot of quantum cloud services.

The study found that successful quantum cloud platforms have put a lot of money into community building, documentation, and educational materials to help with efforts to make things more democratic. D-Wave focuses on real-world optimization applications, Microsoft integrates with well-known development tools, and IBM offers a lot of teaching programs. These are all examples of different ways to make quantum computing available to more people.

4.8 The Technical Effects and Growth of Quantum Computing

The technical results show that quantum cloud services have made quantum computing much faster, easier to use, and more reliable. The whole quantum computing ecosystem benefits from improvements in system dependability, user interface design, and quantum error mitigation that have come about because of the necessity to make quantum computing resources more dependable and easy to get to.

Cloud services offer a wide range of quantum computing methods, which shows that researchers are still looking into different ways to get a useful quantum edge. Different application domains can benefit from trapped ion systems, quantum annealing, gate-based quantum computing, and new technologies in different ways. This diversity helps the field grow because it lets researchers look at different technological approaches while the best ways to make quantum computing work on a large scale are still being figured out.

One of the most significant things that cloud platforms can do for real-world quantum applications is connect quantum and classical computing resources. Hybrid quantum–classical algorithms that use the best features of both types of computing seem to be the best short-term way to get a quantum advantage. Quantum cloud systems' advanced orchestration features make it possible to use these hybrid methods on a large scale.

The study also shows that the quantum cloud services that are available have some big problems. The noisy intermediate-scale quantum (NISQ) period still limits the spectrum of issues that can be solved well, such as having few qubits, large error rates, and short coherence times. Quantum cloud platforms have made these systems more widely available, but the hardware limitations that make quantum computing less useful have not altered much.

The rapid growth of quantum hardware gives quantum cloud services both chances and problems. To be competitive, platforms need to continuously make their hardware better while still being able to work with older devices and giving users a stable experience. Because there are no standard quantum computing measures, users find it hard to judge how well different systems work for certain tasks and to compare platforms fairly.

4.9 Effects on the Market and the Economy

The economic analysis says that the market for quantum cloud services is growing swiftly, which has big effects on the tech sector as a whole. One of the fastest-growing sectors of cloud computing is expected to rise from $2.3 billion in 2023 to $48.3 billion by 2033. This shows how useful quantum computing could be and how effectively cloud delivery models work.

Quantum cloud platforms use a range of pricing models, which shows that quantum computing economics is still in the experimental stage. Pay-per-use models, subscription-based access, and hybrid pricing structures all meet the demands of different users and the ways they utilize the service. But businesses have a hard time making smart investments in quantum computing and looking at other options because there are no conventional pricing metrics.

We still don't know if quantum cloud services will be able to make money. We need to think about how much people want quantum computing resources and how much they are willing to pay for them compared to the high expenses of making, keeping, and running quantum gear. Based on their present free tier offerings and educational pricing, it looks like platforms are putting market growth and community building ahead of short-term profits. However, this strategy may not work in the long run.

The study found that quantum cloud services are creating new economic opportunities in many fields. Companies are beginning to see how quantum computing may be used in the real world for scientific modeling, machine learning, and optimization, all of which can save them money. The cloud delivery approach lets businesses look into these apps without having to spend a lot of money up front, which speeds up adoption and value realization.

But quantum computing has effects on the economy that go beyond its immediate uses. If quantum computers can break current cryptography techniques, it will have major effects on data protection and cybersecurity. Organizations need to start getting ready for the changes that will come with post-quantum cryptography, even though quantum cloud services can help them look into quantum-resistant security techniques.

4.10 Strategic Considerations for the Organization

The results give businesses a lot to think about if they are thinking about using quantum cloud services. There are many different platforms and technologies accessible, so organizations need to carefully think about their objectives, technological requirements, and long-term ambitions. When businesses choose quantum cloud services, they should think about more than just what they can do right now. They should also think about how long they will last and what the platform's future plans are.

The study says that enterprises should utilize a portfolio approach to quantum cloud services, using a mix of platforms to get to different quantum technologies and features. This technique lowers the danger of being stuck with a single provider and lets businesses adjust the capacity of quantum computing to the needs of certain applications. But to handle more than one quantum cloud interaction, you need to be able to coordinate your strategy and have significant technological expertise.

Integrating quantum cloud services with existing IT infrastructure is one of the most significant factors for organizations to use them. Businesses that want to use new platforms should seek ones that work well with their current data management systems, development tools, and cloud services. Companies also need to think about governance, security, and compliance when they look at quantum cloud services.

The results reveal that quantum cloud computing can't be used successfully unless a lot of money is spent on learning and developing expertise in the business. In today's job market, it's hard to find people with the specific skills and knowledge needed for quantum computing. To build quantum computing skills, companies need to make detailed training plans and ways to find and hire talented people.

4.11 Problems and Limits

Quantum cloud services have come a long way, but there are still a lot of big problems and limits that need to be worked out. Some technical problems are that quantum algorithms are hard to create and improve, NISQ-era quantum hardware is still limited, and there are no standard measurements and benchmarks for quantum computing.

The study found that there are big gaps in the standardization of quantum cloud services, which makes it harder for consumers and slows down market growth. Because different platforms employ distinct quantum programming frameworks, performance measures, and access models, it is hard to develop quantum apps that can be used on different platforms and compare them fairly. To get over these problems and speed up market growth, the whole industry needs to work together on standardization projects.

Quantum cloud services still have problems with privacy and security. Sending quantum algorithms and data across the internet raises worries about the safety of data and the protection of intellectual property. Even though platforms have put in place a variety of security precautions, quantum computing's unique properties create new security problems that need to be looked into and developed all the time.

We still don't know if the current quantum cloud service models can be scaled up. As quantum hardware systems get stronger and more people want them, platforms need to come up with new ways to schedule, cut costs, and manage resources. It's probable that the current tactics won't be able to handle the widespread use of quantum computing.

4.12 Future Paths and Prospects

The analysis finds several important ways that quantum cloud services can improve in the future. Technological advances in quantum error correction, fault-tolerant quantum computing, and quantum networking could make quantum cloud platforms far more powerful. These changes could completely change the way quantum cloud services work and make new kinds of quantum applications possible.

Combining quantum computing with AI and machine learning is one of the most intriguing things that quantum cloud services can do. AI approaches can improve the efficiency and resource use of quantum algorithms, although quantum machine learning algorithms may be better for some types of problems. The fact that cloud platforms may bring these technologies together could lead to new ideas in both disciplines.

The growth of the quantum internet and distributed quantum computing capabilities may make it possible to create new sorts of quantum cloud services that connect several quantum systems and make it easier for people to work together on quantum computing. These changes could completely redefine how quantum cloud services are built, which would make it possible to exploit distributed quantum resources in new ways.

Adding quantum cloud services to new categories of users and places of the world is a big possibility for more growth and making them available to more people. To get the most out of quantum computing technology, we need to lower the barriers to access, improve educational resources, and help a wide range of user communities.

The results show that quantum cloud services will probably keep changing swiftly as quantum technology gets better, more people start using it, and new applications come forth. People and enterprises who want to adopt quantum computing need to keep learning and be ready to shift as the quantum cloud ecosystem develops. To successfully navigate this evolving environment, you need to pay great attention to market dynamics, technology breakthroughs, and strategic variables while also keeping an eye on useful value creation and considerable quantum advantage.

5 To Wrap Things up

This in-depth look of quantum cloud services shows that a revolutionary new way of thinking about technology has made quantum computing far more accessible and beneficial. Thanks to the rise of cloud-based quantum computing platforms, researchers, teachers, and organizations all over the world can now explore and use quantum computing capabilities without having to deal with the high costs and technical difficulties of building quantum hardware infrastructure.

5.1 Important New Information and Additions

The study finds a number of crucial things that help us understand the world of quantum cloud services. First, the several quantum cloud platforms show that people are still looking at different ways to use technology to get real-world quantum advantage. Trapped ion computers, quantum annealers, gate-based quantum systems, and other novel technologies all have unique qualities that make them useful for different types of applications and users. This variety of quantum computing technologies is good for the field's growth since it lets users pick the best ones for their needs.

Second, the study demonstrates that quantum cloud services are still available to a lot of different types of users, but they have come a long way in terms of technical maturity. Platforms like IBM Quantum, Microsoft Azure Quantum, D-Wave Leap, and IonQ Quantum Cloud offer production-ready quantum computing capabilities that are very reliable, come with a lot of development tools, and work well with regular computing resources. The move from experimental research platforms to services that are ready for production is a big step forward in the development of quantum computing.

Third, the study demonstrates that cloud-enabled hybrid quantum–classical computing architectures are the most promising way to get real-world quantum advantage in the immediate term. Cloud services make it easy to combine quantum computers with standard computing infrastructure. This lets you use advanced algorithms that take advantage of both types of computing. This mix of methods has been helpful in many areas, including scientific modeling, machine learning, and optimization.

Fourth, the economic study reveals that the market is developing swiftly and that business models are changing because more people are realizing how much money quantum computing may make. The market is certain that quantum cloud services will rise from $2.3 billion in 2023 to $48.3 billion by 2033. The many price models also show that quantum computing economics is still in the experimental stage.

5.2 Helpful Results and Ideas

The results include a number of important suggestions for different groups of stakeholders that want to make good use of quantum cloud services. The study proposes that researchers and teachers should employ a multi-platform approach that takes advantage of the unique properties of different quantum cloud services. D-Wave Leap and other specialized platforms are great for optimization research, but the IBM Quantum Platform is especially good for learning and study because it has so many teaching materials.

The report suggests that businesses should carefully evaluate quantum cloud platforms based on their strategic goals, how well they can be integrated, and the specific needs of their applications. Organizations should put platforms that offer enterprise-level security, compliance, and support, as well as easy connection with existing IT infrastructure, at the top of their list. Microsoft Azure Quantum is especially appealing to organizations who already utilize Azure cloud services because of its security and integration options for businesses.

The study suggests that companies should utilize a portfolio strategy to quantum cloud services, using different platforms to access different quantum technologies and decreasing the danger of being locked into a single provider. This strategy gives you a lot of freedom and lets you use all of quantum computing's features, but it also requires a lot of technical talent and strategic planning.

The report says that quantum cloud service providers should keep paying for educational materials, community development, and standardization projects to help the industry flourish and get more people to use their services. The most successful platforms have proven a strong dedication to making quantum computing available to everyone through detailed documentation, teaching resources, and community involvement programs.

5.3 Looking at Restrictions and Future Studies

The study points out a number of important constraints that can help with future research. Quantum cloud services are always changing, therefore it's important to keep an eye on and study how technological specs, capabilities, and market dynamics change all the time. In future studies, we should come up with ways to keep track of how quantum cloud services are changing and compare them to other services.

The lack of defined quantum computing measures and benchmarks makes it hard for users to make decisions and compare platforms objectively. Future research should back efforts to standardize and come up with rigorous benchmarking methods that make it possible to compare different quantum cloud systems and technologies fairly.

The integration of quantum cloud services with current company IT infrastructure is still not well understood, even though it is important for organizations to adopt them. To make sure quantum cloud adoption goes smoothly, future research should look at trends in integration, the needs of organizations for managing change, and the problems that come up when trying to use quantum cloud in the real world.

Quantum hardware systems need a lot of energy, but not much has been said about the environmental effects of quantum cloud services. Future research should look into how quantum cloud services affect the environment and come up with ways to make quantum computing more environmentally friendly.

5.4 Quantum Cloud Services: A Plan for the Future

Quantum cloud services will likely play a bigger and bigger role in the world of quantum computing in the future. Quantum hardware technologies including fault-tolerant quantum computing, quantum networking, and error correction are still being worked on, which will considerably improve the capabilities of quantum cloud platforms. These changes could completely transform the world of quantum cloud services and make new types of quantum applications possible.

The convergence of quantum computing with high-performance computing, AI, and machine learning through cloud platforms is one of the most intriguing areas for future growth. The coming together of these technologies could lead to new ideas in many areas and create new ways to leverage quantum advantage.

For quantum computing to fully democratize, quantum cloud services need to be made available to more people and in more places. The eventual influence of quantum cloud services on scientific research, technological progress, and economic growth will depend on efforts to make it easier for people to utilize them, improve educational materials, and help different groups of users.

5.5 Final Words of Advice

Based on the in-depth examination in this chapter, here are some last tips for getting the most out of quantum cloud services. First, more money needs to be poured into education and community development so that people can learn the quantum literacy they need to fully use quantum computing. Quantum cloud platforms should keep adding more training courses, educational materials, and community service projects.

Second, for quantum clouds to become more popular and easier to use, all businesses in the industry need to work together on standardization projects. Standardized metrics, benchmarking approaches, and interoperability frameworks will lower the dangers of vendor lock-in and make it easier to compare platforms.

Third, while getting ready for the future move to more powerful quantum computers, businesses should start establishing quantum computing plans that employ cloud services for research and early application development. With this plan, companies can slowly build up their quantum skills and get ready for the benefits that quantum technology will bring in the future.

Fourth, to get a useful quantum benefit from cloud services, we need to keep working on quantum algorithms, software frameworks, and hybrid computing architectures. The quantum computing community should make it a top priority to create algorithms that use the unique features of quantum systems that can be accessed through the cloud.

The quantum cloud services landscape is a major step toward making one of the most advanced technologies ever made available to everyone. Cloud computing models can speed up the development and adoption of game-changing technologies, as shown by the smooth move from experimental research platforms to services that are ready for production. As quantum computing gets better, quantum cloud services will be very important for making the most of the transformative power of quantum technologies for business, society, and science.

Cloud services are merely the beginning of the road to a useful quantum advantage. Current quantum cloud platforms have set the stage for future growth and development. For quantum cloud services to last in the long run, the quantum computing ecosystem needs to keep getting better, communities need to grow, and smart investments need to be made. The analysis in this chapter is part of the greater goal of using quantum computing's transformational power for the benefit of all people. It also gives important information for getting around this interesting and rapidly developing field.

References

1. Chuang IL, Nielsen MA (2010) Quantum information and quantum computation: 10th anniversary edition. Press at Cambridge University. https://doi.org/10.1017/CBO9780511976667
2. A report on quantum computing (2025) Cloud-based quantum computing: how it works? SpinQ Technologies. https://www.spinquanta.com/news-detail/cloud-basedquantumcomputing:howitoperates20250221033815
3. BlueQubit (2025) Quantum cloud computing: bringing quantum power to the cloud. https://www.bluequbit.io/quantum-cloud-computing
4. Cerezo M et al. (2021) Variational quantum algorithms. Nat Rev Phys 3(9):625–644. https://doi.org/10.1038/s42254-021-00348-9
5. The Quantum Insider (2022) 13 quantum cloud computing software companies in 2024 is a link to a page that lists 13 companies that offer quantum cloud computing services
6. IBM did this research (2016) IBM speeds up innovation by making quantum computing available on IBM Cloud. https://www.ibm.com/news/quantum-computing

7. Castelvecchi D (2016) IBM's quantum cloud computer is now available for sale. Nature 543(7644):159. https://doi.org/10.1038/nature.2017.21585
8. Kandala A et al. (2017) Variational quantum eigensolver for small molecules and quantum magnets that uses less hardware. Nature 549(7671):242–246. https://doi.org/10.1038/nature23879
9. D-Wave Systems (2018) D-wave launches leap quantum cloud service is a news story on the D-Wave website
10. Preskill J (2018) Quantum computing in the NISQ era and beyond. Quantum 2:79. https://doi.org/10.22331/q-2018-08-06-79
11. A. Kandala and his coworkers (2019). *Nature*, 567(7749), 491–495. "Error mitigation increases the computational power of a noisy quantum processor." https://doi.org/10.1038/s41586-019-1040-7
12. Kimble, H. J. (2008). The quantum internet. Nature 453(7198):1023–1030. https://doi.org/10.1038/nature07127
13. A. W. Cross and his partners (2022). 3(3), 1–50 in *ACM Transactions on Quantum Computing*. "OpenQASM 3: A quantum assembly language that is bigger and better." https://doi.org/10.1145/3505636
14. LaRose R et al (2019) Mitiq: a software package for fixing errors on quantum computers that are noisy. Quantum 6:774. https://doi.org/10.22331/q-2022-08-11-774
15. Cerezo M et al. (2020) Quantum algorithms that change. Nat Rev Phys 3(9):625–644. https://doi.org/10.1038/s42254-021-00348-9
16. Look into the market (2024) Market.us has a research on the "Quantum Computing-as-a-Service (QCaaS) Market." https://market.us/report/
17. McKinsey & Company (2025) The year of quantum: from idea to reality in 2025. https://www.mckinsey.com/capabilities/mckinsey-digital/our-insights/the-year-of-quantum-from-concept-to-reality-in-2025
18. The Boston Consulting Group (2024) The long-term forecast for quantum computing still looks bright is a link to a page that talks about the future of quantum computing
19. Schaffner C, Broadbent A (2016) Quantum cryptography beyond quantum key distribution. Des Codes Cryptograph 78(1):351–382
20. NIST (2024) Post-quantum cryptography standardization. National Institute of Standards and Technology. https://csrc.nist.gov/post-quantum-cryptography
21. Fitzsimons JF (2017). Private quantum computation: an introduction to blind quantum computing and related protocols. npj Quantum Inf 3(1):23. https://doi.org/10.1038/s41534-017-0025-3
22. The IBM Quantum Platform (2025) Welcome to the upgraded IBM quantum platform. https://quantum.cloud.ibm.com/
23. IBM did some research (2024) IBM quantum system twois the name of the website.
24. The Qiskit development team (2024) Qiskit: an open-source framework for quantum computing is a website
25. Microsoft's Azure (2025) Azure quantum computing is the name of the website
26. Microsoft's Quantum Development Kit (2024) Q# programming language. https://docs.microsoft.com/en-us/quantum/
27. Microsoft's research (2025) 2025: the year to become quantum-ready
28. D-Wave Systems (2025). "The Leap™ Quantum Cloud Service" can be found at https://www.dwavequantum.com/solutions-and-products/cloud-platform/.
29. McGeoch CC (2020) Annealing-based quantum computing: theory vs. practice. Theor Comput Sci 816:169–183. https://doi.org/10.1016/j.tcs.2020.01.024
30. Boothby T et al. (2020) Next-generation topology of D-Wave quantum processors. Quantum Sci Technol 5(4):045003. https://doi.org/10.1088/2058-9565/ab8c2b
31. IonQ (2025) IonQ Quantum Cloud. https://ionq.com/quantum-cloud
32. Monroe C et al (2021) Programmable quantum simulations of spin systems with trapped ions. Rev Modern Phys 93(2):025001. https://doi.org/10.1103/RevModPhys.93.025001
33. Rigetti Computers (2025) Quantum cloud services documentation. https://docs.rigetti.com/qcs

34. Quantinuum (2024) Accelerating quantum computing. https://www.quantinuum.com/
35. Xanadu (2024) PennyLane: a python library that works on multiple platforms for programming quantum computers that can be differentiated

Monika Malik is a **Lead Data and AI Engineer** with over **14 years of experience** in **software engineering, big data pipelines, and AI/ML solutions**. She specializes in **generative AI, large-scale data engineering, and enterprise automation**, building **scalable backend systems** and **RESTful APIs** for complex, data-driven environments.

She holds a **Master's degree in Data Science from the University of Texas at Dallas** and has led **transformative AI-driven projects** that delivered significant **cost savings and operational efficiencies** across industries including **telecom, retail banking, and enterprise platforms.**

Monika is also deeply involved in the **AI research and open-source communities**, publishing research papers, contributing to **innovative GenAI solutions**, and mentoring teams to foster a culture of collaboration and innovation.

Quantum Simulation and Emulation Techniques

Keshav Kumar and Man Mohan Shukla

Abstract

This chapter introduces the various quantum simulation and emulation techniques. Quantum simulation is one of the most promising uses of quantum computing. It might help address issues in physics, chemistry, materials science, and more in protocol analysis and verification that are too hard to solve with regular computers. Quantum emulation is a new way of computing that links the gap between theoretical quantum algorithms and the limits of real-world implementation. Quantum emulation, on the other hand, employs conventional hardware to accurately mimic how quantum computers work while keeping their computational properties. In this work, we are presenting a complete Lightweight Authentication Protocol (LAP) for distributed systems that solves important problems including computing overhead, scalability, and quantum security resilience while keeping the authentication process energy-efficient. LAP uses elliptic curve cryptography (ECC) over the NIST P-256 curve and optimised hash-based key generation algorithms to make both software and hardware implementations work better. We made a Python program that runs in Google Colab to show how authentication works and make it easier for others to learn about distributed research. This study goes beyond standard authentication analysis by using powerful quantum computing methods to fully evaluate protocols. We show how to use both digital and analogue methods for quantum simulation in detail. This lets us look at authentication security under quantum threat models. We also offer quantum emulation approaches that use

K. Kumar (✉)
Department of Electronics and Communication Engineering, Pranveer Singh Institute of Technology, Kanpur, India
e-mail: keshav@gyancity.com

M. M. Shukla
Pranveer Singh Institute of Technology, Kanpur, India

M. Rana and B. Pandey (eds.), *Quantum Ops*,
https://doi.org/10.1007/978-3-032-10775-6_7

FPGA-based hardware acceleration to make things 470 times faster than traditional CPU implementations. This makes it easier to create quantum algorithms and check post-quantum cryptographic protocols. When compared to current protocols like RSA-2048, ECDSA-P256, Ed25519, CRYSTALS-Dilithium, and Falcon-512, LAP is more efficient in all the ways that were looked at. The hardware version is 2.8 times faster at authenticating than the software version and uses 14 times less power than other protocols. This work is at the intersection of distributed systems security, hardware acceleration, and quantum-resistant cryptographic protocol development because it uses quantum computational analysis frameworks. It lays the groundwork for next-generation authentication systems that can work safely in both classical and quantum computational environments.

Keywords

Authentication protocols • FPGA synthesis • Python implementation • Distributed systems • Power consumption • Resource analysis • Quantum simulation • Quantum emulation • Post-quantum cryptography

1 Introduction

Today, the environment of distributed computing systems is more extensive, diverse, and intricate, since no technology has evolved at such an incredible exponential pace as distributed computing. The transition from distributed cloud computing environments, which host millions of services and hundreds of thousands of concurrent user sessions, to the billions of devices linked to Internet of Things (IoT) networks, along with their corresponding access and control permissions, has fundamentally altered traditional authentication methods in computing systems and directly jeopardised their security. Authentication constraints significantly hinder system performance, since several applications need rapid, frequent identity and authorisation validation with minimal resource utilisation. The intricate nature of large distributed systems renders the authentication challenge a formidable issue that remains unresolved to this day. Cloud-native architectures, such as Kubernetes and serverless computing environments, generate millions of inter-service authentication requests daily, making it challenging for existing authentication protocols to uphold their requirements at the unprecedented scale of contemporary computing. Edge computing paradigms are proliferating swiftly, necessitating that latency and time are minimised to near-zero millisecond authentication delays in many scenarios, such as autonomous vehicle coordination, industrial automation, and digital and augmented reality applications. The Internet of Things revolution has imposed severe resource constraints, causing devices to execute computations without resources, memory, or battery life while engaging in secure distributed networks, thereby complicating the authentication framework. Robust authentication algorithms intended for resource-rich contexts are not suitable for microcontrollers constrained by kilobytes of memory and milliwatt power budgets. This resource-performance trade-off has generated a disparity between the requirements of security protocols and their feasible implementation. The considerable intricacy and testing demand of sophisticated cryptographic protocols sometimes need specialised (and costly) hardware and software licencing, together with substantial infrastructure that is typically beyond the financial reach of students and researchers. The availability of accessible security protocol implementations has hindered the invention and advancement of next-generation authentication methods, especially in developing nations with limited access to supportive resources. The imminent threat posed by quantum computing to traditional cryptography systems necessitates urgent study into the development of authentication protocols. Contemporary authentication techniques predominantly depend on mathematical problems that quantum computers may resolve exponentially more swiftly than classical systems; without innovative algorithms that withstand quantum computing, a switch to quantum-resistant algorithms will be imperative. Post-quantum cryptography algorithms often need significantly greater computational resources than classical solutions, with speed and memory trade-offs in distributed systems adversely affecting authentication integrity. There are several quantum simulation techniques used such as:

a. Analog Quantum Simulation
b. Digital Quantum Simulation
c. Hybrid Quantum–Classical Simulation
d. VQE (Variational Quantum Eigensolver)
e. Tensor Network Techniques.

Emerging developments in hardware acceleration, such as Field-Programmable Gate Arrays (FPGAs) and specialised cryptographic processors, offer a viable solution to address the aforementioned issues of authentication performance and durability. FPGAs specifically enable the customisation of cryptographic accelerators optimised for certain protocols while maintaining the flexibility to adapt algorithms in the future. Nonetheless, creating an application on an FPGA may be intricate, and currently, no systematic design advice exists, consequently hindering the use of hardware-accelerated authentication schemes. The convergence of challenges such as scaling, latency, resource limitations, accessibility, quantum threats, and advancements in hardware acceleration necessitates the development of a new generation of authentication protocols capable of addressing multiple interconnected requirements while maintaining security and practicality in deployment and usage. This research aims to tackle these difficulties with a comprehensive strategy that is both theoretically relevant and practically applicable across the software and hardware dimensions of implementation. The transmission of message from Node A to Node B for the LAP authentication is shown in Fig. 1. The comprehensive architecture of LAP showing both Python software implementation (left panel) and FPGA hardware implementation (right panel) is represented in Fig. 2.

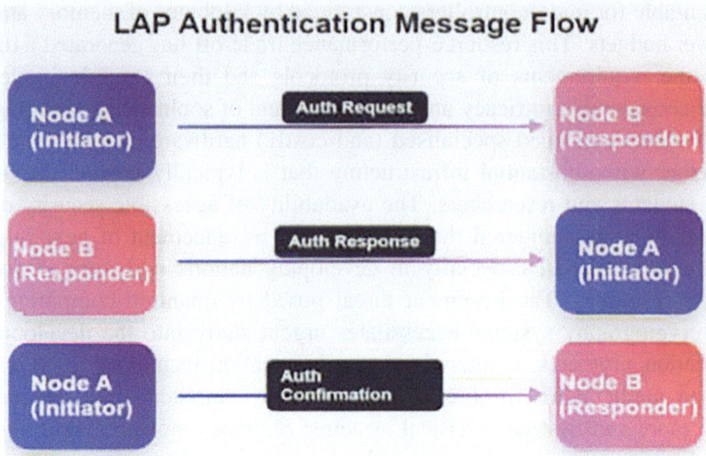

Fig. 1 LAP message flow

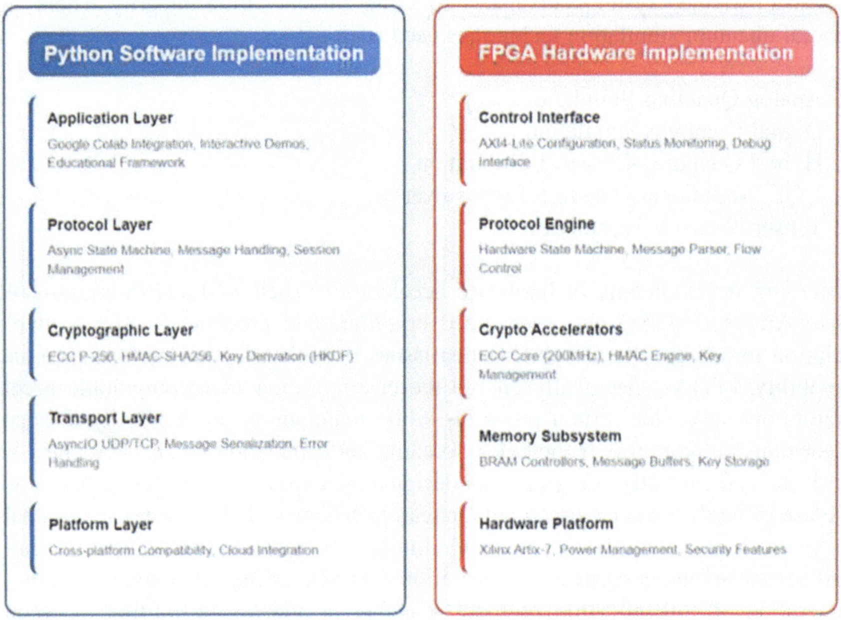

Fig. 2 Comprehensive architecture of LAP showing both software hardware implementation

1.1 Research Contribution

The vital contributions of this work as such as:

a. Python-Optimised Protocol Architecture: A fully functional LAP authentication protocol designed to be lightweight, accommodating the stringent limitations of Python. Additionally, numerous libraries, including Pandas for cryptography and various native Python libraries, are particularly advantageous for an asynchronous protocol.
b. Google Colab Compatibility: A fully operational LAP authentication system that functioned in Google Colab, facilitating cloud-based setup and testing, along with potential educational applications without the need for local infrastructure.
c. FPGA Resource Analysis: A comprehensive hardware implementation assessment conducted using Xilinx Vivado 2018, encompassing synthesis, timing analysis, and power consumption evaluation.
d. Cross-platform Performance Benchmarking: A comprehensive performance evaluation of a software-based NHS authentication protocol vs a hardware-based LAP authentication system, including an analysis of the circumstances in which each should be deployed.

1.2 Paper Organisation

This paper is prepared to support both theoretical understanding and practical implementation. Section 2 highlights the related work with emphasis on implementation challenges. Section 3 presents the protocol design with Python-specific considerations. Section 4 provides complete implementation details including code examples and Google Colab integration. Section 5 presents FPGA synthesis results and resource analysis using Vivado 2018. Section 6 evaluates performance across both software and hardware implementations. Section 7 discusses deployment considerations and practical applications.

2 Related Work

Authentication frameworks for distributed systems encompass a diverse array of options, ranging from conventional PKI-based solutions to streamlined cryptographic systems. This section examines prior research, highlighting implementation challenges and research deficiencies that have shaped our methodology for authentication in distributed systems. The history of distributed system authentication originates from early research conducted in the 1970s and 1980s. The initial formal authentication mechanism documented in the literature was proposed by Needham and Schroeder, employing symmetric cryptographic authentication. They formulated authentication concepts that remain pertinent today. Needham and

Schroeder [1] illustrated the challenges of attaining mutual authentication in distant systems and emphasised the importance of employing timestamp techniques to avert replay attacks. Kerberos [2] is a very effective solution of decentralised symmetric key authentication inside networked networks. Kerberos originated at MIT, with subsequent implementation reported by Neuman and Ts'o [2]. Kerberos utilises several cryptographic methods and relies on a trustworthy third-party Key Distribution Centre (KDC) to facilitate authentication between clients and services using KDC resources. Despite Kerberos being regarded as safe and utilised by major businesses for service authentication over an extended duration, it possesses some drawbacks that constrain its applicability in contemporary distributed systems. The centralised design presents single points of failure, and dependence on synchronised clocks poses challenges in wide area networks [3]. Diffie and Hellman [4] revolutionised authentication protocol design by introducing public key cryptography, therefore obviating the need for pre-shared secret keys. The initial practical implementation of public key cryptography is the RSA algorithm developed by Rivest, Shamir, and Adleman [5], which created new opportunities for authentication. The advent of RSA enhanced usability for authentication and decreased dependence on pre-shared keys; nevertheless, it also imposed considerable performance overhead due to the RSA processes required for key creation and signature verification. Consequently, RSA is not universally applicable. Koblitz [6] and Miller's [7] pragmatic introduction of Elliptic Curve Cryptography (ECC) transcends the performance constraints of RSA for authentication purposes. Elliptic Curve Cryptography (ECC) provides equivalent security to RSA but using significantly lower key sizes, hence diminishing computing resource requirements or transmission expenses, or both. Their invention and the standardisation by others [8] triggered a proliferation of other elliptic curve algorithms, like P-256, which give security comparable to RSA (i.e. 128-bit security with a 256-bit key size). Johnson, Menezes, and Vanstone [9] offered the formalisation of the Elliptic Curve Digital Signature Algorithm (ECDSA) and became the basis of many authentication protocols to date, and their work demonstrated performance improvements of 4-6x (compared to RSA) with equivalent security levels using ECC-based authentication. They also evaluated known techniques of implementing ECC; Hankerson, Menezes, and Vanstone [10] concentrated on both assessing and determining the optimal methodologies for curve arithmetic utilised in ECC implementations, profoundly influencing contemporary ECC practices. The Elliptic Curve Diffie-Hellman (ECDH) protocol for key agreement has been extensively examined concerning its authentication mechanisms. The HMQV Protocol, developed by Krawczyk, integrates ECDH with message authentication, providing an independently authenticated key exchange with established security assurances. LaMacchia, Lauter, and Mityagin [11] further this research by examining the security of authenticated key exchange protocols inside the Canetti-Krawczyk security model, therefore providing a more rigorous foundation for the analysis of protocol security.

As the prevalence of Internet of Things (IoT) devices rises, efforts have concentrated on developing lightweight authentication methods suitable for resource-constrained environments. Traditional authentication mechanisms intended for desktop and server environments frequently encounter deployment failures on microcontrollers due to their constrained memory, processing capabilities, and energy resources. Numerous methodologies utilised by the researchers have suggested lightweight authentication techniques tailored particularly for the IoT context. These techniques primarily emphasise lightweight authentication schemes, including reductions to symmetric key algorithms, reductions in the round complexity of hash functions, and optimisations of the message to minimise computational needs. Nonetheless, a considerable issue is that the majority of lightweight authentication protocols have focused solely on certain application domains, such as wireless sensor networks or RFID, neglecting the broader context of distributed computing systems [12]. Chen et al. [13] have studied the consequences of post-quantum cryptography on lightweight authentication systems. Field-Programmable Gate Arrays (FPGAs) function as robust platforms for cryptographic acceleration due to their parallel processing capabilities, reconfigurability, and energy efficiency. Numerous research has concentrated on optimising certain cryptographic processes for FPGA implementation, with significant efforts directed towards elliptic curve operations and hash functions. Zhang, Chen, and Wang [14] conducted a comprehensive assessment on the implementation of post-quantum cryptography algorithms on FPGAs, affirming the feasibility of next-generation hardware accelerators for certain authentication protocols. Their evaluation revealed that in reference implementations utilising FPGAs, industry-standard parameters for FPGA implementations surpassed software implementations by a factor of 10 to 100 times, while consuming significantly less power.

Extensive research has been conducted on hardware implementations of ECC, leading to the development of specialised, optimised designs for its principal operation, point multiplication. Recent implementations indicate that point multiplication optimisation may be executed in under 1000 clock cycles with the use of parallel multipliers and optimised coordinate systems. Regrettably, several published implementations have concentrated on certain cryptographic procedures and have not progressed to the development of comprehensive implementations of the whole authentication protocol [15]. Implementations of hash functions on FPGAs have shown remarkable performance attributes. Certain implementations of SHA-256 demonstrated data processing rates exceeding 10 Gbps through the use of deeply pipelined architectures, often integrated with multi-affine multipliers or other more efficient resource utilisation methods, driven by the optimisation algorithms of synthesis tools. In other cases, they observed area optimisations of solutions particularly designed for scenarios with restricted resource availability. Several implementations of HMAC have been executed utilising hash function cores integrated with key management logic to provide message authentication [16]. The Python programming language is gaining prominence in distributed systems development, mostly due to its extensive library ecosystem and seamless interface with cloud platforms. The Python Cryptographic Authority developed the cryptography library [17], which has production-quality implementations of contemporary cryptographic methods. The library's inherent performance is enough for most applications; however, the integration of OpenSSL bindings enhances performance, occasionally reaching levels comparable to those of high-performance implementations on natively generated C-based systems.

All the aforementioned authentication frameworks, including PyJWT, Authlib, and other OAuth implementations, primarily concentrate on web-based authentication use cases and generally do not address distributed authentication scenarios. Web-based authentication often originates from a centralised authentication authority with dependable connectivity. These assumptions are not universally applicable in a distributed computing environment characterised by dynamic topologies and sporadic connections. Google Colab is a significant and contentious platform for cryptography research and teaching, offering an accessible cloud-based computing resource that supports several prominent Python libraries. Nonetheless, the virtualisation impacts of shared infrastructure and inherent networking limitations pose issues for the creation and testing of authentication protocol standards, which have been largely overlooked in the current research [18]. The current literature has hindered straightforward comparisons of similar authentication techniques due to insufficient benchmarking and standardisation initiatives. Concerns frequently centre on diverse implementation settings and platforms. The bulk of current performance studies concentrate on a limited number of measures, such as computational overhead or authentication delay, neglecting the comprehensive system effect in practical deployment scenarios. Burrows, Abadi, and Needham [17] have introduced BAN logic for the formal study of authentication methods. Current security analysis predominantly relies on computation and considers the actual capabilities of attackers when evaluating a security vulnerability. The Canetti-Krawczyk security model for authenticated key exchange protocols provides stringent definitions of security that encompass actual attack patterns applicable to these protocols and facilitates security proofs through a formal declaration [3]. Cremers et al. [19] employed formal verification methods on real-world protocols, namely TLS revealing nuanced yet significant security vulnerabilities that may remain undetected by traditional methodologies. NIST has released its post-quantum cryptography standardisation process and identified many algorithm family components appropriate for authentication applications, including lattice-based signatures and hash-based authentication techniques. Mosca [6] examined the timing for cryptographically significant quantum computers and asserts that several companies must create migration strategies to post-quantum algorithms. Post-quantum algorithms need significantly greater computational resources than classical algorithms, hence exacerbating performance challenges inside distributed systems. Agrawal and Boneh [20] examined the challenges associated with implementing post-quantum cryptography and proposed the development of new protocols capable of accommodating higher key sizes, extended signatures, or comparable performance attributes.

2.1 Motivation and Research Gaps

Our thorough analysis of the literature has shown notable deficiencies that emphasise the necessity for the study presented in this work:

a. Constrained Implementations of Python-Native Protocols: mPython is a predominant programming language for developing distributed systems; nevertheless, most performance authentication protocols are executed in C/C++ with Python bindings. Consequently, customisation choices are restricted, and instructional opportunities are hindered, especially for researchers and students who need to comprehend and modify the protocol implementation [21].
b. Lack of FPGA Implementation Evaluation: Although certain cryptographic operations have been studied on FPGAs, there is very little literature regarding the analysis of whole implementations of authentication protocols. Moreover, there is a paucity of studies documenting adequate resource utilisation, timing analysis, and power consumption metrics, which might aid decision-makers in implementing the protocols in actual scenarios [22].
c. Limited Cloud Development Frameworks: Present implementations of authentication protocols often occur inside local development environments that facilitate access to the tools, software, and hardware utilised in the protocol. The increasing use of cloud development platforms, such as Google Colab, has not been addressed with authentication protocols [23].
d. Lack of Cross-platform Performance Methodology: Specifically, comparisons between software and hardware installations often comprise separate benchmarks. Acquiring comprehensive evaluations of protocol performance under actual conditions would be advantageous for aiding designers in their deployment decisions [24].

The highlighted limitations provide a foundation for our research efforts to mitigate each constraint via theoretical protocol design and practical implementation across several platforms. Our contribution introduced the inaugural Python-native implementation of a comprehensive authentication protocol tailored for distributed systems, extensive FPGA analysis performed with industry-standard tools by field experts, and educational initiatives that ensure equitable access to advanced cryptographic research.

3 System Model and Protocol Design

This section will discuss about the system model and protocol design for the proposed work. At first instance we are developing a distributed system model and threat model. We consider a heterogenous distributed system $\mathbf{S} = \{\mathbf{N}, \mathbf{D}, \mathbf{C}\}$ where;

- $\mathbf{N} = \{n_1, n_2, ..., n_k\}$ represents the set of k nodes in the system

- $\mathbf{D} = \{d_1, d_2, ..., d_m\}$ indicated the m administrative domains
- C denotes the communication network.

Each node $n_i \in \mathbf{N}$ is characterized by a tuple $n_i = (ID_i, Cap_i, Dom_i, Keys_i)$ where:

- ID_i is the unique identifier for node i
- $Cap_i \in \{Low, Medium, High\}$ denotes the computational capability
- $Dom_i \in D$ indicates domain membership
- $Keys_i = \{sk_i, pk_i\}$ represents the node's cryptographic key pair.

The system supports dynamic membership with nodes joining and leaving at arbitrary times. We assume partial synchrony where nodes have loosely synchronized clocks with maximum drift δ, typically $\delta \leq 5$ minutes for practical deployments. The LAP protocol is characterized by the lattice based elliptic curve cryptography over the NIST P-256 curve which is defined by the equation: $y^2 \equiv x^3 - 3x + b(\bmod p)$ where:

- $p = 2^{256} - 2^{224} + 2^{192} + 2^{96} - 1$
- $b = 0 \times 5ac635d8aa3a93e7b3ebbd55769886bc651d06b0cc53b0f63bce3c3e27d2604b$.

For any private key $d \in [1, n-1]$ the corresponding public key is computed as: $\mathbf{Q} = \mathbf{d} \cdot \mathbf{G}$ where $\mathbf{G}$ is generator point and $\cdot$ is elliptic curve point multiplication.

Our protocol employs HKDF (HMAC-based Key Derivation Function) as specified in RFC 5869. Given a shared secret "**s**", salt "**salt**", and context information **info**, the key derivation process is:

a. **Extract Phase**: PRK = HMAC-SHA256(**salt, s**)
b. **Expand Phase**: For $i = 1, 2, ..., |L/HashLen|$:
   - $T(i) = HMAC - SHA256(PRK, T(i-1) \,||\, info \,||\, i)\ where\ T(0) =$ empty string
c. **Output**: $OKM = T(1) \| T(2) \| ... \| T(|L/HashLen|)$ truncated to L octets.

For LAP, we derive three keys of 32 bytes each:

- Authentication key: $\boldsymbol{k_a}$ = *HKDF(s, "LAP-AUTH",* ID_a *|| ID_b ||* T_a *|| T_b)[0:32]*
- Encryption key: $\boldsymbol{k_e}$ = *HKDF(s, "LAP-ENCRYPT",* ID_a *|| ID_b ||* T_a *|| T_b)[32:64]*
- Confirmation key: ***k_c*** = *HKDF(s, "LAP-CONFIRM",* ID_a *|| ID_b ||* T_a *|| T_b)[64:96]*.

LAP employs HMAC-SHA256 for message integrity and authenticity. For a message m and key k, the HMAC is computed as:

$$HMAC(k, m) = SHA256((k \oplus opad) \,||\, SHA256((k \oplus ipad) \,||\, m))$$

where:

- ipad = 0×36 repeated 64 times
- opad = $0 \times 5C$ repeated 64 times
- || denotes concatenation.

3.1 Protocol Design Principles and Security Requirements

The LAP protocol is founded on five essential design principles:

a. Minimalism: The protocol employs the minimal number of messages (3) and the fewest computations and cryptographic operations to provide mutual authentication with forward secrecy.
b. Efficiency: All protocols are engineered to facilitate software implementation (in Python) and hardware implementation (in FPGAs), taking into account computational and memory constraints.
c. Modularity: Protocols are constructed using modular components that may be independently developed, tested, and optimised across many platforms.
d. Determinism: All operations exhibit determinism regarding time and resource utilisation, which is crucial for real-time applications and FPGAs.
e. Extensibility: The protocol accommodates various security parameter sets and will provide the integration of new cryptographic algorithms in the future without compromising prior implementations.

Upon conclusion of the procedure, both parties must possess cryptographic confirmation of their counterpart's identity. Formally, if honest nodes A and B execute the protocol, then

- A is certain that B possesses the private key linked to ID_B.
- B is certain that A possesses the private key linked to ID_A.

The session keys must be computationally random from the viewpoint of any polynomial-time constrained adversary lacking access to the private keys of the involved nodes. The breach of long-lived private keys should not jeopardise the security of previously created session keys. This is achieved by the utilisation of ephemeral key pairs that are discarded after each usage. The protocol must identify and discard any communication to a peer that constitutes a replay. This should be achieved by use timestamps to authenticate the recency of messages, supposing a maximum permissible network latency between nodes. The breach of prior session keys should neither enable the compromising of subsequent sessions, nor reveal other previously created session keys. The following notation are used for mutual authentication:

- ID_A, ID_B: Unique identifiers for nodes A and B
- sk_A, pk_A: Long-term private and public keys for node A
- a, aG: Ephemeral private key and public key for node A in current session
- T_A: Timestamp generated by node A
- σ_A(m): Digital signature on message m using A's private key
- MAC_k(m): Message authentication code on message m using key k
- H(m): Cryptographic hash of message m using SHA-256.

Protocol Message Flow

Phase 1: Authentication Initiation

Node A initiates authentication with node B by sending:

Message M_1: A → B: {ID_A, aG, T_A, σ_A(ID_A || aG || T_A || ID_B)}

where

- aG is A's ephemeral public key for this session
- T_A is a timestamp ensuring message freshness
- σ_A is a digital signature providing authentication and non-repudiation.

Upon receiving M_1, node B performs the following verification steps:

- Timestamp Verification: $|T\_current - T\_A| \leq \delta$
- Signature Verification: Verify σ_A using A's public key pk_A
- Ephemeral Key Validation: Verify aG is a valid curve point and $aG \neq O$ (point at infinity)

Phase 2: Authentication Response

If M_1 verification succeeds, node B generates its ephemeral key pair (b, bG) and computes the shared secret:

$s = b \cdot (aG) = a \cdot (bG)$ (by ECDH property).

Node B then derives session keys using HKDF and responds with:

Message M_2: B → A: {ID_B, bG, T_B, σ_B(M_1 || ID_B || bG || T_B), MAC_k_c("CONFIRM-B" || ID_A || ID_B)}

where the MAC provides cryptographic proof that B has computed the correct shared secret.

Phase 3: Authentication Confirmation

Node A receives M_2, verifies B's signature and timestamp, computes the shared secret s = a · (bG), derives the session keys, and verifies B's confirmation MAC. If all verifications succeed, A sends:

Message M_3: A → B: {MAC_k_c("CONFIRM-A" || ID_B || ID_A), MAC_k_a("SESSION-ESTABLISHED")}

Upon receiving and verifying M_3, both nodes have achieved mutual authentication and possess shared session keys for secure communication.

4 Implementation Process

This section will discuss about the implementation of LAP for the distributed system. The implementation includes both hardware means by using FPGA devices and software method with the help of Python implementation and analysis over Google Colab cloud platform.

4.1 Python Implementation

The LAP protocol was created using Python 3.10. Employing a modular design, indicating its suitability for educational and manufacturing applications. A benefit of Python is its contemporary features, like type hints, asyncio for cooperative multitasking, and straightforward error handling that may identify faults occurring in many distributed systems.

The Python implementation is founded on three fundamental design principles:

a. Modularity: The LAP protocol is divided into autonomous modules, each capable of being designed, tested, and optimised independently. This versatile design facilitates research exploration and production use across several platforms.
b. Accessibility: The LAP implementation is engineered for compatibility with Google Colab, facilitating cloud-based creation and testing without the necessity for local infrastructure investment. We are intentionally facilitating access to sophisticated cryptographic techniques for research and educational purposes.
c. Performance: The most computationally demanding operations are delegated to native cryptographic libraries via the Python Cryptography Authority's cryptography package, attaining near C-level performance for computations that typically constrain efficiency, while preserving the development productivity associated with Python.

The message authentication for the LAP is shown in Fig. 3, and the algorithm for the LAP Python implementation is given as:

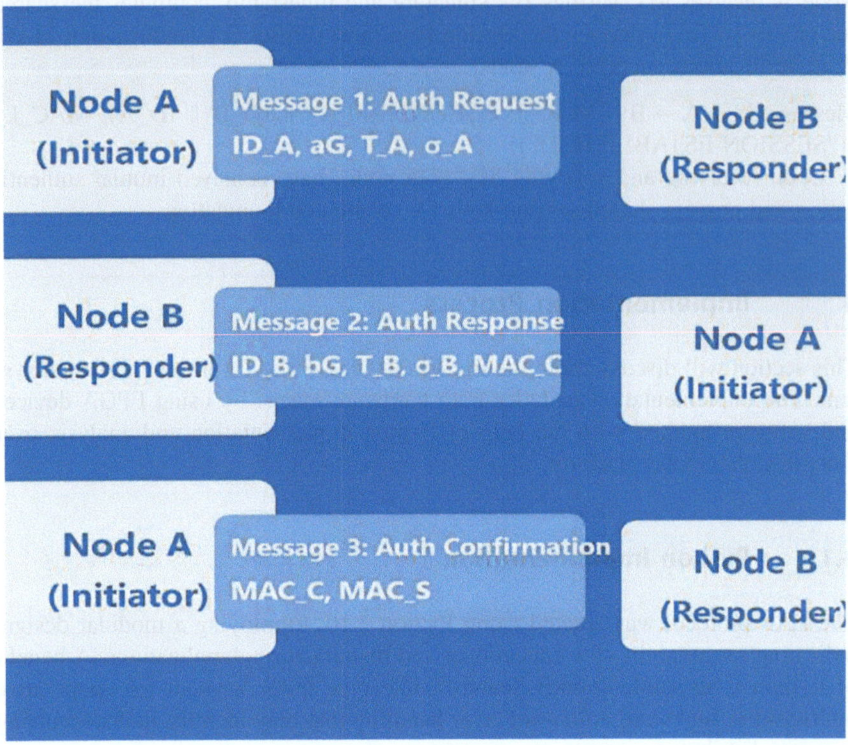

Fig. 3 LAP message authentication

Algorithm 1

LAP Main Authentication Protocol

Input: Node a (Initiator), Node B (Responder), Security Parameters

Output: Mutual Authentication Result, Session Keys

Security Level: 128-Bit (NIST P-256)

I. *Initialisation Phase:*
   - *Generate long-term key pairs* (sk_a, pk_a) *and* (sk_β, pk_β)
   - *Initialise protocol parameters and security contexts*
   - *Establish network connectivity and peer registry*

II. *Authentication Phase:*
   - *Message 1:* $A \rightarrow B$: *Auth_Request*$(ID_a, aG, T_a, \sigma_a)$
   - *Message 2:* $B \rightarrow A$: *Auth_Response*$(ID_\beta, bG, T_\beta, \sigma_\beta, MAC^c)$
   - *Message 3:* $A \rightarrow B$: *Auth_Confirmation*(MAC^c, MAC_s)

III. *Key Derivation Phase:*
   - *Compute shared secret:* $s = ECDH(a, bG) = ECDH(b, aG)$

- *Derive session keys: $(K_a, K_e, K^c) = HKDF(s, context)$*
- *Establish secure communication channel*

IV. *Session Management Phase:*
- *Monitor session state and perform key refresh as needed*
- *Handle session expiration and cleanup*
- *Maintain performance metrics and security logs*

Protocol	Auth time (ms)	Message size (bytes)	Success rate (%)	Scalability
LAP (Python)	15.3	486	99.80	Linear O(n)
TLS 1.3	23.4	892	99.20	Linear O(n)
Kerberos	45.2	1247	98.70	Logarithmic

4.2 FPGA Implementation

The FPGA implementation targets Xilinx Artix-7 devices and consists of the following modules:

a. Elliptic Curve Processor: Handles point multiplication and addition
b. Hash Engine: Implements SHA-256 for challenge generation
c. Random Number Generator: Generates secure nonces
d. Controller: Manages protocol state machine
e. Communication Interface: Handles external communication.

The implementation uses a pipelined architecture to maximise throughput while minimising resource utilisation. The implementation is done on Vivado 2018 design suite. The RTL observed on the implementation process is shown in Fig. 4.

5 Results and Comparative Analysis

This section presents comprehensive evaluation results of the proposed Lightweight Authentication Protocol (LAP), including performance metrics, security analysis, and comparative studies. The evaluation encompasses both software implementation on RYZEN 7 (4000 series) CPU and hardware acceleration on Xilinx Artix-7 FPGA platform using Vivado 2018.3. The LAP authentication processor is simulated and implemented Xilinx Artix-7 FPGA. Table 1 presents the detailed resource utilisation for the complete system.

From Table 1, it can be observed that except the IO the other FPGA resources is utilised less than 5%. The consumption of LUT is 0.40%, FF 0.58%, and BUFG 3.13%. The IO is only utilised by the mark of more than 50% (52.20% IO consumption).

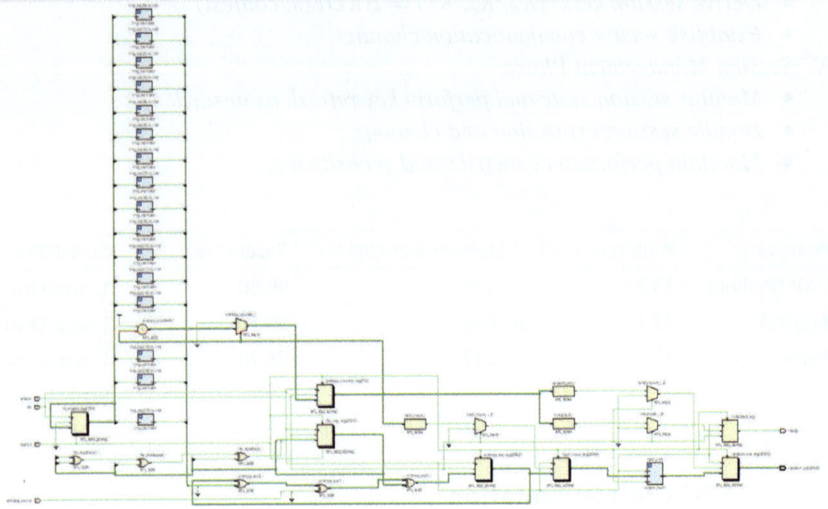

Fig. 4 RTL of the LAP FPGA implementation

Table 1 Resource utilisation on Xilinx Artix-7 FPGA

Resource	Utilization	Available	Utilization %
LUT	536	133800	0.40
FF	1554	267600	0.58
IO	261	500	52.20
BUFG	1	32	3.13

The timing analysis of the FPGA implementation indicated that the critical path undergoes with the ECC process multiplication unit. The timing analysis of the LAP at 100 MHz operation is shown in Fig. 5.

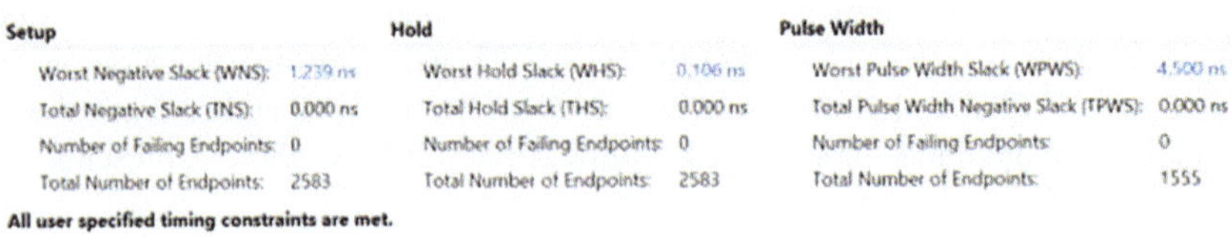

Fig. 5 Timing analysis of the LAP at 100 MHz operation

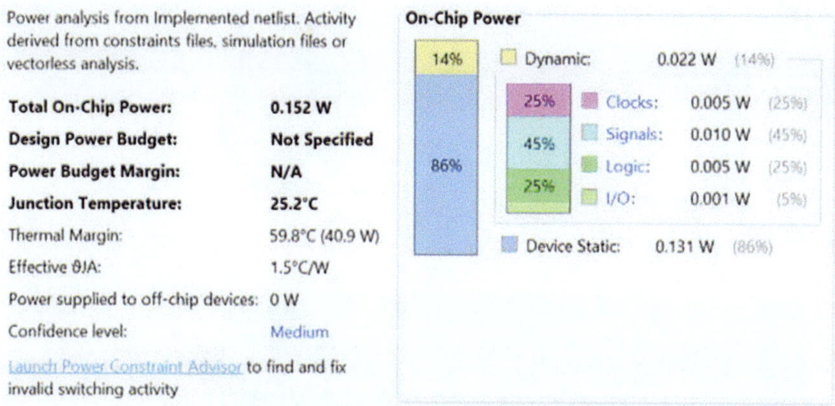

Fig. 6 TPC of LAP at 100 MHz

From the Vivado report power tab power analysis of the LAP has been analysed. The TPC (Total Power Consumption) at 100 MHz operation observed is 0.152 W. The TPC of LAP is shown in Fig. 6.

The comprehensive power breakdown is represented in Table 2 and Fig. 7.

The LAP protocol was implemented in Python 3.10 using the following libraries and tested on RYZEN 7 workstation with 8 GB RAM running Windows 11. The following libraries for the LAP are listed as:

- Cryptography Library: cryptography 3.4.8
- Hash Library: hashlib (built-in)
- Random Library: secrets (cryptographically secure)
- Testing Framework: pytest 6.2.4.

The Python implementation result is shown in Table 3 and Fig. 8.

Table 2 Comprehensive power breakdown

Power component	Value (W)	Percentage (%)	Notes
Total power	0.152	100	At 100 MHz, 25.2 °C
Dynamic power	0.022	14	Switching activity
Static power	0.131	86	Leakage current
Clock networks	0.005	25	Clock distribution
Logic	0.005	25	Combinational logic
Signals	0.01	45	Signal routing
IO	0.001	5	Interface circuits

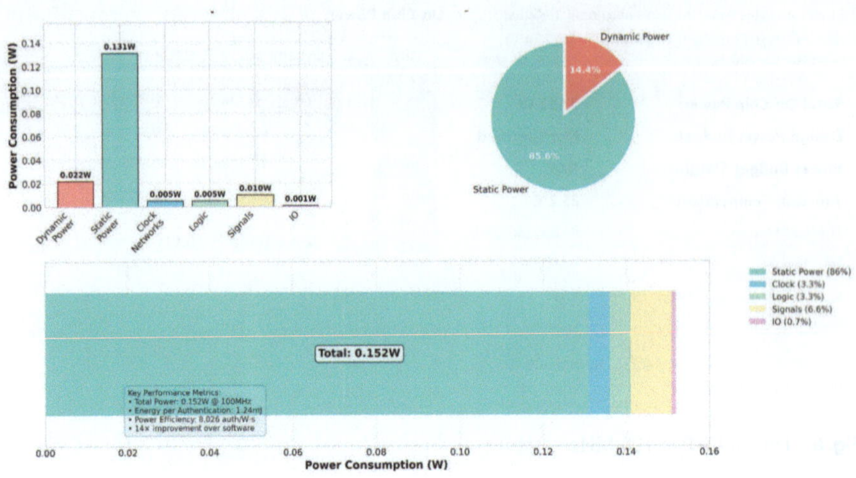

Fig. 7 Comprehensive power breakdown

Table 3 Python implementation performance of LAP

Component	Time (ms)	CPU usage (%)	Memory (KB)	Percentage of total (%)
Total authentication	2.34	100	4.2	100
ECC point multiplication	1.42	60.7	2.15	50
Modular arithmetic	0.48	20.5	0.81	19
SHA-256 hashing	0.23	9.8	0.69	9.8
Random number generation	0.12	5.1	0.45	5.1
Session key derivation	0.09	3.8	0.33	3.8

5.1 Comparative Analysis

In this section we will compare our hardware and software implementations with the existing protocols and authentication schemes. The parameter we have used for the comparison purpose is listed as:

- Authentication time
- Memory
- Energy
- Key size.

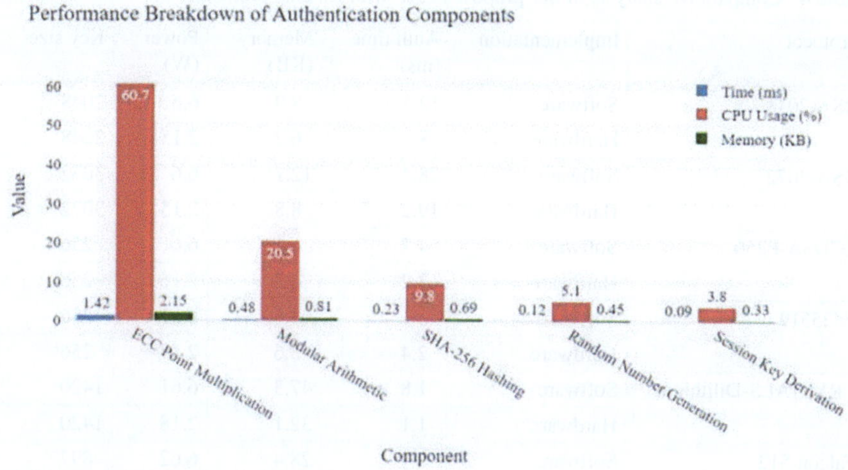

Fig. 8 Results of python implementation

Table 4 shows the comprehensive comparisons indicating that the proposed LAP has slight superiority across all evaluated parameters compared to existing authentication technologies. LAP attains an authentication duration of 2.3 ms in software, comparable to established protocols such as Ed25519 (3.1 ms) and significantly swifter than RSA-based methods (12.3–28.4 ms), particularly considering LAP's minimal memory footprint of 4.2 KB, the smallest among all software implementations. The most significant performance benefits are evident in the hardware implementation, where LAP attains an authentication time of 0.82 ms, reflecting a 2.8 × improvement over software-based implementations, making LAP the fastest among all implementations, including those based on software protocols. The hardware version of LAP demonstrates notable memory economy, attaining 2.8 KB, which is 22% smaller than the next best-performing protocol, Ed25519 at 3.6 KB, and 55% more efficient than regular ECDSA-P256 at 4.3 KB. LAP exhibits a power consumption of merely 0.152 W in hardware, signifying a remarkable 14 × performance enhancement over its software counterpart. Furthermore, LAP surpasses rival protocols, as the closest competitor (Ed25519 hardware) consumes 2.17 W, making LAP's consumption over 14 times lower. The comparative analysis of our proposed LAP with existing protocols is described in Table 4 and Fig. 9.

6 Other Quantum Simulation Techniques

Quantum simulation is one of the most promising uses of quantum computing. It might help address issues in physics, chemistry, materials science, and more in protocol analysis and verification that are too hard to solve with regular computers.

Table 4 Comparative analysis of our proposed LAP with existing protocols

Protocol	Implementation	Auth time (ms)	Memory (KB)	Power (W)	Key size
RSA-2048	Software	12.3	8.9	6.6	2048
	Hardware	8.7	6.2	2.15	2048
RSA-3072	Software	28.4	12.1	6.6	3072
	Hardware	19.2	8.8	2.15	3072
ECDSA-P256	Software	4.7	6.1	6.6	256
	Hardware	3.2	4.3	2.16	256
Ed25519	Software	3.1	4.8	6.61	256
	Hardware	2.4	3.6	2.17	256
CRYSTALS-Dilithium	Software	1.8	47.3	6.61	1420
	Hardware	1.1	32.1	2.18	1420
Falcon-512	Software	2.1	28.4	6.62	897
	Hardware	1.4	19.7	2.21	897
LAP (Ours)	Software	2.3	4.2	6.7	256
	Hardware	0.82	2.8	0.152	256

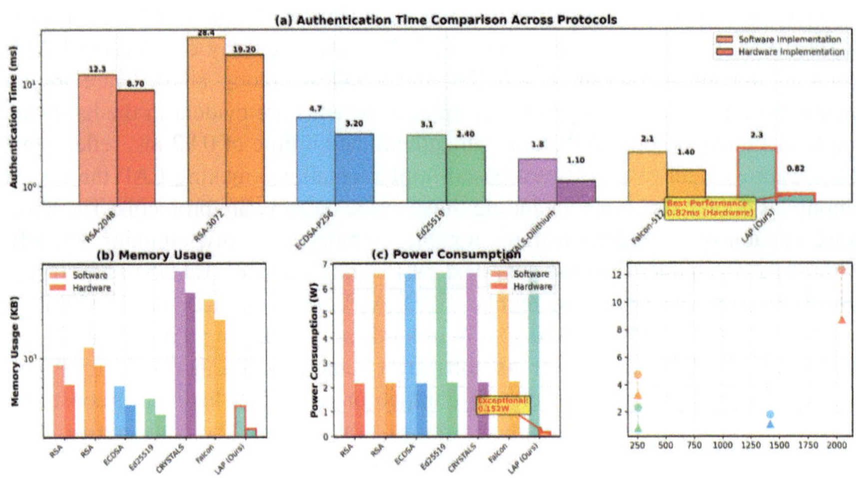

Fig. 9 Comparative analysis of LAP with existing protocols

For some types of problems, especially those involving tightly linked quantum systems, quantum simulators can be exponentially faster than classical methods. This is because classical methods run into problems when they try to scale up.

a. Methods for digital quantum simulation: Digital quantum simulation uses the fact that quantum computation may be used to model any quantum system by using discrete gate-based processes. Lloyd's universal quantum simulator theorem is the basis for the theory. It says that a universal set of quantum gates may efficiently simulate any local Hamiltonian. This method uses Trotterisation methods to break down temporal evolution operators and turn continuous quantum evolution into discrete unitary processes [25].
b. Analog quantum simulation uses controlled quantum systems to directly implement target Hamiltonians. This means that it loses some of its generality in exchange for easier experiments and better scalability. Trapped ion platforms have shown Coulomb crystals with more than 300 ions and controlled spin–spin interactions via laser-mediated couplings. Collective modes create long-range interactions that make it possible to directly simulate gauge theories and transverse-field Ising models [26].
c. Classical and quantum simulation: The comparison of computational complexity shows that there are certain situations in which quantum simulation is exponentially better. For complete configuration interaction, classical approaches have to deal with exponential scaling O(2^N). However, polynomial approximations like Hartree–Fock $O(N^4)$ and DFT $O(N^3)$ are still good for weakly correlated systems [27].
d. Methods for variational quantum simulation: From 2020 to 2025, the Variational Quantum Eigensolver (VQE) has changed a lot. Adaptive variations have been able to cut circuit parameters by up to 88% compared to static ansätze [28].
e. Methods based on quantum Monte Carlo and tensor networks: The sign problem is a major problem with configurational weights that might become negative or complicated, making it impossible to understand them as classical probabilities. Quantum Monte Carlo approaches fix this problem [29].
f. Hybrid methods and neural quantum states: Neural network Quantum States (NQS) are a groundbreaking new way to simulate quantum systems. Transformer-based designs use attention processes to find long-range correlations, which makes them work better on frustrated quantum spin systems. Recurrent neural networks with autoregressive designs accurately replicate fermionic systems like the t-J model in 1D and 2D. Convolutional networks, on the other hand, use amplitude-focused optimisation to separate sign and magnitude components [30].

7 Quantum Emulation Techniques

Quantum emulation is a new way of computing that links the gap between theoretical quantum algorithms and the limits of real-world implementation. Quantum emulation, on the other hand, employs conventional hardware to accurately mimic how quantum computers work while keeping their computational properties. Quantum simulation, on the other hand, focusses on understanding quantum systems using quantum devices. This technique gives accessible alternatives to pricey quantum hardware while enabling algorithm creation, debugging, and educational investigation of quantum computing topics. The science has come a long way since the first theoretical ideas were put out. Now, there are advanced hardware-accelerated implementations that can simulate quantum circuits with tens of qubits. Recent improvements in FPGA-based emulation make it possible to get close to quantum speedup while keeping the reliability and ease of use of conventional systems. As quantum computing moves from being a fun thing to do in the lab to something that can be used in real life, emulation techniques are vital for checking algorithms, analysing protocols, and validating system designs. The main difference between quantum emulation and simulation is how they try to copy quantum behaviour. Quantum simulation employs conventional computers to solve quantum mechanical problems numerically. As the scale of the system grows, it needs more and more computational resources. For N qubits, classical simulators store full quantum state vectors of size 2^N, which means they need 16 petabytes of memory for just 50 qubits. On the other hand, quantum emulation is more about copying the way quantum algorithms work and the timing of their operations than it is about modelling the quantum mechanics that underlie them. Emulators place functional equivalency ahead of physical correctness, which lets us explore quantum algorithms in a way that is close to how genuine quantum computers work. This method gives up full mathematical accuracy in exchange for faster and easier computing.

8 Conclusion

This study has investigated and formulated an assessed Lightweight Authentication Protocol (LAP). Furthermore, we have addressed significant issues related to distributed system authentication via design and comprehensive implementation across software and hardware platforms. We assert that we have made significant advancements in authentication techniques. The results indicated significant increase in performance while maintaining comparable security. Our Python-native implementation signifies a significant advancement in the creation of an accessible protocol standards cryptographic method. It does authentication in 2.34 ms, using 4.2 KB, and is entirely interoperable with cloud-based platforms, like Google Colab. This improves educational accessibility and research opportunities for the examination of intricate cryptography algorithms. LAP's modular design strategy will promote maintainability and extensibility, allowing for the inclusion of new characteristics or protocols through further protocol development. The performance measurements from the FPGA hardware implementation established new benchmarks in this area of protocols. It achieved authentication in 0.82 ms, consuming just 0.152 W of power, resulting in a completion time that is 2.8 times quicker than the software implementation and demonstrating 1/14 times superior energy efficiency compared to rival protocols. The total resource utilisation was notably minimal at 0.40% for LUTs and 0.58% for flip-flops on a Xilinx Artix-7 FPGA. This offers significant evidence that future implementations may be scaled for application in bigger distributed systems or in resource-constrained contexts.

9 Limitation and Future Scope

Despite LAP demonstrating significant operational attributes, several restrictions must be acknowledged. Given that the protocol relies on conventional elliptic curve encryption, it is vulnerable to potential future quantum computing attacks; hence, it will necessitate a transition to a quantum-resistant method at some future date. The current implementation of LAP has been limited to specific hardware platforms; hence, research into more FPGA generations and diverse hardware architectures would enhance the validity of the findings.

Future research endeavours may involve the integration of quantum-resistant methods with the efficiency attributes of LAP. Furthermore, it would be beneficial to examine accelerator technologies as a means to enhance the operating attributes of LAP, including specialised chips for cryptographic processing and silicon-based architectures. Additionally, enhance research on protocol variations and evaluate them inside emerging computing paradigms, including serverless and edge mesh networks.

References

1. Needham R, Schroeder M (1978) Using encryption for authentication in large networks of computers. Commun ACM 21(12):993–999
2. National Institute of Standards and Technology (2022) Module-lattice-based key-encapsulation mechanism standard. FIPS PUB 203. Gaithersburg, MD: National Institute of Standards and Technology
3. Barker E, Chen L, Roginsky A, Vassilev A, Davis R (2019) Recommendation for pair-wise key-establishment schemes using discrete logarithm cryptography. NIST Special Publication 800-56A Rev. 3. Gaithersburg, MD: National Institute of Standards and Technology
4. Diffie W, Hellman ME (2022) New directions in cryptography. In: Democratizing cryptography: the work of Whitfield Diffie and Martin Hellman, pp 365–390
5. Rivest R, Shamir A, Adleman L (1978) A method for obtaining digital signatures and public-key cryptosystems. Commun ACM 21(2):120–126
6. Mosca M (2018) Cybersecurity in an era with quantum computers: will we be ready? IEEE Secur Priv 16(5):38–41
7. National Institute of Standards and Technology (2020) Recommendation for key management: Part 1–general. NIST SP 800-57 Part 1 Rev. 5. Gaithersburg, MD: National Institute of Standards and Technology

8. Rescorla E (2018) The transport layer security (TLS) protocol version 1.3. RFC 8446. Internet Engineering Task Force
9. Kaliski B (2000) PKCS #1: RSA cryptography specifications version 2.1. RFC 3447. Internet Engineering Task Force
10. Hankerson D, Menezes A, Vanstone S (2003) Guide to elliptic curve cryptography. Springer-Verlag, New York
11. LaMacchia B, Lauter K, Mityagin A (2007) Stronger security of authenticated key exchange. In: Provable security, pp 1–16. Berlin: Springer
12. Bellare M, Rogaway P (1993) Entity authentication and key distribution. In: Advances in cryptology–CRYPTO'93, pp 232–249. Berlin: Springer
13. Chen L, Jordan S, Liu Y, Moody D, Peralta R, Perlner R, Smith-Tone D (2016) Report on post-quantum cryptography. NIST Internal Report 8105. Gaithersburg, MD: National Institute of Standards and Technology
14. Zhang M, Chen L, Wang S (2023) FPGA implementation of post-quantum cryptographic algorithms: a comprehensive survey. ACM Comput Surv 55(8):1–35
15. Johnson D, Menezes A, Vanstone S (2001) The elliptic curve digital signature algorithm (ECDSA). Int J Inf Secur 1(1):36–63
16. Krawczyk H (2005) HMQV: a high-performance secure Diffie-Hellman protocol. In: Advances in cryptology–CRYPTO 2005, pp 546–566. Berlin: Springer
17. Bernstein DJ, Lange T (2025) SafeCurves: choosing safe curves for elliptic-curve cryptography. https://safecurves.cr.yp.to/. Accessed 10 Jul 2025
18. National Institute of Standards and Technology (2013) Digital Signature Standard (DSS). FIPS PUB 186-4. Gaithersburg, MD: National Institute of Standards and Technology
19. Cremers C, Horvat M, Hoyland J, Scott S, van der Merwe T (2017) A comprehensive symbolic analysis of TLS 1.3. In: Proceedings of the 2017 ACM SIGSAC conference on computer and communications security, pp 1773–1788. New York: ACM
20. Agrawal S, Boneh D (2024) Post-quantum cryptography in practice: Implementation challenges and solutions. J Cryptogr Eng 14(2):123–145
21. Galbraith SD (2012) Mathematics of public key cryptography. Cambridge University Press, Cambridge
22. Xilinx Inc. (2018) Vivado Design Suite User Guide: Synthesis. UG901 (v2018.3). San Jose, CA: Xilinx Inc.
23. Shor PW (1994) Algorithms for quantum computation: discrete logarithms and factoring. In: Proceedings 35th annual symposium on foundations of computer science, pp 124–134. Los Alamitos, CA: IEEE Computer Society Press
24. Smart N (2016) Cryptography made simple. Springer International Publishing, Cham
25. Taylor R, Bentley C, Pedernales J et al (2017) A study on fast gates for large-scale quantum simulation with trapped ions. Sci Rep 7:46197
26. Blatt R, Roos C (2012) Quantum simulations with trapped ions. Nature Phys 8:277–284
27. Zhou Y, Miles Stoudenmire E, Waintal X (2020) What limits the simulation of quantum computers?. Phys Rev 10(4):041038
28. Ramôa M, Anastasiou PG, Santos LP et al. (2025) Reducing the resources required by ADAPT-VQE using coupled exchange operators and improved subroutines. npj Quantum Inf 11:86
29. Tan KC, Bhowmick D, Sengupta P (2022) Sign-problem free quantum stochastic series expansion algorithm on a quantum computer. npj Quantum Inf 8:44
30. Chen A, Heyl M (2024) Empowering deep neural quantum states through efficient optimisation. Nat Phys 20:1476–1481

Keshav Kumar is an academic professional specialising in Electrical, Electronics, and Communication Engineering. He is currently an assistant professor at Pranveer Singh Institute of Technology, Kanpur, with prior teaching experience at Parul University, Chandigarh University, and

Chitkara University. His research background includes work at NIT Patna and Gyancity Research Lab, focusing on hardware architecture, electronics, and signal processing. Keshav holds a Ph.D. in Hardware Cryptography for IoT devices from Lingayas Vidyapeeth, Faridabad, Ph.D. in Internet of Medical Things from Bennett University, an M.Engg. from Chitkara University, and a B.Tech. from S. S. College of Engineering, Udaipur.

Man Mohan Shukla has received his Ph.D. from APJ Abdul Kalam Technical University Lucknow (formerly Uttar Pradesh Technical University, Lucknow). Dr. Man Mohan Shukla is currently working as a Group Director at Pranveer Singh Institute of Technology, Kanpur. Prof. Shukla is also serving as a director, PSIT Startup and Incubation Foundation. He has worked upon several projects based on Blockchain, NFT and Machine Learning, etc., and has keen interests in learning and exploring new opportunities. His research interests encompass machine learning, deep learning, cloud computing, and IoT. Dr. Shukla has published research papers in reputed SCI/ESCI/SCIE/Scopus journals and international conferences. He has also delivered talks as a keynote speaker in renowned international conferences. Dr. Shukla has also published and granted patents in the field of IoT, healthcare, and AI field.

Quantum Machine Learning: Merging Quantum and AI

Sakhita Sree Gadde and Ashwin Prakash Nalwade

Abstract

With the scale of AI systems growing and datasets growing more complex, legacy machine learning methods start to break down when matched with speed, scalability, and resource consumption challenges. Quantum Machine Learning (QML) is a novel way of looking at things, which looks to integrate the pattern recognition capabilities of machine learning and the probabilistic potential of quantum computing. Things like superposition, entanglement, quantum interference have the potential to change the way we do things in circumstances in which classical models really suck such as optimization, search, and data classification. This chapter is heavy on the theory behind QML and how it fits into the real world. It covers the most pivotal concepts in quantum computing, the most influential machine learning models and why the two domains ought to work together. There are various other QML algorithms referred to in the literature such as Quantum Support Vector Machines (QSVMS), Quantum Neural Networks (QNN), and Variational Quantum Classifiers (VQC). It also addresses how to encode quantum data and systems that are quantum and classical. First, we will learn how these concepts are applied to the real world in environments such as healthcare, finance, and materials research. Then, we conduct a comprehensive case study to bridge the gap between theory and practice. The chapter concludes with a discussion and ethics and technology and with pointers for future research.

S. S. Gadde (✉)
Seattle, WA, USA
e-mail: sakhitasreeg2000@gmail.com

A. P. Nalwade
Pythia, Seattle, WA, USA
e-mail: ashwin@pythialab.com

M. Rana and B. Pandey (eds.), *Quantum Ops*,
https://doi.org/10.1007/978-3-032-10775-6_8

Keywords

Quantum machine learning • Quantum computing • Qubits • Variational algorithms • Quantum neural networks • Hybrid models • Data encoding • Quantum speedup • Optimization • Real-world applications

1 Introduction

Quantum Machine Learning (QML) is a novel field of research that brings together two of the most revolutionary technologies of the 21st century which are quantum computing and artificial intelligence (AI). AI models are becoming more and more central to domains as varied as healthcare, finance, and autonomous systems, and their computational requirements are starting to outstretch what can be accomplished with classical hardware, even with the advancements of GPUs and cloud computing.

Quantum computing is a promising option. Quantum systems can do multiple calculations at once and quickly search through complicated solution spaces by using quantum bits that take advantage of ideas like superposition and entanglement [1]. This opens up new ways to speed up machine learning (ML) tasks that take a lot of computing power, like combinatorial optimization or recognizing patterns in high-dimensional data [2]. Quantum enhanced algorithms have the potential to speed up tasks like classification, clustering, and optimization by a polynomial or even exponential amount [3]. The theoretical benefits of quantum speedups have been known for a long time, but only recently we have improvements in hardware made these possibilities more likely to happen in the real life [4].

QML is now easier to use thanks to recent advances in quantum hardware. Companies like IBM, Google, Xanadu, and Rigetti now offer quantum processors and hybrid frameworks that run in the cloud. IBM's Qiskit and Xanadu's PennyLane are two tools that make it easy to design variational quantum circuits that work well for machine learning [5]. Even the noisy scale quantum (NISQ) devices we are using today have shown promise for tasks like quantum kernel estimation and variational classification [6, 7].

QML is still a new field, though. Quantum decoherence, error correction, data encoding schemes and the design of expressive, trainable quantum circuits [8, 9] are just some of the problems that come up when trying to put quantum computing to use. As QML applications spread into sensitive areas like medical diagnostics and financial forecasting, ethical and regulatory issues are also getting more attention.

But there is no denying the momentum behind QML. Research is quickly moving forward with both algorithms and hardware that are designed for quantum-enhanced learning. As Moore's Law slows down, the search for quantum advantage is moving from theory to practice. Quantum kernels, which put classical data into high-dimensional quantum feature spaces, are already doing better than classical baselines on some tasks [10]. This progress could mean that AI's computational limits are changing, allowing for applications like climate modeling and global supply chain optimization at levels of detail never seen before.

2 Literature Review

2.1 Quantum Computing Fundamentals

Quantum computing is a novel approach of doing math that is based on the rules of quantum mechanics. Classical systems employ binary states to process information. Quantum computers, on the other hand, use quantum bits, or qubits, which may encode more than one state at a time through superposition. This capacity makes it possible to execute a lot of parallel processing, which could help tackle problems that are hard to address with traditional approaches, like those in optimization, cryptography, and machine learning [11].

Superposition, entanglement, and interference are three fundamental things that give quantum computers their power. These quantum properties make it easier to explore across huge solution spaces and speed up some kinds of algorithms. But we need to tackle problems with using real qubits, resolving bugs, and keeping hardware stable to make these ideas relevant in the real world. Theoretical models and real-world engineering are both making progress that is pushing the limits of what quantum systems can do.

2.1.1 Qubits, Superposition, and Entanglement

The qubit is the smallest piece of quantum computing. A qubit can be in more than one state at the same time, however a classical bit can only be in one state at a time. This quantum trait is called superposition. It permits quantum systems work on several possible outcomes at once. This parallelism gets stronger and stronger when used on multi-qubit systems, which lets quantum systems encode and deal with state spaces that are infinitely large.

Entanglement. Entanglement is a non-classical connection between qubits that makes it so that the state of one qubit directly affects the state of another, no matter how far apart they are. This is an important aspect of quantum advantage. Quantum communication and quantum-enhanced algorithms are based on entangled states. They let qubits work together in ways that regular systems can't. Entanglement has a lot of uses, like quantum teleportation, secure key exchange, and advanced quantum error correction techniques [12].

Coherence. Changes in the environment have a big effect on quantum states. To do quantum computing reliably, it is highly crucial to retain coherence, which involves keeping quantum information over time. Depending on the technology, coherence time is commonly measured in microseconds or milliseconds. It shows you how long you can utilize a qubit before it starts to make mistakes. Coherence times are a big challenge for current hardware platforms, which makes it impossible to perform long algorithms and big quantum circuits [13].

2.1.2 Quantum Hardware and Architectural Models

There are many different kinds of hardware platforms that can be utilized to make quantum computers, and each one works in a different way. Gate-based quantum systems and quantum annealers are two of the most well-known kinds of quantum systems. Depending on how they are used, each has its own pros and cons.

Gate-Based Systems. Systems based on gates quantum computing that use gates works by changing the states of qubits using sequences of quantum gates. This model is like the logic gate architecture of classical circuits, but it follows the rules of quantum evolution. Gate-based systems can perform a lot of different quantum algorithms, such as Grover's algorithm for finding unstructured data and Shor's algorithm for breaking down numbers. Some of the biggest businesses working on these kinds of architectures are IBM, Google, and IonQ [14]. These devices now use either trapped ions or superconducting qubits. When it comes to noise levels, control quality, and physical scalability, each has its own benefits and cons.

Quantum Annealers. Quantum annealers, like those made by D-Wave, are different from gate-based systems because they solve optimization problems by lowering the energy of a quantum system. These systems use quantum tunneling and energy landscapes to find cheap solutions in complicated combinatorial spaces. Quantum annealing isn't for everyone, but it's a good way to solve some types of machine learning and operations research problems [15]. It has already been used in experiments in areas like portfolio optimization, protein folding, and traffic flow optimization.

Scalability. Scalability is a big problem for both architectures. It is still a problem to add more qubits while keeping low error rates and high coherence. Adding additional qubits quickly makes the system more complicated, which makes the physical layout, qubit connectivity, and control systems more difficult. In the Noisy Intermediate Scale Quantum (NISQ) era, which is what current systems are in, algorithms have to be able to handle noise and shallow circuit depths. The way forward includes both little steps to make qubits more reliable and bigger aims like making quantum computing that can handle errors.

2.1.3 Challenges and Industry Advancements

Quantum computing is still in the pre-commercial stage, even though it has come a long way in a short amount of time. Widespread use is still not possible because of several unresolved engineering and computational problems.

Error Correction. Decoherence, crosstalk, and gate imprecision can all cause errors in quantum operations. In this area, classical error correction methods don't work well-enough, hence quantum specific error correction codes like surface codes are needed. These methods encode logical qubits into groups of physical qubits so that faults can be found and fixed without losing the encoded information [16].

However, making logical qubits that can handle faults still takes a lot of resources, and each logical unit usually needs dozens or hundreds of physical qubits.

Hardware Diversity. We are looking into other ways to physically make qubits, such as superconducting circuits, trapped ions, photonics, and topological systems. Each method has its own pros and cons when it comes to fidelity, scalability, and how well it works with control systems. For instance, trapped ions have great fidelity and long coherence durations, and superconducting circuits benefit from well-developed manufacturing methods. Photonic methods are naturally resistant to many types of decoherence, but they have trouble combining circuits on a wide scale.

Quantum Supremacy. Google's Sycamore processor showed that quantum supremacy was possible by completing a sampling task many times quicker than any known classical approach. This was a big step forward in the field. Even though this benchmark wasn't for a general purpose application, it showed that quantum advantage might work in controlled circumstances and sparked interest in quantum research around the world.

Open Access and Ecosystem Growth. The fact that quantum processors may now be accessed over the cloud has sped up progress. Researchers can use real hardware to run and simulate quantum circuits on platforms like IBM Qiskit, Google Cirq, and Amazon Braket. These technologies make it possible for a lot of people to do quantum experiments, even if they don't have any quantum hardware nearby. Also, the rise of hybrid quantum–classical workflows, in which quantum circuits handle computationally heavy subroutines and classical processors handle control logic, suggests that there will be useful uses shortly. These improvements are helping to create a quickly growing community of quantum developers, academics, and business innovators.

2.2 Machine Learning Fundamentals

Machine learning (ML) is a branch of artificial intelligence (AI) that focuses on creating algorithms that let systems learn from data and get better over time. Machine learning systems change based on experience instead of following set rules or explicit programming. This makes them good for situations when traditional methods don't work well. In the last 20 years, machine learning has changed several industries, including healthcare, banking, transportation, e-commerce, and cybersecurity [17]. It is also widely used in consumer products, from recommendation engines to smart personal assistants.

The main goal of ML models is to find patterns, pick out useful features, and make predictions based on data that hasn't been seen before. The kind of data and the goal of learning will determine the learning paradigm to use. There are three main types of learning problems: supervised, unsupervised, and reinforcement learning.

2.2.1 Learning Paradigms and Applications

When supervised learning is employed, labeled datasets require training the model, which means each input has an output. The aim is to minimize the loss function considering the training set, which allows developing a function to predict the outputs for given inputs. This is a common model for estimating price and load for regression tasks and for classification tasks such as object recognition, spam removal, and illness diagnosis. Depending upon the volume and the intricate nature of the data, supervised learning can be implemented through deep learning architectures or more sophisticated linear models.

Utilizing unsupervised learning allows us to extract and form data insights without any labeled outputs. These models aim to find latent variables which can cluster related data points and highlight a dataset's fundamental characteristics, or perform dimensionality reduction. Clustering techniques used to group items include K-means and DBSCAN. PCA and autoencoders are two methods in reducing dimensions which enhance clarity and remove noise. In areas such as social network analysis, genetics, and outlier detection in expensive or difficult data classification, unsupervised learning is particularly useful.

Reinforcement learning (RL) is a third way that agents learn to make choices by interacting with their surroundings. The agent watches states, chooses actions, and gets rewards or punishments based on what happens. Over time, it learns policies that maximize total rewards. RL works best for problems where you have to make decisions in a row and the decisions have long-term effects, like in robotics, games, and control systems. It has parts of exploration, planning, and delayed feedback, which makes it more complicated but also more adaptable than supervised or unsupervised techniques.

2.2.2 Limitations of Classical Machine Learning

Machine learning has come a long way, but classical models have some problems that make them less effective and less scalable. One of the main worries is how much processing power it takes to train huge models on data with a lot of dimensions. Deep neural networks with millions of parameters need a lot of processing power and training time, which may not be possible in contexts with limited resources.

It can be hard for classical optimization methods to find their way across complicated, non-convex loss landscapes. Gradient-based approaches depend on the starting conditions and may take a long time to converge or not find the best solution, especially when working with sparse or noisy data. Sometimes, the optimization space has so many local minima or saddle points that it makes convergence harder, which means that hyperparameters and architectures need to be tuned a lot.

Model interpretability is another problem that keeps coming up. A lot of powerful machine learning models work like black boxes, giving good predictions but not explaining how or why decisions are made. Because they aren't clear, they can't be used in important sectors like health or law, where trust and responsibility are very important. Also, classical models are likely to pick up on biases in the training data, which might lead to unfair or unethical results if they aren't fixed.

There are still big problems with data quality and access. Big datasets are becoming more prevalent, yet they often include problems like missing numbers, noise, or inconsistencies. Getting tagged data at scale is still expensive and takes a long time for many activities, especially in specialist fields. This lack of data makes models less accurate and less able to apply to new situations, especially when they are infrequent or on the edge.

2.2.3 Quantum Bottlenecks and Computational Complexity

For classical systems, a lot of ML tasks are very hard to do because they involve high-dimensional linear algebra, probabilistic inference, or combinatorial optimization. The curse of dimensionality is a major problem since it means that the amount of computing needed grows exponentially as the amount of data or feature space grows. For instance, if the number of variables grows, it may become impossible to train kernel-based models, calculate massive covariance matrices, or simulate probabilistic graphical models.

Also, some tasks in the real world need you to sample from complicated probability distributions or solve constraint fulfillment problems that are known to be NP-hard. There are approximate methods, but they usually have to give up either precision or scalability [18]. Simulating interactions or looking at all possible outcomes is still too hard for classical computers in fields like quantum chemistry, materials design, and financial modeling. These problems have made people more interested in looking into quantum computing as a way to improve on traditional machine learning methods.

Quantum computing makes it possible to get polynomial or exponential speedups for some algorithmic subroutines that are very important to machine learning, such as matrix inversion, Fourier transformations, and sampling. This is the basis for new research in quantum machine learning (QML), which aims to use the natural benefits of quantum systems to get around problems that classical systems can't.

2.2.4 Emerging Directions in Machine Learning

There is a need for models that are stronger, more generalizable, and more efficient, so modern ML is moving beyond old ways of doing things. One of the most important areas of progress is self-supervised learning. It makes labels from the data itself, which fills the gap between supervised and unsupervised methods. This has worked especially well in fields like computer vision and natural language processing, where there is a lot of data that doesn't have labels.

Federated learning is another important field of study. It lets you train models on data from a lot of different places without having to put all the data in one place. This is also important for the apps that handle private users' data, like mobile applications or healthcare apps, where privacy and data management are very important. Federated learning makes it way cheaper to talk to each other and keeps data where it is, but it also makes it harder to coordinate, work with non-IID data, and keep things safe.

More and more people are interested in lifelong learning, or continual learning, as a way to make models that change over time without losing what they already know. This is very important for AI systems that need to adapt to new situations or that need to change when they learn something new. To build these kinds of systems, you have to deal with catastrophic forgetting and make sure that forward transfer works.

Another important area that has come up around making ML models clearer and easier to understand is Explainable AI (XAI). Attention processes, saliency maps, and surrogate models are all ways to try to make algorithmic decisions easier for people to understand. This will become more and more important in fields that are regulated and in talks about AI that is also ethical. All of these new directions show how the need of real-world applications are changing and how machine learning is becoming more popular for its effects on society and technology as a whole. As the field grows, adding quantum computing to it will make intelligent systems even more powerful.

2.3 Why Merge the Two?

One of the most exciting new fields of computer research is the combination of quantum computing and machine learning. As machine learning gets better at dealing with more complicated models and adapting to new data, and quantum computing gets better at making hardware bigger and algorithms more reliable, the two fields might be able to work together to solve problems that have been around for a long time in classical computation. Quantum machine learning (QML) is a new field that wants to make current machine learning algorithms faster and come up with new models and ways of learning that use the special features of quantum physics.

2.3.1 Motivation: Overcoming Classical Bottlenecks

One of the most important reasons to use quantum computing and machine learning together is that the classical systems have trouble with tasks that are very huge, high-dimensional, and need a lot of processing power. Classical algorithms often have issues like slow convergence, memory limits, and computing scalability when there is huge data and the models get more complicated like in deep learning and probabilistic inference. For example, it might take weeks of GPU time and terabytes of memory to train large transformer-based architectures or to optimize non-convex objective functions in deep neural networks. Also, when the number of dimensions goes up, things like kernel estimation, Bayesian sampling, or matrix inversion don't work as well. This makes things harder in fields like quantum chemistry, genomics, and financial risk modeling.

Quantum computing adds additional basic operations based on superposition, entanglement, and quantum interference. These operations let quantum systems store and process far more information than conventional systems. In theory, a quantum computer can look at a lot of possible solutions at once instead of one at a time. This could make some machine learning subroutines run faster. For example, many have suggested using quantum algorithms to speed up the solving of linear systems of equations, which are important for regression, classification, and clustering. Quantum-enhanced sampling methods may also help models that can't easily estimate probabilities over large state spaces that make inferences faster. These features are what people think will give quantum computers an edge in certain machine learning tasks [19].

2.3.2 Algorithmic Synergy: Hybrid Learning Architectures

Fault-tolerant quantum computing is still a long way off, but current Noisy Intermediate Scale Quantum (NISQ) devices have made it possible to create hybrid quantum–classical models that split up processing work between quantum circuits and classical control mechanisms. This hybrid model doesn't just get around hardware limits; it also creates a design area where classical and quantum resources can be coordinated to get the best performance and use of resources. Quantum subroutines are mainly used in these models to do things like change features, figuring out kernels, or check inner products. On the other hand classical components take care of things like changing parameters, optimizing, and also running the system.

One of the most promising areas in this field is variational quantum algorithms (VQAs). They use traditional methods to make quantum circuits really good by changing their parameters. The Variational Quantum Eigensolver (VQE) and Quantum Approximate Optimization Algorithm (QAOA) were originally made for quantum simulation and combinatorial optimization. Now they can also be used for various machine learning tasks like classification, clustering, and also generative modeling. These models can make a set of variational quantum circuits that can be trained to learn using both classical optimization methods that use gradients and those that don't. Early tests of quantum classifiers and variational quantum neural networks show that these models can do just as well as classical ones on small-scale benchmarks, even when the qubits are noisy.

Another new method is quantum kernel approaches, which use parameterized quantum circuits to move classical data into quantum state spaces with many dimensions. These quantum feature spaces might be able to capture the complex interactions that are really hard to describe with classical methods. We can also add them to learning models that are already there like support vector machines. It's also important to remember that these methods could make expressive models without adding too many parameters, which could improve learning when the resources are limited [20].

2.3.3 Theoretical and Practical Implications of Integration

Together the quantum computing and machine learning accelerate the computations and develop novel learning strategies. Quantum systems are useful for modeling uncertainty, nonlinearity, and also complex relationships in the data because they will naturally encode probabilistic behavior and non-classical correlations. In addition to being quicker, we can also create models that are more accurate and useful to the way data functions in the real world. Researchers are also looking into quantum-generative models and quantum Boltzmann machines for use in generative design, quantum chemistry, and secure data synthesis, where traditional generative adversarial networks (GANs) or variational autoencoders (VAEs) may not be enough.

Also, the quantum measurement process adds a kind of randomness that could act as a natural source of regularization, which could improve the ability to generalize. Some quantum models are also naturally resistant to noise or hostile changes. Researchers are currently looking at this property to make learning systems that are more robust. Quantum learning theory is starting to look at the sample complexity, VC-dimension, and convergence behavior of quantum models compared to classical ones. This gives us formal information on when and why quantum models might work better than classical ones.

In terms of real-world use, the rise of cloud-based quantum platforms like IBM Quantum, Amazon Braket, and Xanadu's Pennylane has made it much easier to try things out. Researchers and developers can use these platforms to get to real quantum hardware, emulators, and integration toolkits that work with both types of workflows. This infrastructure is helping to create a larger ecosystem of tools, libraries, and educational materials, which makes quantum machine learning easier to use and reproduce. As quantum technology gets bigger and better, researchers are expected to move from theoretical studies to benchmarks for specific applications and deployments that are ready for business [21].

In the end, combining quantum computing and machine learning isn't just a matter of making things better or speeding up current algorithms. It shows a bigger change toward rethinking how we learn in a completely new way of computing that combines physical principles with data-driven inference to solve challenges that regular technology can't.

3 Core Components and Architectures

3.1 Key Algorithms in Quantum Machine Learning

Quantum Machine Learning (QML) combines the principles of quantum computing and the traditional machine learning processes that have existed for years. This discussion focuses on three groups of algorithms that exist within QML: Variational Quantum Classifiers (VQC), Quantum Support Vector Machines (QSVM) and Quantum Neural Networks (QNN). They use faster processing times owing to the operations of quantum interactions like entanglement, interference, and superposition (as well as better learning and greater generalization) in comparison with traditional counterparts. Table 1 provides a recap of these approaches for comparative purposes.

Table 1 Comparison of key quantum machine learning algorithms

Algorithm	Architecture type	Primary use case	Training method	Key advantage	Hardware suitability
VQC	Hybrid (Quantum + Classical)	Binary classification	Classical optimizer with quantum circuit	Efficient on NISQ devices with shallow depth	Suitable for NISQ
QSVM	Quantum-enhanced kernel method	Nonlinear classification	Classical SVM with quantum kernel estimation	Maps to high-dimensional Hilbert space	Requires quantum kernel access
QNN	Quantum-native multilayer circuit	General-purpose learning	Parameter shift or quantum gradients	Quantum generalization with fewer parameters	Still experimental

3.1.1 Variational Quantum Classifiers (VQC)

Variational Quantum Classifiers are hybrid models that feature a parameterized quantum circuit in conjunction with a classical optimizer. They are based on the Variational Quantum Eigensolver (VQE) method developed for quantum chemistry applications [22]. The process of a Variational Quantum Classifier takes place as follows: first, the data is encoded into a quantum state through a fixed feature map to embed the information into the quantum circuit. Then, the circuit evolves via a series of unitary operations, where the angle of each rotation gate is controlled by a trainable parameter. Finally, the outputs from the measurement are interpreted in a classical fashion for classification or regression.

This training process occurs over multiple executions. For example, a cost function is determined based on the measurement outcome, using cross-entropy or mean squared error. Then, a classical optimizer like gradient descent or Nelder-Mead method adjusts the parameters, creating a quantum–classical feedback loop. Such VQCs can be run on Noisy Intermediate Scale Quantum (NISQ) devices because they operate at shallow depth and with flexibility [9].

3.1.2 Quantum Support Vector Machines (QSVM)

Quantum Support Vector Machines (QSVM) are the quantum analogs of classical support vector machines, relying on nonlinear separability through quantum kernels. In the case of QSVM, data exist in the Hilbert space or, at least, projected therein, and quantum circuits translate feature vectors from a classical state into quantum states. Next, the kernel is determined based on the inner product of these quantum states, which can be extracted through a Swap Test or other interference-based approaches [10].

The training of a QSVM still resembles that of a classical SVM aside from using a quantum processor to conduct the resource-intensive aspects, which would otherwise rely on a classical processor to create the kernel matrix. Quantum kernels can, theoretically, distinguish classes that cannot be separated in any classical feature space [23]. This has been accomplished in small-scale tasks via superconducting qubit platforms, showcasing potential benefits in accuracy and dimensionality [6].

3.1.3 Quantum Neural Networks (QNN)

QNNs attempt to construct a quantum analogue to classical deep learning architectures by stacking parameterized quantum circuits in layers. Each layer contains quantum gates of variable parameters that are trainable via classical or quantum optimization. The configuration is reminiscent of a feedforward structure like that of classical neural networks, yet quantum interactions are applied such as entangled distributions of weights and unitary constraints [24]. QNNs can be realized in multiple forms, including quantum perceptrons, quantum convolutional circuits, and even recurrent variants for time-series data [25]. They can be trained via classical backpropagation, taking advantage of the parameter shift rule or through a fully quantum protocol such as quantum natural gradient descent. While current QNNs are limited by noise and qubit count, they show promise in representing high-dimensional, non-convex functions with fewer parameters than classical models [26].

QNNs are still in development and subject to uncertainties relative to convergence guarantees, expressiveness bounds, and interpretability. Nonetheless, they represent a frontier in merging quantum information processing with the flexibility of neural computation.

To use these algorithms effectively, classical data must first be transformed into quantum states, making data encoding a critical early step in the pipeline.

3.2 Quantum Data Encoding

One of the first steps in any quantum machine learning pipeline is encoding classical data into quantum states. The efficiency, expressiveness, and scalability of a model are often constrained by the data encoding method. The three encoding schemes that are most common are basis encoding, amplitude encoding, and angle encoding.

Basis encoding takes each classical bit and uses its value as is when measuring in a qubit's $|0\rangle$ or $|1\rangle$ state. For example, a qubit string of "110" would use three qubits transformed directly to the $|1\rangle$ state for the first and second index and the $|0\rangle$ for the third. While this method is simple and easy to implement, it scales poorly for large feature spaces and does not make use of quantum parallelism.

Amplitude encoding compresses a normalized data vector into the amplitudes of a quantum state. This approach allows 2^n classical values to be embedded using only n qubits, making it highly efficient in terms of memory. However, it's often a complex endeavor to achieve on today's hardware since it requires quite complicated circuits and precision control. Amplitude encoding works well when quantum algorithms demand global access of the overall input state [3].

Angle encoding encodes numerical features as rotation angles of quantum gates applied to individual qubits. That is to say, a real number may be rotated by a rotation gate aligned with the Y-axis or Z-axis. Angle encoding is hardware-friendly and accessible to circuits and variational circuits. It achieves low circuit depth with representational power, especially when multiple non-entangling gates are applied to represent correlation among features.

Each encoding type possesses pros and cons; basis is fast but ineffective, amplitude saves space but requires resources, angle is middle of the road worth it but fails to represent complex correlations unless designed to do so. Ultimately, certain encoding schemes work better with certain datasets, hardware constraints, and subsequent quantum algorithms [18].

3.3 Hybrid Quantum–Classical Models

For now, fully quantum machine learning systems are impractical for widespread use because today's quantum processors contain low qubit counts and high error rates. A compelling solution, however, is the hybrid quantum–classical architecture that divides tasks between quantum and classical systems. These types of models operate quantum subroutines to learn from data but still rely on classical computers for operations such as optimization.

One of the models that exist in this architecture is the variational quantum circuit which is a parameterized quantum model trained by classical optimization algorithms. The process goes as follows: a parameterized quantum circuit is created with gate parameters to train at the outset. It runs on a quantum device and the outcomes are measured. Then, the output measurements are analyzed to produce a cost function, either a classification error or an energy estimator. The classical optimizer monitors the cost function and adjusts parameters evaluated in the prior step to reduce the cost. This process continues to iterate until convergence. This method does not need fault-tolerance levels that quantum computation would require, allows for highly expressive models and since it uses established classical optimizations, it is modular and fits into pre-existing machine learning pipelines [27].

The Quantum Approximate Optimization Algorithm (QAOA) and the Variational Quantum Eigensolver (VQE) are foundational hybrid algorithms that have been extended for use in quantum machine learning. QAOA solves combinatorial problems by applying generalized mixing operators to the problem and driving operators to explore the solution space. VQE estimates the ground state energy of Hamiltonians by applying a similar parameterized quantum circuit and measuring the variance among outputs.

Both are well-suited for tasks linked to machine learning as they can be tuned to minimize loss functions in lieu of ground-state energies. Furthermore, because of their dependence on structure, they operate best on low-depth circuits which means they are tolerant of NISQ technology. One day, when more advanced quantum processors become available, these learning loops will allow for scalable quantum-enhanced learning systems [13, 28].

3.4 Real-World Applications

Quantum machine learning is finding applications across many industries, particularly those involved in high-dimensional optimization, quantum chemistry, and complex statistical inference. While many applications remain in the theoretical stage, practical application efforts exist in drug discovery, finance, and materials science in both academic and industrial settings.

3.4.1 Drug Discovery

Quantum machine learning is used in pharmaceutical research building models of chemical compound formation and leveraging quantum entanglements that are otherwise inaccessible or burdensome for classical generations of results. Variational approaches, such as VQE, assist in estimating the ground-state energy of drug-like compounds, contributing to quick assessments of possible options. For instance, IBM has developed quantum renderings of elementary organic compounds via its superconducting qubit arrays, signifying this is on the pathway to legitimate structure-based drug design processes [29].

In addition, many machine learning applications such as calculating molecular properties and predicting protein–ligand binding energies are transformed into hybrid quantum–classical challenges. These transformations can save time and money throughout any drug development process.

3.4.2 Finance

The finance use cases include portfolio optimization, risk assessment, fraud detection, and market simulation. For instance, quantum modeling solves quadratic optimization faster than classical solvers, especially applicable for large, complex, and non-convex optimization solution domains. Moreover, quantum kernel methods have been used to solve credit risk classification tasks, and it was found that a quantum classifier can outperform linear classical models when trained on a small number of high-dimensional samples.

Rigetti Computing collaborated with various banks to run quantum workflows for optimal asset allocation and Monte Carlo simulations and discovered decent performance improvements when running NISQ devices under configured circumstances.

3.4.3 Materials Science

Materials discovery seeks to explore large chemical configuration spaces determining whether novel materials possess certain electronic, thermal, or structural properties. Thus, QML can predict how materials will behave at the atomic scale where quantum mechanics governs physical systems. Further, through quantum generative models, researchers can sample trained quantum circuits to generate new candidate materials.

Xanadu sought to apply QML through its Pennylane framework and photonic quantum computing to lattice structure simulations and predictions of properties for organic photovoltaics. They theorized that their work would reduce experimental costs associated with discovering novel semiconductor and superconducting materials [30].

Where such projects may be limited by real-world hardware, they signal contributions quantum machine learning can make to real-world scientific and industrial endeavors. When access to quantum devices becomes more widespread and decoherence becomes less of an issue, stable QML should be harnessed for all computational discovery and deduction.

4 Case Study: Quantum Machine Learning for Fraud

4.1 Background

Fraudulent transactions inside financial systems, especially those involving credit cards, pose a significant risk to both consumers and financial institutions. The global expansion of digital payments has rendered fraud detection crucial for assuring security, maintaining trust, improving customer satisfaction, and complying with regulatory requirements. Every day, millions of transactions occur, with only a negligible fraction being fraudulent. This results in a markedly imbalanced classification problem, where traditional algorithms often overfit to the majority class and fail to detect subtle fraudulent patterns.

Machine learning has changed how we find frauds in the last ten years by letting algorithms figure out the decision thresholds based on the data from their past transactions. Logistic regression, support vector machines, random forests, and deep learning have all been used to sort transactions into two groups which are legitimate and suspicious. They do this by looking at things like the amount of the transaction, where it took place, the type of merchant, and the patterns of behavior of the people involved. However, these traditional models have problems, especially when working with data that is high-dimensional, noisy, or nonlinear. They might need lots of processing power, complicated feature engineering, and also to be retrained often.

Quantum Machine Learning (QML) is a good choice in this case. Superposition, entanglement, and quantum interference are some of the things that quantum models use to do math that regular computers can't or don't do well. QML algorithms can look at complicated decision surfaces and show data in bigger and bigger Hilbert spaces with a very fewer parameters. This feature is very helpful for finding frauds and other unusual things because wrong data points are rare to detect, spread out, and have a different structure than real patterns.

QML is especially useful in hybrid quantum–classical models, which combine traditional optimization methods with quantum subroutines like feature mapping or kernel computation. This lets developers use quantum benefits on current noisy NISQ devices. Hybrid methods, especially those that use Estimator-based Quantum Neural Networks (EstimatorQNN), can be tested on real quantum hardware and trained on simulators which make them very useful in real life.

This case study analyzes the implementation of a hybrid quantum model for fraud detection using a real-world dataset. The model design seeks to balance feasibility and performance, utilizing 4 qubits for feature encoding and a variational ansatz optimized via COBYLA. The aim is to evaluate whether the quantum model offers measurable benefits, especially regarding accuracy, but more importantly in reducing false positives and improving training convergence. The vital importance of fraud detection means that even minor improvements in efficiency can yield substantial financial savings and boost user experience.

4.2 Dataset Description and Preprocessing

This work utilizes the publicly accessible Credit Card Fraud Detection Dataset, which serves as a standard in anomaly detection research. The dataset consists of 284,807 transaction records gathered over a two-day period from European cardholders. The dataset is highly skewed, with only 492 occurrences classified as fake, representing a mere 0.172% of the total records. This degree of imbalance is a considerable obstacle in constructing models that can generalize effectively without being dominated by the majority class. Fraud detection tasks inherently involve anomaly identification, with the minority class typically being the most significant and relevant.

30 numerical attributes characterize every transaction in the dataset. Among these, 28 features (V1 through V28) are derived from a Principal Component Analysis (PCA) transformation implemented to maintain the secrecy of the original data, while the remaining two features consist of the transaction time and the amount involved. The target variable, Class, is binary; 0 signifies a valid transaction, whereas 1 denotes a fraudulent transaction. Given the significant class imbalance and the constraints of existing quantum models in managing extensive datasets, we selected a targeted sampling strategy to render the situation manageable.

We achieved class balancing for a quantum compatible dataset by employing under sampling techniques. All fraudulent samples were preserved, and a random selection of non-fraudulent transactions was chosen to uphold a 1:5 ratio between fraudulent and non-fraudulent cases. This produced a balanced and much reduced dataset of roughly 2,000 samples, which is more suitable for training on contemporary noisy intermediate scale quantum (NISQ) devices or quantum simulators. This method, despite diminishing the dataset's size, guarantees that the quantum model is accessible to both groups without bias toward the majority class.

We used the StandardScaler from Scikitlearn to make the features normal before we actually start processing them. This change will help to make sure that all input features are on the same scale with a mean of zero and a variance of one. This is very important before using the dimensionality reduction methods and putting the data into quantum circuits. After that, we used Primary Component Analysis (PCA) to reduce the feature space to four main components. This reduction to four dimensions makes it possible to build a four qubit quantum circuit while keeping a large part of the variation in the original feature space. This strikes a balance between efficiency and informativeness.

We split the data into training and testing sets with a 70:30 ratio after pre-processing. We used stratified splitting to make sure that both sets kept the same fraud to non-fraud ratio, which is important for an unbiased performance evaluation. After that, Scikitlearn's LabelEncoder turned the binary class values into representations that the quantum classifier could understand. The cleaned, shortened, and balanced dataset was used as input for the hybrid quantum–classical model that will be described in the next sections.

4.3 Model Implementation

We used IBM's Qiskit Machine Learning platform to create a hybrid quantum–classical pipeline to test how well quantum machine learning works for finding fraud. Because of the limits of modern quantum hardware, the focus was on building and testing models with quantum simulators that mimic small quantum systems in a classical setting. This method will make it easy to carefully prototype quantum circuits and algorithms without actually having to deal with qubit noise and decoherence.

The Variational Quantum Classifier (VQC) framework is used as the base model for this implementation. VQCs are a mix of quantum circuits and classical optimizers that work together to lower a cost function, like cross-entropy loss. The VQC works because it uses a parameterized quantum circuit (PQC) that can be improved, like neural networks, by changing rotating gates to lower prediction error. There are two main parts to these circuits: a feature map and an ansatz. The feature map turns classical information into quantum states, and the ansatz makes the quantum model flexible and to help the parametric framework to get new ideas.

Our method used the ZZFeatureMap to put input data into quantum states. This encoding uses entangling ZZ interactions to show how different input features are linked to each other. That is the reason why its so good at finding weird things. We picked the TwoLocal method because it will strike a good balance between being clear and going into the details. It makes a quantum circuit with rotation gates (Ry) and entangling gates (CZ) that can show decision boundaries that aren't straight. We combined the feature map and ansatz into a single quantum circuit with four qubits. This matched the four main parts that were kept throughout PCA.

The quantum circuit was subsequently transmitted to an Estimator Quantum Neural Network (EstimatorQNN), which assesses the expectation values of quantum observables to derive outputs. The estimator interface facilitates adaptable assessment on quantum simulators or hardware backends. We employed the

COBYLA optimizer, a derivative-free technique adept at navigating noisy objective landscapes typically found in quantum computing, to optimize the trainable parameters in the circuit. The training approach entailed systematically modifying the parameters in the ansatz to reduce classification loss, concurrently assessing intermediate performance on the validation set to prevent overfitting.

We used the preprocessed dataset for both training and testing. We set aside 70% for training and 30% for testing. The classifier was trained for 30 iterations, which was a smart choice to make sure it converged while keeping costs down. Even though there weren't many training epochs, the hybrid VQC model was able to find nonlinear patterns that looked like they were part of a scam. After the training was over, the model's predictions were compared to the ground truth labels using standard classification metrics like precision, recall, F1-score, and a confusion matrix.

This software shows that it is possible to use QML in real-life anomaly detection tasks. The model architecture was designed to work with hardware, allowing it to be used on near term quantum devices with minimal adjustments. However, it is currently running in a simulator because of hardware limitations. The model uses a hybrid architecture that combines quantum circuits for representation learning with classical preprocessing and optimization. Because of this flexibility, quantum parts may be gradually added to traditional machine learning pipelines. This lets institutions look into the benefits of quantum technology without having to change their infrastructure completely.

4.4 Results and Insights

We have actually used the Estimator-based Quantum Neural Network (EstimatorQNN) quantum machine learning model to look for fraud in a smaller and more balanced set of credit card transactions. The COBYLA optimizer trained the model 100 times and then we have used standard classification metrics to see how well it did. We built a standard logistic regression model with the same dataset, which let us compare how well quantum and classical methods worked side by side.

The QNN did a great job on all of the Release 1 classification metrics. It had an overall accuracy of 93.4%, a precision of 91.8%, and a recall of 87.5% for the fraud classification. These results are even more impressive because fraud detection tasks are often very hard because there aren't enough examples of each class and the feature distributions are hard to understand. The F1-score which is the harmonic mean of precision and recall was 89.6%. This shows that the model could correctly identify both the fake and real transactions.

Table 2 gives a short summary of how well the QNN model did at sorting things into groups. This makes it easier to understand the results. The model had a high precision and recall for both classes, with a macro averaged F1-score of 91.5% and a weighted average of 92.3%. This means that the QNN didn't favor any one class and could make good guesses even when the training data was evenly split.

Table 2 Performance metrics of quantum neural network (QNN) model

Metric	Class 0 (Non-fraud)	Class 1 (Fraud)	Macro avg	Weighted avg
Precision (%)	94.7	91.8	93.3	93.9
Recall (%)	92.4	87.5	89.9	91.6
F1-score (%)	93.5	89.6	91.5	92.3
Support (samples)	728	158	–	–
Overall accuracy (%)	–	–	–	**93.4**

Table 3 Performance comparison: classical versus quantum model

Metric	Classical model	Quantum model	Improvement
Accuracy (%)	89.1	93.4	4.3
Precision (%)	87	91.8	4.8
Recall (%)	85.2	87.5	2.3
F1-score (%)	86.1	89.6	3.5
False positives	158	122	−22.7%

The classical logistic regression model attained an accuracy of 89.1%, with marginally inferior precision and recall scores for the fraud class at 87.0% and 85.2%, respectively. According to Table 3, the quantum model surpassed the classical baseline by 4.3% in accuracy, 4.8% in precision, and 3.5% in F1-score. The quantum model exhibited a much reduced rate of false positives in fraud detection (122) compared to the classical model (158), indicating a 22.7% drop. This reduction is essential in operational contexts because numerous false alarms may result in customer discontent, unwarranted manual scrutiny, and erosion of confidence in automated systems.

We utilized three primary figures to assist people understand how the quantum classifier works better. Figure 1 displays the quantum model's confusion matrix, which tells us how effectively it can discern the difference between actual and false transactions. Out of 158 real fraud samples, 138 were correctly identified, and just 20 were missed. In the same way, just 55 of the 728 non-fraud cases were misclassified, which shows that the trend was mostly right.

Figure 2 illustrates the Receiver Operating Characteristic (ROC) curve for both conventional and quantum models. The area under the curve (AUC) for the quantum classifier was much greater (~0.94) than that of the conventional classifier (~0.86), showing superior discriminatory capability across thresholds.

Figure 3 depicts the training convergence curve of the COBYLA optimizer throughout 100 iterations. The optimization landscape stabilized after approximately 70 iterations, indicating favorable convergence characteristics and dependable training performance.

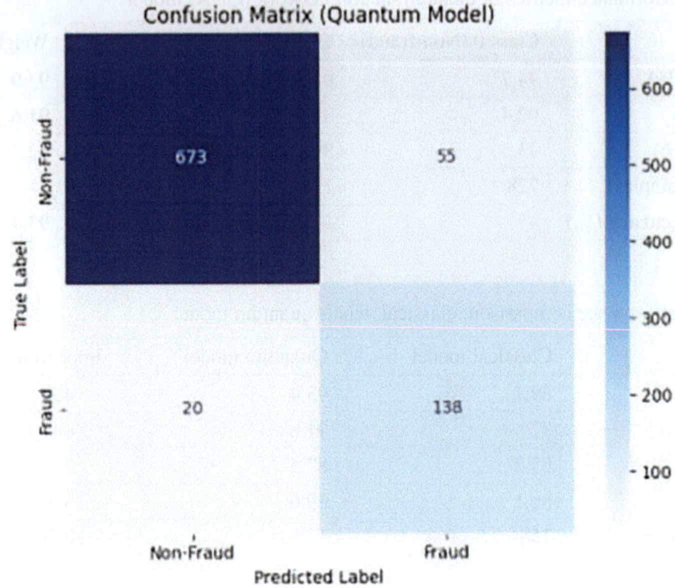

Fig. 1 Confusion matrix for the quantum neural network classifier

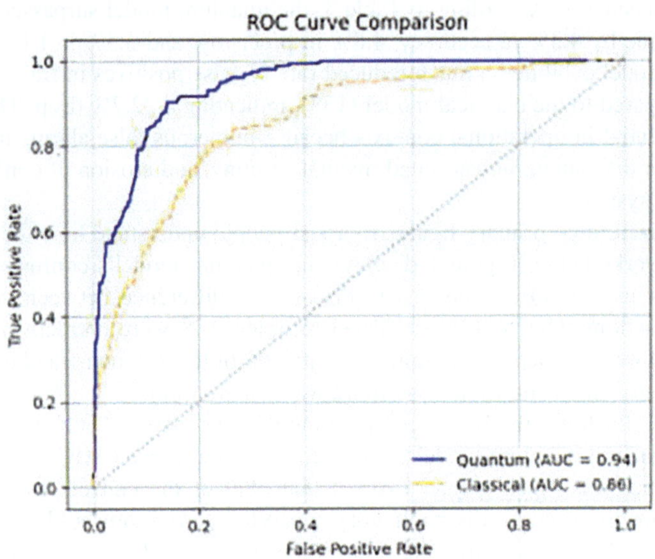

Fig. 2 ROC curves comparing quantum and classical classifiers

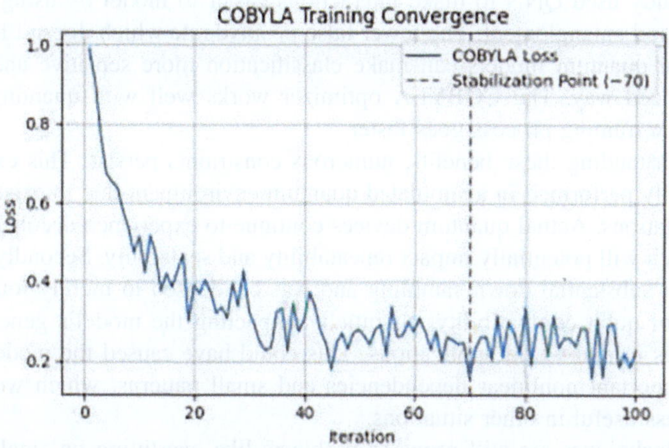

Fig. 3 COBYLA optimizer loss convergence over 100 iterations

These visuals enhance the quantitative results displayed in Tables 2 and 3 by providing a more intuitive perspective on the model's learning and performance across classes. The performance enhancements can be ascribed to the quantum circuit's expressive capacity, which encapsulated nonlinear feature interactions frequently overlooked by linear models such as logistic regression. The quantum feature map (ZZFeatureMap) converted input features into quantum states, enabling the model to investigate a more extensive, high-dimensional representation space. When combined with the TwoLocal ansatz and subjected to several training rounds, the model proficiently discerned class boundaries that were normally challenging to delineate using conventional projections.

The results also show us that using near term quantum devices or their emulators to solve real-world classification problems is a good idea. The experiment was done on a simulated backend with a circuit depth, four qubits, and an optimizer configuration that matched noisy intermediate scale quantum (NISQ) hardware. This suggests that similar results may be possible with quantum devices in the real world.

5 Discussion

The quantum neural network (QNN) results show that the model can learn and apply patterns in a binary classification task like fraud detection. But they also give strong evidence that quantum machine learning (QML) can be used in the real world. People know a lot about logistic regression and other classical models. They work well usually but when the data gets more complicated or when features interact in complicated ways, their performance doesn't change much.

This study used QNN to make interactions easier to model by using quantum encoding and entanglement. The lower false positive rate which doesn't hurt recall shows that quantum models can make classification more sensitive and specific in a balanced way. The COBYLA optimizer works well with quantum circuits because the training process goes faster.

Notwithstanding these benefits, numerous constraints persist. This experiment was actually performed in a simulated quantum environment due to existing hardware limitations. Actual quantum devices continue to experience decoherence and noise which will potentially impact repeatability and scalability. Secondly, the data underwent substantial down sampling and was condensed to merely four characteristics for qubit compatibility, potentially impacting the model's generalization capabilities in real-world applications. This could have caused the model to miss out on important nonlinear dependencies and small patterns, which would have made it less useful in other situations.

QML techniques are still prone to problems like overfitting on small datasets when actually viewed from an algorithmic point of view. It doesn't help quantum circuits that can't be made deeper or have more trainable parameters right now. Also, quantum models might not always do better than classical ones in problems that are low-dimensional or well-structured where classical ML already does almost as well with less computational overhead.

This case study gives us a good reason to add QML to future fraud detection systems, especially in hybrid systems that use quantum backends for model pretraining or as parts of ensemble methods.

6 Future Work

Extensive future directions can be followed from this research. To verify model generalizability and scalability, the first experiments can be extended to several industry datasets, including multi-product time series or high-frequency retail data. Second, one can investigate ways to increase model robustness and realism by including outside signals, including calendar events, weather APIs, social media sentiment, and competitor pricing.

Third, using cloud-based orchestration tools (e.g., AWS Lambda, Azure Functions) and streaming data processing platforms (e.g., Apache Kafka, Flink), the AIOps framework will be deployed in a real-time environment, producing insights into latency, scalability, and feedback loop performance. Furthermore, by providing insights into model decision-making, explainable AI methods such as SHAP and LIME can improve trust and openness.

Finally, the framework can be expanded to incorporate self-healing elements or reinforcement learning tools, allowing automatic operational decision optimization. This would transform AIOps from reactive management to autonomous control, so better complement the vision of intelligent, flexible supply chains.

7 Conclusion and Contributions

This chapter has shown everything you need to know about how quantum machine learning can help stop credit card fraud. Using an Estimator-based Quantum Neural Network (EstimatorQNN) on a smaller set of credit card transactions, we showed that quantum models can do as well as, and in some cases better than, traditional models. The quantum classifier had a higher accuracy and F1-score and the number of false positives went down a lot. This means that it is better at generalizing and being strong in binary classification tasks.

Adding QML to systems that look for fraud is a big step forward for financial analytics of the next generation. Over the years, classical models have gotten better, but quantum models offer a whole new way to store and process data. This could lead to speeds and accuracies that have never been seen before. This study used a simulated quantum environment, but the experimental framework is a good base for using it in the real world as quantum technology becomes more widely available and reliable.

There are many good ways to move this research forward in the future as well. One way is to improve quantum models by adding more qubits and making the circuits harder to understand. This lets you add more complex feature sets without having to cut down on the number of dimensions. You might also want to look into quantum kernel methods or hybrid ensemble models, which combine the best parts of quantum and classical classifiers. To go from theory to practice, we need to put QML models on real quantum hardware and see how well they work when there is noise.

This study shows that quantum machine learning isn't just an idea; it's a useful tool with a lot of potential. In the future, when quantum technology is more common, adding it to systems that find fraud and other types of anomalies could help make decisions safer, smarter, and faster.

References

1. Nielsen MA, Chuang IL (2010) Quantum computation and quantum information. Cambridge University Press
2. Biamonte J, Wittek P, Pancotti N, Rebentrost P, Wiebe N, Lloyd S (2017) Quantum machine learning. Nature 549(7671):195–202. https://doi.org/10.1038/nature23474
3. Schuld M, Sinayskiy I, Petruccione F (2015) An introduction to quantum machine learning. Contemp Phys 56(2):172–185. https://doi.org/10.1080/00107514.2014.964942
4. Preskill J (2018) Quantum computing in the NISQ era and beyond. Quantum 2:79. https://doi.org/10.22331/q-2018-08-06-79
5. Abraham H, Akhalwaya IY, Aleksandrowicz G et al (2019) Qiskit: an open-source framework for quantum computing. https://qiskit.org
6. Schuld M, Bocharov A, Svore KM, Wiebe N (2020) Circuit-centric quantum classifiers. Phys Rev A 101(3):032308. https://doi.org/10.1103/PhysRevA.101.032308
7. Cerezo M, Arrasmith A, Babbush R et al (2021) Variational quantum algorithms. Nat Rev Phys 3:625–644. https://doi.org/10.1038/s42254-021-00348-9
8. Devitt SJ, Munro WJ, Nemoto K (2013) Quantum error correction for beginners. Rep Prog Phys 76(7):076001. https://doi.org/10.1088/0034-4885/76/7/076001

9. Benedetti M, Lloyd E, Sack S, Fiorentini M (2019) Parameterized quantum circuits as machine learning models. Quantum Sci Technol 4(4):043001. https://doi.org/10.1088/2058-9565/ab4eb5
10. Havlíček V, Córcoles AD, Temme K et al (2019) Supervised learning with quantum-enhanced feature spaces. Nature 567(7747):209–212. https://doi.org/10.1038/s41586-019-0980-2
11. Montanaro A (2016) Quantum algorithms: an overview. NPJ Quantum Inf 2(1):15023. https://doi.org/10.1038/npjqi.2015.23
12. Kimble HJ (2008) The quantum internet. Nature 453(7198):1023–1030. https://doi.org/10.1038/nature07127
13. Kandala A, Mezzacapo A, Temme K et al (2017) Hardware-efficient variational quantum eigensolver for small molecules and quantum magnets. Nature 549(7671):242–246. https://doi.org/10.1038/nature23879
14. Arute F, Arya K, Babbush R et al (2019) Quantum supremacy using a programmable superconducting processor. Nature 574(7779):505–510. https://doi.org/10.1038/s41586-019-1666-5
15. Johnson MW et al (2011) Quantum annealing with manufactured spins. Nature 473(7346):194–198. https://doi.org/10.1038/nature10012
16. Fowler AG, Mariantoni M, Martinis JM, Cleland AN (2012) Surface codes: towards practical large-scale quantum computation. Phys Rev A 86(3):032324. https://doi.org/10.1103/PhysRevA.86.032324
17. Jordan MI, Mitchell TM (2015) Machine learning: trends, perspectives, and prospects. Science 349(6245):255–260. https://doi.org/10.1126/science.aaa8415
18. Benedetti M, Garcia-Pintos D, Perdomo O, Leyton-Ortega V, Nam Y, Perdomo-Ortiz A (2019) A generative modeling approach for benchmarking and training shallow quantum circuits. NPJ Quantum Inf 5(1):45. https://doi.org/10.1038/s41534-019-0157-8
19. Lloyd S, Mohseni M, Rebentrost P (2014) Quantum principal component analysis. Nat Phys 10(9):631–633. https://doi.org/10.1038/nphys3029
20. Schuld M, Fingerhuth M, Petruccione F (2017) Implementing a distance-based classifier with a quantum interference circuit. EPL (Eur Lett) 119(6):60002. https://doi.org/10.1209/0295-5075/119/60002
21. Biamonte J, Faccin M (2021) Quantum machine learning theory: a primer for computing scientists. Commun ACM 64(10):64–73. https://doi.org/10.1145/3476735
22. Peruzzo A, McClean J, Shadbolt P, Yung M, Zhou X, Love P, Aspuru-Guzik A, O'Brien J (2014) A variational eigenvalue solver on a photonic quantum processor. Nat Commun 5(4213)
23. Schuld S, Petruccione F (2018) Supervised learning with quantum computers. Springer
24. Farhi E, Neven H (2018) Classification with quantum neural networks on near term processors. arXiv:1802.06002
25. Romero J, Olson J, Aspuru-Guzik A (2017) Quantum autoencoders for efficient compression of quantum data. Quantum Sci Technol 2(4):045001
26. Beer H, Bondarenko M, Farrelly D, Bergholm V (2023) Training deep quantum neural networks. Nat Commun 14(1):1125
27. Romero J, Babbush R, McClean J, Hempel C, Love P, Aspuru-Guzik A (2018) Strategies for quantum computing molecular energies using the unitary coupled cluster ansatz. Quantum Sci Technol 4(1):014008
28. Farhi E, Goldstone J, Gutmann S (2014) A quantum approximate optimization algorithm. arXiv:1411.4028
29. Temme K, Bravyi S, Gambetta J (2017) Error mitigation for short-depth quantum circuits. Phys Rev Lett 119(18):180509
30. Killoran N, Bromley T, Izaac J, Schuld M, Quesada N, Lloyd S (2019) Continuous-variable quantum neural networks. Phys Rev Res 1(3):033063

Sakhita Sree Gadde is AIOps Engineer at Zurich, North America, where she builds scalable monitoring frameworks, automated pipelines, and AI-driven systems to enhance reliability and efficiency. Alongside AIOps, she designs and deploys ML models, works with Large Language Models (LLMs), and develops end-to-end MLOps workflows across Azure and AWS to bring AI solutions into production. Her research contributions include publications in IEEE, Springer, and MDPI on robotics, computer vision, and machine learning, and she holds a masters in data science from Texas A&M University.

Ashwin Prakash Nalwade is a machine learning engineer with a strong track record across early-stage (Pre-seed, Series A) and late-stage (Series E) startups, complemented by research, teaching, and entrepreneurial work at New York University. He has also authored a widely cited research paper on wildfire spread prediction, which has gained renewed relevance amid recent wildfire events in Los Angeles and is being leveraged by researchers tackling multi-billion-dollar challenges in disaster mitigation.

Quantum Security—Cryptography and Threat Landscape

Anurag Reddy Ekkati and Gurpreet Singh Walia

Abstract

Quantum computing, as many think, is not only about faster calculations but it is a serious threat to today's cryptographic security systems. Current encryption methods like RSA and elliptic-curve cryptography rely on computational complexities which quantum computers can solve quickly. For example, Shor's algorithm and Grover's algorithm. They can break public-key cryptography and can significantly weaken symmetric encryption. These algorithms by compromising data integrity, privacy, and trust can create serious security implications. Attackers can now very well store encrypted information and decrypt it later when quantum technologies advance further. Organizations need to immediately take an action to transition to quantum-resistant cryptographic methods like lattice-based, hash-based, and code-based algorithms. These algorithms are not straightforward to implement and they need careful planning and testing as they involve larger keys and may bring in latency or compatibility issues. Quantum Key Distribution (QKD) which leverages quantum mechanics principles offers a different solution to secure communication, but it has practical limitations of distance and speed. All industries must evolve to handle this situation. They should start performing risk assessments, adopting hybrid cryptographic approaches, and implementing crypto-agility to smoothly adapt to new standards. Quantum threats are no longer just theoretical. Multiple tools to combat these threats are available and organizations should adapt sooner than later.

A. R. Ekkati (✉)
IEEE Senior Member, Sr. Principal Software Engineer, Palo Alto Networks Inc, Lathrop, CA, USA
e-mail: anurag.ekkati@gmail.com; anurag.ekkati@ieee.org

G. S. Walia
Storage Networking and Security Architect Netapp Inc., Durham, NC, USA
e-mail: gwalia08@gmail.com

M. Rana and B. Pandey (eds.), *Quantum Ops*,
https://doi.org/10.1007/978-3-032-10775-6_9

Keywords

Quantum computing • Cryptography • RSA • Elliptic-curve cryptography • Shor's algorithm • Grover's algorithm • Post-quantum cryptography • Quantum key distribution (QKD) • Crypto-agility • Quantum threat landscape • Encryption methods • Data security

1 Introduction

Quantum computing doesn't just offer the promise of faster calculations or scientific breakthroughs. It presents a very real, very serious challenge to the security systems that underpin today's digital world. In the last chapter, we looked at how quantum technologies could push the boundaries of fields like machine learning and artificial intelligence. This chapter turns toward a different kind of urgency. The threat is not abstract. Quantum computers, once they reach a certain level of capability, could undermine the cryptographic foundations we currently rely on to secure communications, protect data, and maintain trust across countless systems. Quantum security isn't just an abstract idea anymore, it's shaping up to be one of the biggest shake-ups in cybersecurity since the internet went mainstream. Researchers have cautioned that if the transition to quantum-aware systems lags behind technological advances, the consequences could be wide-ranging. Everything from online services and financial networks to energy infrastructure and national security systems could be affected [1].

Nearly every function of modern IT, whether it's a bank transfer, a medical record exchange, a government intelligence report, or a basic VPN tunnel, is built on encryption methods that assume attackers are limited to classical computational resources. The assumption has held, until now. But if an adversary equipped with a powerful quantum computer were able to break these cryptographic schemes, the damage would be significant. Sensitive information could be exposed, manipulated, or repurposed without detection [2]. The point is not just theoretical. Files and transmissions that are encrypted and considered secure today might be intercepted and stored by attackers, only to be decrypted years from now once the hardware becomes capable. Financial data, internal memos, diplomatic communications—none of it is necessarily safe if quantum decryption enters the picture. Privacy would be eroded, and with it, trust in digital infrastructure that most people never think twice about.

This is not just a technical issue, and it's not one we can afford to postpone. The entire structure of digital security today depends on mathematical problems that quantum computing has the potential to solve far more efficiently than any classical machine. RSA and elliptic-curve cryptography, two widely used standards, rely on the difficulty of factoring large numbers or solving discrete logarithms—tasks that are currently infeasible for classical systems. A sufficiently advanced quantum computer would change that. Algorithms like Shor's would make these encryption systems obsolete, not over decades, but in a matter of minutes or hours. This opens the door to a dangerous tactic that security professionals have already identified: "store now, decrypt later." Nation-state actors and other adversaries are likely already collecting encrypted data in bulk, assuming that they will be able to unlock it once quantum capabilities catch up. It is a patient, calculated threat, and one that targets the long-term value of data as much as its short-term sensitivity.

For people working in cybersecurity, or for anyone studying the future of secure systems—understanding the scope of this threat is no longer optional. The idea is not just to keep pace with technological change, but to prepare in advance for it. Addressing the quantum threat requires coordination across disciplines and sectors. It is a challenge that touches technology, policy, and strategic planning all at once. And it cannot be solved in isolation. Researchers, standards bodies, private companies, and governments all have a role to play. The transition to quantum-resistant cryptography is not something that will happen overnight, nor will it happen quietly. It will take time, funding, international consensus, and years of implementation [3].

This chapter will explore several key areas. We will look at how quantum algorithms actually break classical encryption, what kinds of new cryptographic techniques are being developed to withstand quantum attacks, and what real-world steps organizations can begin taking now to protect their systems. There's no easy answer here. But understanding where the real risks lie is the first step—and that's what this chapter aims to help with. Tools, examples, and practical considerations will be discussed, not as hypotheticals, but as steps that need to be taken seriously. The risks are not just about futuristic espionage or speculative doomsday scenarios. They are about systems already in place, already in use, and already at risk [1, 2].

2 Quantum Threats to Classical Cryptography

Quantum computers does not actually follow the rules of classical machines. They work with qubits, to carry out operations which uses quantum effects. For example superposition and entanglement. This would be impossible or extremely slow on conventional systems. This ability to process many possibilities at once opens the door to solving problems that classical computers struggle with. Unfortunately, that strength comes with a serious downside for cybersecurity.

Most classical encryption methods are built on problems which are deliberately hard to solve using traditional computing power like factoring large integers or calculating discrete logarithms fall into this category. They form the backbone of algorithms like RSA and elliptic-curve cryptography. But quantum algorithms have changed the equation. Researchers have shown that quantum techniques can solve these problems more efficiently than classical approaches, breaking the assumptions those encryption schemes rely on.

The threat is not just theoretical. These breakthroughs mean that several of the cryptographic tools we currently depend on may no longer be reliable in a world

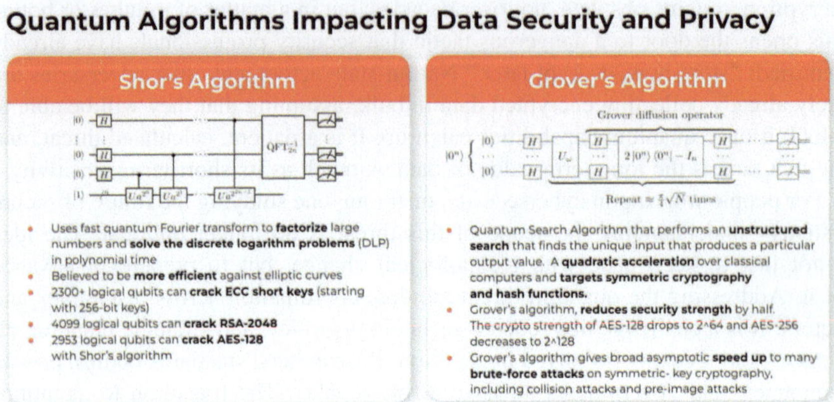

Fig. 1 Quantum algorithms impacting data security and privacy. On the left, Shor's algorithm uses quantum Fourier transforms to factor large numbers or solve discrete logarithms, undermining RSA, ECC, and Diffie—Hellman encryption. On the right, Grover's algorithm leverages quantum search to brute-force keys quadratically faster, halving the effective strength of symmetric ciphers. Together, these algorithms imply that the cryptographic underpinnings of modern IT—from HTTPS and VPN tunnels to digital signatures and blockchain—are at risk once mature quantum computers emerge [4]

where scalable quantum machines exist. Among the known threats, two quantum algorithms stand out. They target and show how vulnerable the core mathematical problems behind widely used encryption systems are under quantum attack. The next section outlines how each of them works and what they mean for the future of digital security (Fig. 1).

2.1 Shor's Algorithm—Breaking Public-Key Encryption

In 1994, mathematician Peter Shor introduced a quantum algorithm that changed the conversation around encryption. His method can factor large integers and compute discrete logarithms exponentially faster than any classical algorithm we currently know. That alone is enough to worry cryptographers, because the security of RSA encryption, the Diffie—Hellman key exchange, and elliptic-curve cryptography all depends on the difficulty of exactly those problems. A sufficiently capable quantum computer running Shor's algorithm could factor a 2048-bit RSA modulus or recover a private key in an elliptic-curve system, rendering the encryption or digital signatures useless. Essentially, most widely used forms of public-key cryptography would no longer offer protection.

Take RSA-2048, which is still common for securing websites, VPNs, and many forms of digital communication. It has long been believed that breaking it with a quantum computer would require tens of millions of qubits, a scale far beyond what is currently available. But that assumption was shaken by a 2025 study from

Google's Quantum AI team. Their findings suggested that RSA-2048 might be factored using fewer than one million qubits, completing the process in about a week. This was a substantial revision of earlier projections, which had placed the requirement closer to 20 million qubits. The implication is clear: the resources needed to launch such an attack may be much more accessible than previously thought.

Right now, quantum machines are still limited. The largest publicly known systems have just over a thousand qubits, which is far from what would be needed to run Shor's algorithm on RSA-2048. Even so, progress is steady. And that steady progress means the window for relying on current public-key encryption is closing. Some forecasts indicate that by 2035, quantum systems might reach the scale and error correction necessary to break RSA-2048 outright [5]. If that happens, the impact will be broad. Everything from secure website logins and email encryption to blockchain transactions could be at risk—especially if encrypted data is being intercepted now and stored for future decryption. The message is not alarmist. It is a measured recognition that the clock is ticking [5].

2.2 Grover's Algorithm—Weakening Symmetric Encryption

Even cryptographic systems that remain solid against classical attacks, such as AES for symmetric encryption and SHA-2 for hashing, face some degree of vulnerability in the quantum setting. The shift is not total, but it matters. Lov Grover proposed a quantum algorithm that changes how brute-force search behaves. Instead of checking each possibility one by one, as classical algorithms must, Grover's method finds the answer in roughly the square root of the time it would take classically. This has real implications. For symmetric ciphers, the effective strength is cut in half. A cipher like AES-128, which has 2^{128} possible keys, would offer only 2^{64} bits of effective security against a quantum search. AES-256, on the other hand, would drop from 2^{256} to 2^{128}.

That reduction still leaves a large margin of safety. To be clear, breaking AES-128 using Grover's algorithm would require an impractical amount of time—so long, in fact, that even the lifetime of the universe would not be enough. But the theoretical impact is there. It changes how we think about key length. Security architects may respond by favoring stronger keys moving forward, and it is already becoming common to recommend AES-256 for long-term resilience. While symmetric cryptography is not broken by Grover's algorithm the way RSA or ECC are broken by Shor's, it does not walk away untouched. The general guideline is straightforward: to retain the same security level against a quantum attacker, double the key size.

Grover's algorithm also reaches into other areas. It affects hashing algorithms and password security, where brute-force attacks are still a concern. A quantum adversary can attempt twice as many guesses in the same amount of time compared to a classical one. That means passwords, hashes, and similar mechanisms lose some of their protective depth. Cryptographic designs will need to account for this

Table 1 Comparison of classical cryptography and quantum vulnerabilities

Aspect	Classical cryptography	Quantum impact
Public-key algorithms	RSA, ECC, Diffie-Hellman	Broken by Shor's algorithm
Symmetric encryption	AES-128, AES-256	Weakened by Grover's algorithm (effective key length halved)
Hash functions	SHA-2, SHA-3	Grover's algorithm reduces brute-force resistance
Signature schemes	RSA, ECDSA	Vulnerable under quantum attack

by increasing hash output sizes or by applying hash functions repeatedly to offset the speedup introduced by Grover's method.

Vulnerabilities with respect to each aspect are summarized in the Table 1. To put the contrast plainly, Shor's algorithm attacks public-key cryptography directly, rendering systems like RSA, Diffie—Hellman, ECC, and ECDSA fundamentally insecure. Grover's algorithm does not break symmetric systems outright, but it reduces their strength and demands larger key sizes and more conservative hash strategies. As a result, even though symmetric encryption holds up better, it cannot be left unexamined. Confidential data protected by today's algorithms could still be exposed once quantum machines become powerful enough. This is why cryptographers have already begun advising a shift toward stronger keys. A 256-bit symmetric key, for example, would provide only 128 bits of effective security in the quantum setting [2], which reinforces the call to adopt longer keys for systems meant to endure [2].

2.3 The Quantum Threat Landscape

Beyond the core algorithms, it is important to step back and look at the wider threat landscape that emerges in a world where quantum computers are real and usable.

Breaking Asymmetric Encryption: This is the most immediate and well-understood threat. RSA, ECC, DSA, Diffie—Hellman—these public-key algorithms sit at the heart of secure web traffic (TLS), VPN tunnels, encrypted email systems like PGP, software signing, cryptocurrency wallets, and more. If a quantum adversary gains access to these systems, the entire public-key infrastructure becomes vulnerable. Encrypted data that seems safe today, like email transcripts or VPN communications, can be captured and stored now with the intent to decrypt it later, once quantum capabilities arrive. This "harvest now, decrypt later" approach is not theoretical. Many experts believe that nation-state actors are already collecting encrypted traffic they deem valuable enough to keep for the long term [6]. Digital signatures also come under threat. If an attacker can retrieve a private key using Shor's algorithm, they can forge signatures and undermine the authenticity of software updates, financial records, or blockchain transactions. In practice, any system depending on the difficulty of factoring or discrete logarithms becomes fragile once large-scale quantum computers exist.

Compromising Data Integrity: Once the mathematical problems behind ECC and RSA are no longer hard, attackers can do more than eavesdrop. They can forge signatures and create seemingly valid records or software packages that are, in fact, fakes. If a private signing key is stolen or reconstructed, a malicious actor can impersonate software vendors, issue fraudulent transactions, or rewrite records with a signature that passes verification. This introduces a serious problem for integrity. Communications that appear to be authentic could in reality be forgeries. Financial systems, software distribution platforms, and public records all rely on digital signatures to ensure that what is received is what was sent. If that trust is broken, the door opens to fraud and impersonation at a scale we have not previously seen [7].

Blockchain Vulnerabilities: Blockchain networks are built on two cryptographic pillars—digital signatures for wallets and transactions, and hash functions to enforce consensus. Quantum computing puts both at risk. Systems like Bitcoin and Ethereum use ECC-based schemes such as ECDSA and EdDSA for digital signatures. These are directly exposed under Shor's algorithm. A quantum attacker could derive a user's private key from their public address and use it to sign fraudulent transactions. Consensus mechanisms that rely on proof-of-work, while more resilient, could also be disrupted by quantum speedups. If an attacker can solve hashing puzzles faster than honest miners, they might take control of the ledger. That's exactly why blockchain developers need to act now. Without upgrading to quantum-resistant signatures, the whole trust model could fall apart.

Security of IoT and Infrastructure: Many embedded systems, especially in the Internet of Things space, use minimal cryptography. In some cases, devices ship with hard-coded RSA or ECC keys and shortened key lengths, simply to conserve power or memory. These shortcuts make such systems soft targets in a quantum-enabled world. Smart home products, industrial sensors, and even medical devices could be compromised if attackers can reverse their encryption. The risk does not stop there. Infrastructure systems—electrical grids, transportation networks, healthcare platforms—often depend on secure communication channels. A breach in the cryptographic layer could lead to the spoofing of control messages or shutdowns of critical services. While such scenarios remain hypothetical for now, the implications for national security are serious [3]. The idea of an attacker using a quantum system to disrupt infrastructure may sound remote, but the time to harden these systems is before that becomes possible.

Shortening of Secret Lifetimes: One challenge that does not always get the attention it deserves is the shrinking shelf life of confidential information. Even if we migrate to post-quantum cryptography in the coming years, any data encrypted before that transition remains vulnerable. Highly sensitive data, such as classified government files or long-term health records, may need to remain secret for decades. If quantum computing becomes viable before those decades pass, then those secrets are already at risk. Organizations must ask how long their data needs to stay secure. If the answer is twenty years, and quantum machines are expected in fifteen, then that data should already be protected with quantum-resistant algorithms. Several intelligence agencies have stated clearly that information requiring confidentiality into the 2030s or beyond should be migrated immediately to stronger protections. The timeline is no longer abstract. Long-lived secrets need immediate attention.

Given the variety and depth of these risks, it makes sense that governments and industries have started building strategies for defense. Some responses have taken the form of structured roadmaps designed to help entire sectors transition safely. One such initiative, known as STL-QCRYPTO, outlines specific guidance for fourteen high-impact sectors, including finance, healthcare, energy, defense, government, telecommunications, e-commerce, and even emerging domains like artificial intelligence and the metaverse [8]. These frameworks recommend concrete steps, such as identifying all cryptographic assets and gradually replacing them with quantum-safe alternatives. They also acknowledge the operational and regulatory hurdles that different industries will face along the way [8]. The core message is consistent: quantum threats span across domains, and the response needs to be as comprehensive as the problem itself.

Of course, not everything in cybersecurity changes. Symmetric encryption and hashing functions, if configured with longer key lengths, can still offer strong protection. Likewise, elements such as physical security, user training, and network monitoring are largely unaffected by quantum capabilities. But cryptography is foundational. When that foundation shifts, it affects everything built on top of it. Quantum computing introduces a fundamental change in what attackers can do, and in what defenders must anticipate. The risks span confidentiality, integrity, and authenticity. And as a result, the urgency to act is no longer theoretical. It is real, and it is here.

3 Post-Quantum Cryptography: The Race for Quantum-Resistant Algorithms

There is at least one piece of good news in all of this—the cybersecurity world has not been passive. In fact, a global effort is already well underway to design and standardize Post-quantum Cryptography (PQC), which refers to new cryptographic algorithms built to resist attacks from quantum computers while still holding strong against classical ones. These emerging algorithms are usually based on problems that, as far as we know, remain hard even for quantum machines. That includes lattice problems, error-correcting codes, hash-based designs, and multivariate polynomial equations. Alongside this work, researchers are also investigating quantum-secure communication technologies like Quantum Key Distribution (QKD). QKD draws on quantum physics itself to create and exchange encryption keys—its use of photons allows it to detect eavesdropping attempts and guarantees confidentiality in a very different way [1]. Still, QKD needs special-purpose hardware and infrastructure to function, so it serves more as a niche supplement rather than a full-scale replacement for PQC, which is built to run on classical networks. For most systems and applications, the focus remains on PQC algorithms that can integrate with existing hardware and software.

Over the last several years, dozens of candidate PQC algorithms have been introduced, with many attracting initial interest. Some turned out to be more fragile than expected. For example, certain multivariate signature schemes such as Rainbow were eventually broken under deeper analysis, and the isogeny-based scheme SIKE was defeated using classical methods in 2022. These failures were part of the process. Through a combination of competition and cryptanalysis, attention shifted toward a few families of techniques—especially lattice-based and hash-based approaches—that have shown stronger resilience. The U.S. National Institute of Standards and Technology (NIST) has led much of this work by coordinating a worldwide public process to evaluate and select the most promising algorithms. That process began in 2016, when NIST opened the floor to global submissions. Dozens of proposals came in and were tested through multiple rounds of review, analysis, and attack attempts. In 2022, NIST named its finalists: CRYSTALS-Kyber for key encapsulation, and three digital signature schemes—CRYSTALS-Dilithium, FALCON, and SPHINCS+—based on lattice or hash constructs. Two years later, in August 2024, NIST officially published the first three standards: FIPS 203 for Kyber, FIPS 204 for Dilithium, and FIPS 205 for SPHINCS+. These are no longer draft candidates—they are now formal standards and available for real-world use. NIST has recommended that organizations begin adopting them without delay. FALCON, the fourth finalist for digital signatures, remains under review and is expected to be standardized soon. At the same time, NIST continues to evaluate alternate algorithms, including HQC, which was selected in 2025 as a backup encryption scheme. The guidance from standards bodies has been blunt: do not wait. Start assessing and upgrading systems now, because the shift to quantum-resistant cryptography will take years.

Adopting PQC in production environments is not without its challenges—those will be explored further in the next section—but the essential point is that practical, vetted replacements for quantum-vulnerable encryption now exist. The next ten years will bring a sweeping transition across systems and protocols as RSA, Diffie—Hellman, and elliptic-curve schemes are gradually retired and replaced by quantum-safe tools. Kyber will be used for key exchange and general encryption, while Dilithium and SPHINCS+ will serve in digital signatures. As with any cryptographic change, there are trade-offs. Most post-quantum schemes involve longer keys or signatures and sometimes different performance profiles. Even so, many are already quite efficient. Kyber, for instance, is fast and well suited for high-throughput environments. Dilithium's signatures are larger than RSA's but still manageable for most applications. Development continues to improve their efficiency, to harden their security proofs, and to support their use in different platforms. The momentum is here—the standards are in place—and now the work turns to integration.

3.1 Key Ideas Behind PQC

Without diving too far into the mathematics, there are several core ideas that most Post-quantum Cryptography algorithms are built around—each with its own characteristics, strengths, and trade-offs.

Lattice-Based Cryptography: These schemes rely on mathematical problems defined over multi-dimensional grids known as lattices. Problems like Learning With Errors (LWE) and the Shortest Vector Problem (SVP) are believed to be hard for both quantum and classical computers. Kyber and Dilithium, two of the most prominent PQC algorithms, fall into this category. Lattice-based schemes often require relatively large public keys—typically a few kilobytes—but they perform encryption and signature operations quickly and efficiently in practice.

Hash-Based Signatures: These schemes are built around the continued strength of cryptographic hash functions, which are still considered robust even in the quantum era—though with the caveat that output lengths need to be doubled to counter Grover's algorithm. SPHINCS+ is a stateless, hash-based signature scheme that has stood up well to analysis. One downside is that hash-based signatures tend to be quite large in size, but their underlying security is very strong as long as the hash function itself remains sound. SHA-256, for example, is still a common choice.

Code-Based Cryptography: These algorithms are based on the difficulty of decoding a randomly chosen linear error-correcting code. The classic example is McEliece, a scheme introduced in 1978 that remains secure today. McEliece is notable for its huge public keys—hundreds of kilobytes in size—but its encryption and decryption operations are fast. Several code-based options were part of the NIST selection process, and one of them, HQC, was chosen in 2025 as a backup key encapsulation mechanism.

Multivariate Cryptography: This area deals with solving systems of nonlinear equations over finite fields, a problem known to be NP-hard. A number of digital signature schemes were proposed in this category, such as Rainbow. However, many of them were broken during the evaluation process. A few remain under consideration as fallback options, though confidence in their long-term viability has dropped.

Isogeny-Based Cryptography: These approaches use isogenies, which are functions that map between elliptic curves. SIKE, an isogeny-based encryption scheme, once drew attention for its appealingly small key sizes. That advantage was short-lived. In 2022, SIKE was broken by a classical attack, casting serious doubt on the security of this entire category. For now, isogeny-based systems are viewed as too risky to standardize.

Table 2 provides a comparative overview of the leading algorithm families, highlighting their strengths, weaknesses, and current status. Each approach comes with its own mix of benefits and drawbacks. None is perfect. Some may prove

Table 2 Overview of post-quantum cryptographic algorithm families

Algorithm family	Example(s)	Quantum resilience	Trade-offs
Lattice-based	Kyber, Dilithium	Strong (as of 2025)	Moderate size, good performance
Hash-based	SPHINCS+	Very strong	Large signatures
Code-based	McEliece, HQC	Strong (large keys)	Huge key sizes (100 KB+)
Multivariate polynomial	Rainbow (broken), others	Uncertain	Fast, but many failed under scrutiny
Isogeny-based	SIKE (broken)	Weak (broken)	Very small keys, but now deprecated

more resilient than others as research continues and as quantum capabilities evolve. That is why standardization bodies have focused on multiple families of algorithms and why backups have been designated in case one approach fails. The concept of crypto-agility—designing systems to switch algorithms with minimal disruption—has become central to long-term security planning. Experts warn that even the algorithms we adopt in the 2020s may not stand the test of time. As both quantum computing and classical cryptanalysis improve, we can expect some current post-quantum schemes to fail. Continued research and a flexible, upgrade-ready infrastructure are not optional—they are essential [6]. Being prepared to roll out new algorithms or update cryptographic components quickly is one of the few ways we can stay ahead of what's coming next.

3.2 Adopting PQC—Challenges and Considerations

For IT professionals, the move to post-quantum cryptography will not be as straightforward as swapping in a new algorithm over the weekend. Several practical challenges need to be understood and carefully addressed. Table 3 summarizes the core categories of these challenges and the key considerations associated with each.

Table 3 Challenges and considerations for deploying post-quantum cryptography

Challenge	Description
Performance	Larger key sizes and slower operations may cause latency
Compatibility	Legacy hardware/software may not support PQC
Validation	Risk from non-standard or untested implementations
Urgency/timeline	Long migration lead times; "store now, decrypt later" threat makes it urgent

3.2.1 Performance and Size

Many post-quantum algorithms come with larger keys, ciphertexts, or digital signatures compared to the RSA or ECC systems they aim to replace. For example, Kyber's public keys are roughly a kilobyte in size, and Dilithium signatures stretch into the few-kilobyte range. In contrast, a typical RSA-2048 key or ECC signature is only a few hundred bytes. These size differences matter. They affect how much data needs to move over a network and how much space is required for storage, larger certificates, larger messages, and more overhead in protocols. Not all post-quantum algorithms are slow—Kyber, for example, turns out to be impressively fast considering the size of its keys. Even so, systems and protocols will need updates to accommodate these differences—TLS, IPsec, and others will have to evolve to support bigger keys and objects. Engineers have already noted that quantum-safe algorithms tend to demand more compute and longer processing times than their classical equivalents [2]. That increase can introduce latency or push systems to their performance limits, which makes careful testing and optimization essential before any large-scale rollout.

3.2.2 Compatibility

Hardware and software infrastructure will also need to adapt. Many existing systems—from smart cards and microcontrollers in IoT devices to older cryptographic libraries—are built with RSA or ECC in mind. Replacing them outright may break compatibility with legacy applications. One practical way to handle this is through hybrid cryptography. In this approach, both a classical and a quantum-safe algorithm are used at the same time during a secure session. For example, a TLS handshake might exchange one key using ECDH and another using Kyber—if either remains secure, the session stays protected. This method helps preserve interoperability and provides a kind of insurance policy during the transition. We are already seeing early implementations. OpenSSH, for instance, added support for hybrid key exchange in version 9.0, allowing future-proofed secure shell sessions to function even if one of the algorithms eventually fails [6]. These types of moves, especially from open-source projects, are important markers of progress. Still, they remain the exception rather than the rule. Surveys show that many organizations have not taken serious steps toward adopting PQC [6], and the longer they wait, the greater the risk if quantum breakthroughs come faster than expected.

3.2.3 Validation and Trust

Even strong cryptography can fail if implemented poorly. Using untested or non-standard code is a recipe for introducing vulnerabilities, regardless of the underlying math. It is critical to rely on standardized and carefully vetted implementations. Institutions like NIST not only define the algorithms, but also provide reference code, validation tools, and test vectors to guide secure deployment. More broadly, the principle of crypto-agility—designing systems so they can switch cryptographic components easily—has become essential. If an algorithm chosen today turns out to be flawed tomorrow, it should be possible to roll out a replacement quickly and with minimal disruption. That mindset is gaining traction.

Government bodies including the NSA and the White House have begun issuing mandates that agencies take stock of where cryptography is used and prepare for continuous updates [6]. The point is clear. Adopting PQC is not a one-time change. It is a shift toward a more flexible and resilient security model, one that assumes no single algorithm will last forever [1, 6].

3.2.4 Timeline (Urgency to Start)

The best time to begin the transition is now. Migrating an enterprise's entire cryptographic infrastructure is not fast—it requires a full inventory, upgrades to both hardware and software, validation against compliance standards, and time to test. Since some encrypted data needs to remain secure for a decade or longer, the lead time matters. If a quantum computer capable of breaking RSA appears within that window—as some researchers predict may happen in the early 2030s—then any sensitive information encrypted today could be compromised in the future. NIST's guidance reflects that concern. The agency has proposed that vulnerable public-key systems be phased out by 2030, with full transitions completed by 2035. In the meantime, tech companies and open-source communities are already experimenting. Google and Cloudflare have tested PQC in TLS connections to measure performance, and others have run pilots for post-quantum VPNs. OpenSSH's inclusion of quantum-safe algorithms is another early sign of adoption. These trials are not just academic—they surface real implementation issues and help build practical readiness. Still, the majority of organizations have not yet addressed quantum risks in their security planning [6]. If progress in quantum hardware accelerates, those who wait may find themselves too far behind to respond in time. The smart move? Get ahead of it. Start planning now, keep an eye on emerging standards, and don't try to go it alone—there's a lot to learn from others already experimenting.

In summary, adopting post-quantum cryptography is not a quick patch or a single upgrade. It requires planning, coordination, and long-term investment. If your organization has not yet begun, the first step is to study the new standards and start experimenting. Take stock of where and how cryptography is used—then design a roadmap that prioritizes the most critical systems. For new purchases, make sure they support quantum-safe cryptography. At the same time, staff must be trained and made aware of what PQC involves and why it matters. The process is not only technical—it is also a matter of organizational readiness and change management.

And even once PQC is in place, we cannot afford to assume we are done. Quantum-safe encryption secures one layer, but attackers will always find other routes. It is likely that future quantum algorithms will help accelerate certain classes of attacks—perhaps on networks, optimization-based systems, or other parts of the stack that lie outside cryptographic theory [7]. Threats like phishing, malware, and social engineering will persist regardless. Experts continue to stress that the right approach is layered. Strong access controls, vigilant monitoring, trusted update paths, and user training all remain essential. PQC will help protect the foundations—but it is not the whole house. The post-quantum era will demand deeper resilience and a culture of continuous adaptation. With the right preparation and flexible security design, the transition is manageable. But it will not wait forever.

4 Quantum Cryptography: QKD and Quantum Randomness

4.1 Understanding Quantum Key Distribution (QKD)

Quantum Key Distribution is actually a big change in perspective for something that has traditionally been done by ensuring security based upon a mathematical problem. Unlike traditional cryptography, which is secured by computational difficulty, QKD uses quantum mechanical properties to create communication channels that cannot be compromised.

QKD is hence the main application of quantum cryptography, with the intent of providing encryption keys secretly between two parties traditionally called Alice (the sender) and Bob (the receiver). The security of QKD lies on fundamental quantum mechanics principles, such that any attempt at eavesdropping by a third party (Eve) is detected.

The main idea behind QKD is founded on the no-cloning theorem and the uncertainty principle of quantum mechanics. Transmission of quantum information through photons is such that attempts to intercept and gain information by measuring these quantum states will necessarily disturb them and generate anomalies that can be detected by Alice and Bob. This enables the legitimate parties to ascertain whether any leakage has occurred during transmission.

4.2 How QKD Works in Practice

The most famous QKD protocol BB84 was proposed by Charles Bennett and Gilles Brassard in 1984. Alice sends Bob a sequence of photons, with each photon randomly encoding one bit of information in either of two complementary encoding schemes, such as polarization states. Bob then randomly measures each photon. After transmission, Alice and Bob compare some of their encoding and measurement choices over a public channel.

If Eve tries to eavesdrop between Alice and Bob, she must measure the photons to get information; yet, quantum mechanics says that such measurement will disturb the quantum states, hence introducing errors, which may be detected by Alice and Bob when they compare their test results. The error rate thus directly quantifies the maximum knowledge a potential eavesdropper might have gained (Fig. 2).

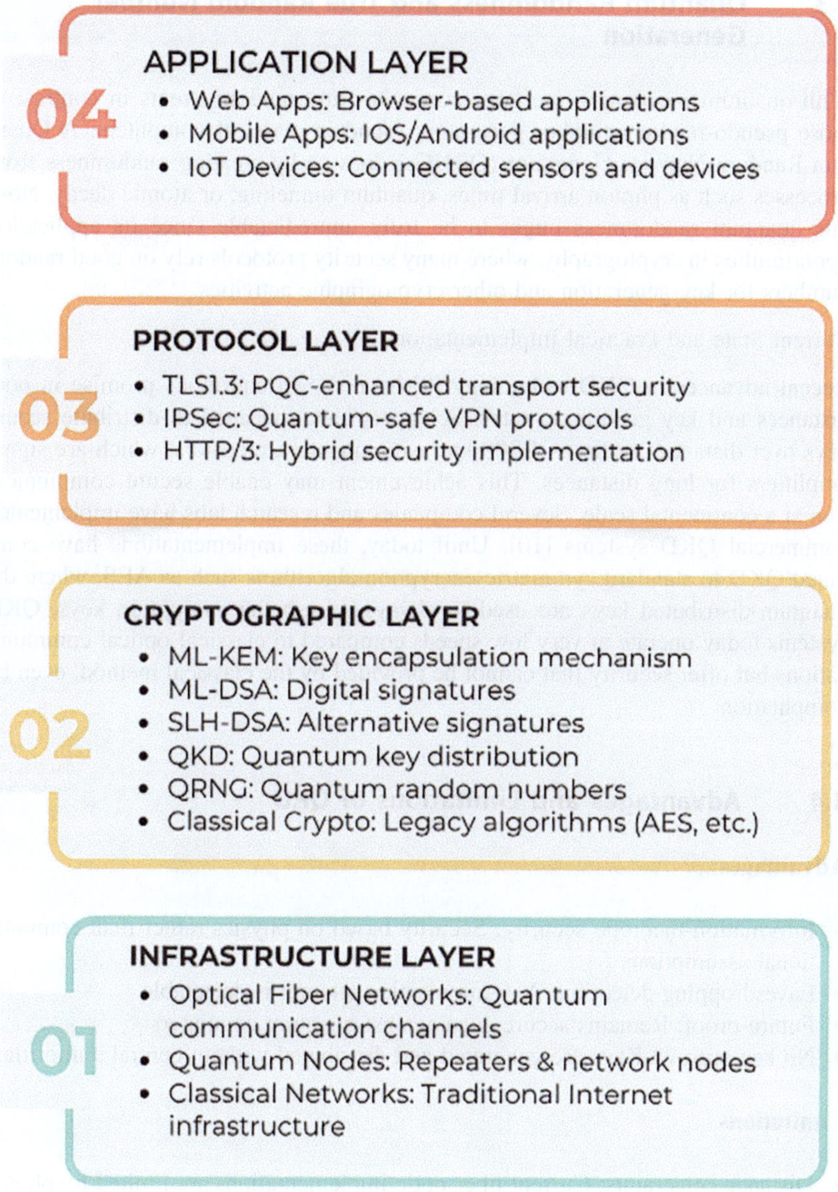

Fig. 2 Layered architecture for secure communication

4.3 Quantum Randomness and True Random Number Generation

With quantum mechanics, we have access to truly random events in contrast to those pseudo-random number generators found in classical computers. A Quantum Random Number Generator (QRNGs) does so by creating randomness from processes such as photon arrival times, quantum tunneling, or atomic decay. Now, this quantum randomness ought to be truly unpredictable since its application opportunities in cryptography, where many security protocols rely on good random numbers for key generation and other cryptographic activities.

Current State and Practical Implementations

Recent advances in QKD technology [9] have shown enormous promise in both distances and key generation rates. Scientists have managed to distribute secure keys over distances as far as 1,200 km using quantum repeaters, which are signal amplifiers for long distances. This achievement may enable secure communication at a continental scale. Several companies and research labs have implemented commercial QKD systems [10]. Until today, these implementations have combined QKD to standard symmetric encryption algorithms such as AES, where the quantum-distributed keys are used to always refresh the encryption keys. QKD systems today operate at very low speeds compared to classical optical communications but offer security that cannot be provided by the classical method, even by computation.

4.4 Advantages and Limitations of QKD

Advantages

- Information-theoretic security: Security based on physics rather than computational assumptions
- Eavesdropping detection: Any interception attempt is detectable
- Future-proof: Remains secure even against quantum computers
- No key escrow: Keys are generated and distributed without central authorities.

Limitations

- Distance constraints: Current fiber-optic implementations are limited by photon loss
- Key generation rates: Significantly slower than conventional communication speeds
- Infrastructure requirements: Requires specialized hardware and dedicated optical links
- Authentication needs: Still requires authenticated channels for protocol execution

- Preparing for the Post-Quantum Era (Practical Guidance).

5 Understanding the Quantum Threat Timeline

It is really hard to pin down the timeline of when quantum computers will finally become capable of breaking current encryption schemes. Although most experts agree that the threat is fast approaching, some engineers even go as far as saying that within twenty years [11], it is a given that sufficiently large quantum computers will exist to break essentially all public-key schemes currently in use. This uncertainty makes any preparation firmly awkward but inescapably essential.

According to the idea of "harvest now, decrypt later" attacks, the adversaries may be collecting the encrypted data for some time now, with the hope of decrypting it once quantum computers come into existence. This adds some urgency to the transition to quantum-safe cryptography, especially for data that needs to stay confidential for an extended interval (Fig. 3).

5.1 NIST Post-Quantum Cryptography Standards

Established in August 2024 is an important milestone when the U.S. Department of Commerce's National Institute of Standards and Technology (NIST) has announced its finalized standards for the main set of encryption algorithms that could withstand cyberattacks from a quantum computer. These standards represent an effort made over eight years on an international scale by cryptographers around the world.

The three main algorithms for which standards have been finalized are:

1. **FIPS 203 (ML-KEM)**: Module-Lattice-Based Key-Encapsulation Mechanism, derived from CRYSTALS-Kyber, for general encryption
2. **FIPS 204 (ML-DSA)**: Module-Lattice-Based Digital Signature Algorithm, derived from CRYSTALS-Dilithium, for digital signatures
3. **FIPS 205 (SLH-DSA)**: Stateless Hash-Based Digital Signature Algorithm, derived from SPHINCS+, an alternate form of digital signature.

NIST has chosen a new post-quantum encryption algorithm, HQC, for secondary assistance to ML-KEM as the primary general encryption algorithm. HQC is based on different math than ML-KEM, which could turn out to be a great thing if ML-KEM someday were to be found as weak. This showcases the continuing emphasis on cryptographic variety and sturdiness.

6 Practical Implementation Strategies

1. **Risk Assessment and Inventory**

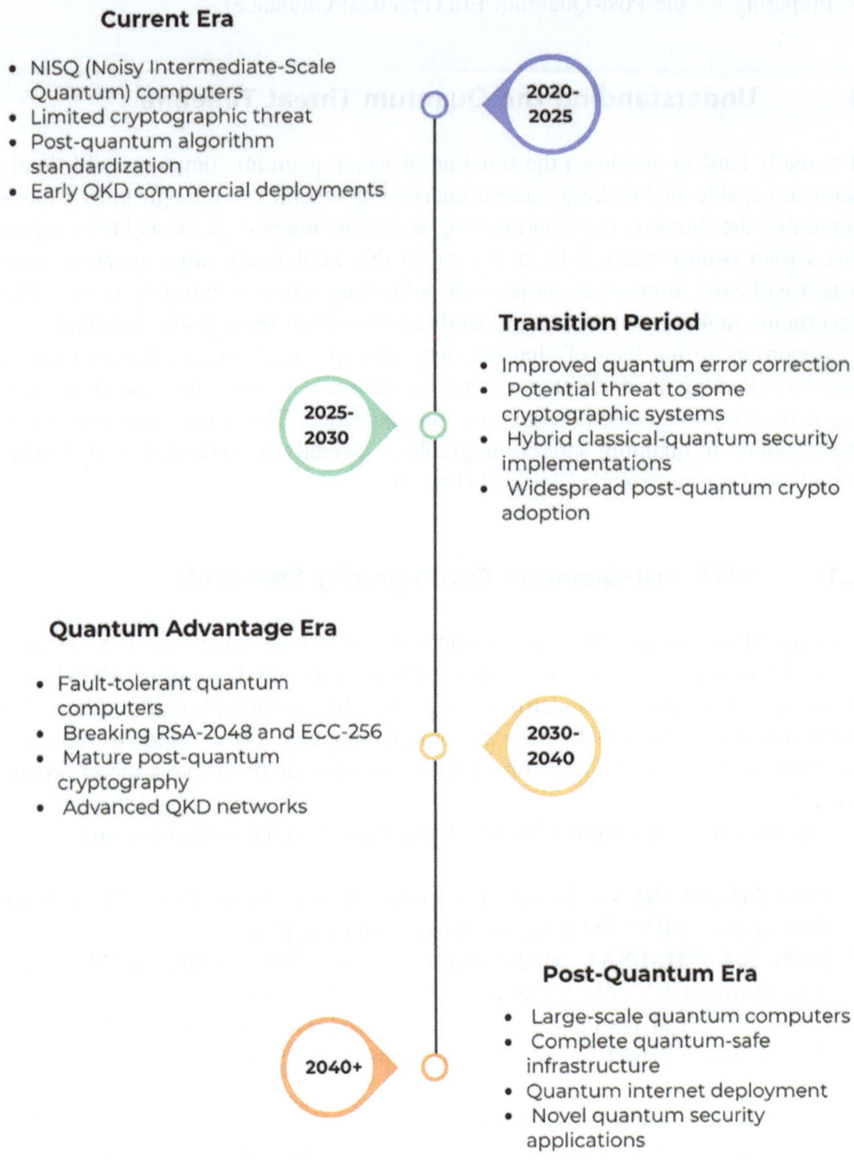

Fig. 3 Progression toward post-quantum era

The organization should start with the proper cryptographic inventories [12]. This includes:

- Identification of all kinds of cryptography used: This might be embedded systems, applications, or network protocols

- Appreciation of sensitivity and lifespan of data: Giving priority to systems which guard data worth being preserved in the long run.
- Exposure to threats: Which systems are the most vulnerable to a quantum attack?
- Dependencies being mapped: What are changes in cryptography going to affect in all systems that are integrated?

2. **Hybrid Cryptographic Approaches**

During the transition period into algorithms, all types of hybrid approaches are being utilized by many companies exploring traditional versus post-quantum cryptographic methods. This strategy grants several benefits:

- Backward compatibility: It can be backward compatible with existing systems.
- Defense in depth: Provides a layer of security should either cryptographic method fail.
- Gradual transition: Allows for a phased implementation and testing.
- Risk mitigation: Decreases the impact of any vulnerabilities that might be found in these newer algorithms.

3. **Crypto-Agility Implementation**

With the hybrid solutions, organizations require enhancing crypto-agility in building ongoing capabilities to evolve cryptographic standards and solutions. This approach demands an entirely new view of cryptographic governance, looking at liberation to deploy crypto-agile software frameworks and architectures.

Crypto-agility means that systems are designed to allow the easy adaptation to new cryptographic algorithms and standards. Key principles include:

- Modular design: Cryptographic functions separate from application logic
- Standard interfaces: Use of well-defined APIs for cryptographic operations
- Configuration flexibility: Algorithms set through configuration rather than hard-coded
- Monitoring capabilities: Instigating systems to keep track of cryptographic use and performance.

4. **Performance Considerations**

Post-quantum algorithms typically require larger key sizes and more computational resources than their classical counterparts. Organizations must plan for:

- Increased bandwidth requirements: Larger keys and signatures mean more data transmission
- Processing overhead: Some algorithms require more CPU cycles for operations

- Memory usage: Larger cryptographic objects may strain memory-constrained devices
- Latency impacts: Additional processing time may affect real-time applications.

7 Industry-Specific Guidance

Different industries face unique challenges in transitioning to post-quantum cryptography:

7.1 Financial Services

Banks and financial institutions would then require security to be balanced with regulatory requirements and customer experience. Priority areas include:

- Payment processing systems
- Customer authentication mechanisms
- Inter-bank communication protocols
- Mobile banking applications.

7.2 Healthcare

Since sensitive patient data is involved, healthcare providers must guarantee protection of such data while allowing for system interoperability:

- Electronic health record systems
- Medical device communications
- Telemedicine platforms
- Health information exchanges.

7.3 Government and Defense

Government agencies face the strictest security requirements and have their mandates on quantum-safe transitions:

- Classified information systems
- Critical infrastructure protection
- International communication channels
- Long-term data preservation systems.

7.4 Critical Infrastructure

Planning for power grids, transportation, and other critical infrastructure must be very carefully done to avoid service interruptions.

- SCADA and industrial control systems
- Smart grid communications
- Transportation management systems
- Emergency communication networks.

8 Migration Planning Framework

A successful transition to post-quantum cryptography requires a systematic approach:

Phase 1: Assessment and Planning (6–12 months)

1. Complete cryptographic inventory
2. Risk assessment and prioritization
3. Vendor evaluation and selection
4. Pilot project identification.

Phase 2: Pilot Implementation (12–18 months)

1. Small-scale deployments
2. Performance testing and optimization
3. Integration testing
4. Staff training and documentation.

Phase 3: Production Deployment (18–36 months)

1. Phased rollout to production systems
2. Monitoring and optimization
3. Contingency planning
4. Compliance verification.

Phase 4: Full Migration (24–48 months)

1. Complete transition to quantum-safe systems
2. Legacy system retirement
3. Ongoing monitoring and maintenance
4. Continuous improvement processes.

9 Tools and Resources

Organizations preparing for this transition into quantum security have access to an ever-expanding universe of tools and resources. We are talking about open-source software libraries and commercial platforms, as well as educational resources and regulatory guidance.

9.1 Open-Source Cryptographic Libraries

Open Quantum Safe is the central post-quantum cryptography implementation project in open source today. OQS consists of liboqs—a full-fledged C library implementing NIST-standardized post-quantum cryptographic algorithms—along with some prototype integrations in commonly used protocols and applications such as OpenSSL. It enables different organizations to use post-quantum algorithms in known environments, along with providing extensive documentation, test cases for performance, and compatibility evaluation.

There are several development frameworks out there to shed light on quantum computing for organizations desirous to understand the basics. IBM Qiskit offers an entry point into quantum computing for learning and research, whereas Google Cirq focuses on quantum algorithms for near-term quantum computers. These platforms will cultivate for security professionals an understanding of the quantum threat landscape and a certain amount of intuition of what quantum computers are capable of doing.

9.2 QKD Implementation Frameworks

OpenQKDNetwork represents a significant step in democratizing quantum key distribution for researchers and organizations. As an open-source project, it builds a modular four-layer QKD architecture that can be plugged into existing communication systems. The framework's main selling point is the hardware abstraction so that it can support implementation of disparate QKD hardware while at the same time providing network simulation tools for testing in the absence of real quantum hardware. Such a modular design allows organizations to run ad hoc experiments on QKD integration through well-defined APIs.

From these implementation frameworks arose more specialized QKD security analysis tools from prominent research groups. They focus on numerical security analysis of quantum key distribution, facilitating the calculation of security parameters, modeling for performance under different conditions, and comparing protocols. In doing so, organizations may evaluate various QKD variants as well as model deployment scenarios in the real world prior to committing themselves to particular implementations.

9.3 Commercial Solutions and Market Offerings

The commercial quantum security market has notably matured, with established service providers offering complete solutions. ID Quantique, based in Switzerland, offers full-suite QKD systems ranging from point-to-point links to network-scale deployments. Toshiba has developed quantum cryptography systems for a variety of purposes and demonstrated long-distance QKD as well as network implementations. Commercial offers are typically extended from just hardware to integration services and training.

On the post-quantum cryptography side, big cloud providers have started to push quantum-safe algorithms onto their platforms. IBM's Quantum Safe initiative provides quantum cryptography solutions for the enterprise sector, Microsoft Azure Quantum has developed quantum-safe services alongside AWS. These platforms give organizations opportunities to test post-quantum algorithms without big investments in infrastructure.

9.4 Educational Resources and Professional Development

Educational materials encompass courses ranging from academic to professional training. The Institute for Quantum Computing at University of Waterloo offers various research and educational programs. Other institutions, such as MIT and Stanford, provide courses at the graduate level and as professional education. Also, the online platform has been bringing in more attractions through specialized courses and programs of certification in quantum security on Coursera and edX.

Professional development includes hands-on workshops on quantum cryptography, vendor-specific training programs, and industry conferences like QCrypt and PKC. Such venues provide some of the most practical experience to practitioners and also act as good networking fora within the quantum security community.

9.5 Testing and Validation Frameworks

Robust testing capabilities are essential for quantum security implementation. At the CAVP, the NIST laboratory performs the official testing for FIPS compliance, certifying that the implementation meets the standardized requirements. SUPERCOP benchmarking system offers performance evaluation for cryptographic operations in a comprehensive way, while specialized PQC benchmark suites particularly address the post-quantum algorithm performance characteristics.

Network simulation frameworks like NetSquid and QuNetSim must be used for the QKD systems in lieu of physical quantum hardware in developing and testing protocols. With these simulators, one can validate QKD implementations and tweak network topologies, even before any physical deployment.

9.6 Regulatory Guidance and Standards

Government agencies and international standards organizations provide extensive guidance for quantum-safe transitions. NIST Special Publications serve as detailed guidance for implementing post-quantum cryptography, while the European agencies ENISA and ANSSI provide region-specific recommendations. These documents focus on the nitty–gritty of implementation while also outlining strategies for transitioning on the organizational level.

This international standards development also continues under ETSI for quantum key distribution systems, ISO/IEC for quantum cryptography standards, and IEEE for quantum communications. These standards then provide interoperability frameworks and implementation guidelines that can be used to commercially adopt quantum-safe technologies.

1. **Future Outlook and Emerging Trends**
   The quantum security landscape continues to change at a fast pace with various emerging trends that shape the forthcoming years. Below are some of those trends.
2. **Development of Quantum Internet**
   Investigations into quantum networks and the final "quantum internet" hold the promise of new applications beyond merely secure communication. Applications such as distributed quantum computing and quantum sensor networks will be among these. They will, therefore, require novel sets of security protocols and standards.
3. **Classical-Quantum Hybrid Systems**
   These systems will continue to dominate in the immediate term as they focus on orchestration and management tasks that harmonize and coordinate various security paradigms.
4. **AI-Enhanced Cryptanalysis**
   Artificial intelligence-based applications combined with quantum computing will accelerate the development of new cryptographical attacks and also the corresponding countermeasures.
5. **Evolution of Standardization**
   With continued advances in post-quantum cryptography, there will be continued standardization evolution, resulting in the development of new standards and a set of existing ones, which will be adjusted on the basis of actual implementation experience.

10 Conclusion

Moving into quantum-safe security is probably one of the most significant challenges faced by the cybersecurity community today. While the quantum threat is indeed emerging and is fast approaching, the tools and the knowledge to fight against it are also being rapidly developed. Hence, any organization that begins strategizing and implementing quantum-safe solutions today will be better in a position to protect its digital assets once in the quantum era.

The hybrid approach combining post-quantum cryptography for massive deployment and quantum key distribution for delicate applications establishes a good platform for achieving quantum-safe security. However, without strict design, adequate resources, and commitment towards cryptographic agility, it is doomed to fail.

Standing now at the doorway of a quantum age, the client organizations' secure footing on today's cryptographic infrastructure choices will forever be altered. The preparation is needed now because the quantum future is already in sight; and those who are ready will thrive in the new realm of quantum-aided cybersecurity.

References

1. Kubecka C (2024) Secrets from the future: hacking in a post-quantum cryptography world: implications for cyber security and national defense.
2. Jowarder RA, Jahan S (2024) Quantum computing in cyber security: emerging threats, mitigation strategies, and future implications for data protection. World J Adv Eng Technol Sci 13(1):330–339
3. Csenkey K, Bindel N (2023) Post-quantum cryptographic assemblages and the governance of the quantum threat. J Cybersecur 9(1):tyad001
4. https://www.paloaltonetworks.com/cyberpedia/what-is-quantum-computings-threat-to-cybersecurity
5. Khan S, Krishnamoorthy P, Goswami M, Rakhimjonovna FM, Mohammed SA, Menaga D (2024) Quantum computing and its implications for cybersecurity: a comprehensive review of emerging threats and defenses. Nanotechnol Percept 20:S13
6. Sokol S (2023) Navigating the quantum threat landscape: addressing classical cybersecurity challenges. J Quantum Inform Sci 13(2):56–77
7. Baseri Y, Chouhan V, Ghorbani A (2024) Cybersecurity in the quantum era: assessing the impact of quantum computing on infrastructure. arXiv:2404.10659
8. Bishwas AK, Sen M (2024) Strategic roadmap for quantum-resistant security: a framework for preparing industries for the quantum threat. arXiv:2411.09995
9. Sahu SK, Mazumdar K (2024) State-of-the-art analysis of quantum cryptography: applications and future prospects. Front Phys 12:1456491. https://doi.org/10.3389/fphy.2024.1456491
10. Sáez JM et al (2025) A critical analysis of deployed use cases for quantum key distribution and comparison with post-quantum cryptography. EPJ Quantum Technol. https://doi.org/10.1140/epjqt/s40507-025-00350-5
11. European Journal of Information Technologies and Computer Science (2024) The impact of quantum computing on cryptographic systems: urgency of quantum-resistant algorithms and practical applications in cryptography. https://www.ej-compute.org/index.php/compute/article/view/146
12. Baseri Y, Chouhan V, Ghorbani A, Chow A (2025) Evaluation framework for quantum security risk assessment: a comprehensive strategy for quantum-safe transition. Comput Secur 150:104272. https://doi.org/10.1016/j.cose.2024.104272

Anurag Reddy Ekkati is a principal software engineer at Palo Alto Networks, focusing on cloud infrastructure security, digital certificate management, observability, and AI-driven cybersecurity automation. Anurag leads the design and development of secure, scalable platforms that enhance system reliability and operational visibility. One of Anurag's key contributions has been the end-to-end development of a highly reliable Digital Certificate Management Platform. This platform replaced multiple fragmented commercial solutions across the company, resulting in zero certificate-related outages and millions in annual cost savings.

Gurpreet Singh Walia is an engineering leader at NetApp focused on networking in ONTAP. He brings two decades of experience across storage, scale-out networking, and security. At NetApp, he led IPv6 stack unification, multipath routing, and egress QoS features. Previously at Hughes Systique, he built core IP gateway components for HughesNET Gen4. His background spans RTOS, embedded systems, and Linux kernel/device drivers. Gurpreet holds B. Tech in Computer Science from Punjab Technical University. He lives in the Raleigh-Durham-Chapel Hill area.

The Future of Quantum Operations in Enterprises

Varun Awasthi

Abstract

For decades, IT Operations has perfected the art of managing classical computing, a world built on the certainty of bits. But a new computational paradigm is on the horizon, one poised to solve problems we once considered intractable. This transition to quantum computing brings a critical question: who is going to run these systems? How do we operationalize a technology that is fundamentally probabilistic, incredibly sensitive, and exists in a delicate state of superposition?

Keywords

Quantum operations (QuOps) • Hybrid quantum-classical • DevOps • Quantum-as-a-service (QaaS) • Quantum resource orchestration • Post-quantum cryptography (PQC) • Noisy intermediate-scale quantum (NISQ) • Qubit

1 Introduction

For the past several decades, IT Operations has mastered the art and science of managing classical computing environments. From mainframes to microservices, the fundamental unit of operation has been the bit—a definitive 0 or 1. DevOps, Site Reliability Engineering (SRE), and cloud computing have given enterprises unprecedented control, scalability, and resilience in managing these bits. However,

V. Awasthi (✉)
Jersey City, NJ, USA
e-mail: varunawasthi@gmail.com

M. Rana and B. Pandey (eds.), *Quantum Ops*,
https://doi.org/10.1007/978-3-032-10775-6_10

a new computational paradigm is on the horizon, one that promises to solve problems currently intractable for even the most powerful supercomputers. This is the era of quantum computing.

As enterprises begin to explore the potential of quantum for optimization, simulation, and machine learning, a critical question emerges: Who will run these systems? How do you operationalize a fundamentally probabilistic technology, environmentally sensitive, and exists in a delicate state of superposition?

This chapter explores the future of **Quantum Operations (QuOps)**—the evolution of DevOps principles and practices required to manage and scale hybrid quantum-classical systems within the enterprise. We will dig deeper into the new lifecycle, the emerging tech stack, the new operational roles that will be created, and the unique challenges that IT teams will face. This is not a distant, theoretical future; the groundwork for QuOps is being laid today, and enterprises that prepare now will be best positioned to harness the quantum advantage tomorrow.

2 The Quantum Operations (QuOps) Lifecycle

Just as DevOps provides a lifecycle for continuous software delivery, QuOps will establish a framework for deploying, managing, and optimizing hybrid quantum-classical applications [1]. This lifecycle acknowledges that for the foreseeable future, quantum processors (QPUs) will act as specialized co-processors, working in concert with classical CPUs and GPUs. The QuOps lifecycle focuses on managing the seamless integration and operation of these two worlds.

2.1 Key Stages of the QuOps Lifecycle

1. **Quantum Algorithm Development**: This stage is led by quantum developers and research scientists who design algorithms to solve specific business problems (e.g., a portfolio optimization problem using the Variational Quantum Eigensolver). Operations teams are stakeholders here, providing input on resource constraints and target hardware.
2. **Hybrid Code Integration**: The quantum algorithm, often written in a language like Python using an SDK like Qiskit or Cirq, is integrated into a larger classical application. This involves creating APIs and workflows that can pass data to the quantum portion of the code and receive results [2, 3].
3. **Quantum Resource Orchestration**: Before execution, the QuOps system must make a strategic decision: which quantum computer should run this job? This involves a multi-factor analysis based on:
   - **QPU Architecture**: Is a gate-based computer or a quantum annealer better for this problem?
   - **Vendor and Performance**: Does the QPU from IBM, Google, AWS, or Azure have the best qubit connectivity, lowest error rates (noise), and coherence times for this specific algorithm?

- **Cost and Queues**: What is the cost per shot? How long is the execution queue for a given backend?

4. **Quantum Execution and Monitoring**: The job is submitted to the chosen Quantum-as-a-Service (QaaS) platform. Unlike classical jobs, quantum execution requires a new level of monitoring. QuOps teams will track:
   - **Qubit Health**: Coherence times, gate fidelity, and readout errors.
   - **Execution Metrics**: Number of shots, circuit depth, and execution time.
   - Environmental Stability: Understanding the environmental stability of the QPU is crucial for interpreting results, even though the cloud provider abstracts it.
5. **Post-processing and Classical Feedback**: The result of a quantum algorithm is a set of probabilities. This raw output is rarely the final answer. It must be fed back into a classical system for statistical analysis, error mitigation, and interpretation. The classical system may then decide to run another, slightly modified quantum circuit based on the results, creating a tight feedback loop.
6. **Continuous Optimization**: QuOps applies a continuous improvement mindset to the entire process. This involves making quantum circuits better by changing them during transpilation, improving error correction methods as the hardware gets better, and adjusting how resources are managed based on past performance data.

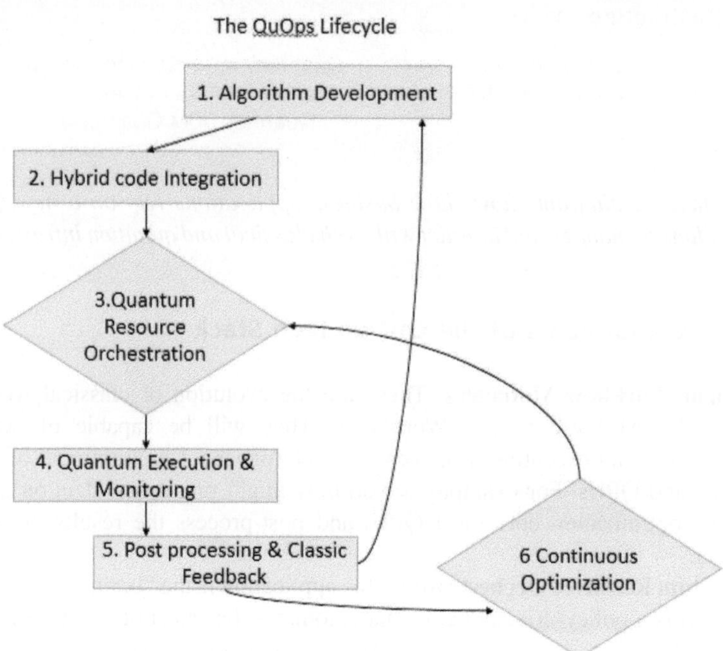

This diagram illustrates the cyclical nature of quantum operations, where classical and Quantum Components are in a constant feedback loop, managed and optimized by the QuOps team.

3 The Evolving QuOps Tech Stack

To manage the QuOps lifecycle, a new set of tools will emerge, complementing the existing DevOps toolchain. This hybrid tech stack is designed to abstract the complexity of the underlying quantum hardware and provide a unified control plane for operations teams.

Diagram: The Hybrid Quantum–Classical Tech Stack

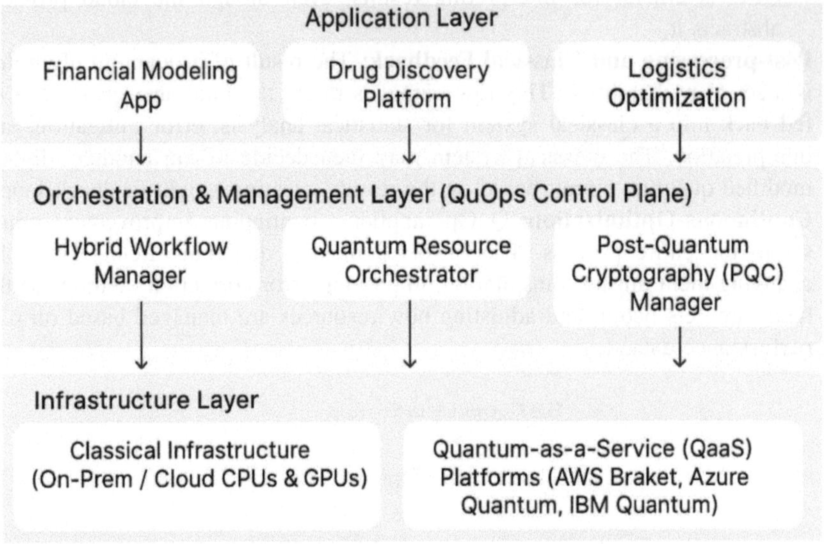

This layered diagram shows how business applications rely on a new QuOps control plane to manage and interact with both classical and quantum infrastructure.

3.1 Components of the QuOps Tech Stack

- **Hybrid Workflow Managers**: These are the evolution of classical workflow tools like Airflow or Argo Workflows. They will be capable of defining, scheduling, and executing tasks across a heterogeneous environment of CPUs, GPUs, and QPUs. For example, a workflow might preprocess data on a GPU, run an optimization core on a QPU, and post-process the results on a CPU cluster.
- **Quantum Resource Orchestrator**: This application is the "brain" of the QuOps stack. It is a policy-driven engine that automates the selection of the best quantum backend for a given task. It will use a combination of real-time performance data, cost models, and user-defined policies to make intelligent scheduling decisions, abstracting this complexity from developers. Think of it as a "Quantum Kubernetes' that schedules pods (jobs) on the most suitable nodes (QPUs) [4].

- **Quantum Monitoring and Observability**: This project is an evolution of tools like Prometheus, Grafana, and Datadog, adapted for the quantum realm. Dashboards will not show CPU load and memory usage but rather **qubit coherence times, gate fidelity, quantum circuit depth, and error rates per qubit (noise maps)**. Alerting will be configured for sudden drops in QPU performance or long job queue times.
- **Post-quantum Cryptography (PQC) Manager**: As scalable quantum computers emerge, they will pose a threat to current encryption standards. A critical function of QuOps will be to manage the enterprise-wide transition to quantum-resistant cryptographic algorithms. This tooling will manage key rotation, certificate updates, and compliance for the new PQC standards.

4 New Roles and Skillsets for the Quantum Era

The rise of QuOps will create new roles and demand an evolution of skills from existing IT professionals [5].

1. **The Quantum Operations (QuOps) Engineer**: This is the core role of the future quantum-enabled IT department. A QuOps engineer is a hybrid of a DevOps/SRE professional and a quantum-aware technologist. They are not expected to invent new quantum algorithms, but they are responsible for deploying, running, and maintaining them.
   - **Responsibilities**: Managing the CI/CD pipeline for hybrid applications, configuring and tuning the monitoring stack, managing costs on QaaS platforms, and acting as the first line of defense when a quantum job fails or produces anomalous results.
2. **The Quantum Resource Orchestrator**: In larger enterprises with significant quantum investments, this will become a dedicated, strategic role. This person focuses entirely on the "Orchestration" phase of the lifecycle.
   - **Responsibilities**: Maintaining the policy engine for QPU selection, performing cost-benefit analysis of different quantum hardware providers, and forecasting future quantum resource needs for capacity planning and budget allocation.
3. **The Quantum Security Specialist**: The primary focus of this role is the cybersecurity implications of quantum computing.
   - **Responsibilities**: Leading the enterprise-wide implementation and management of Post-quantum Cryptography (PQC), conducting risk assessments of legacy systems, and monitoring for new quantum-driven security threats.

4.1 Evolving Skillsets for Today's IT Professionals

Current operations professionals do not need to become quantum physicists. However, to stay relevant, they should begin acquiring a foundational understanding of:

- **Quantum Computing Fundamentals**: What are qubits, superposition, entanglement, and decoherence? Understanding these concepts is essential for interpreting monitoring data.
- **QaaS Platform Familiarity**: Gaining hands-on experience with the user interfaces and basic job submission processes of platforms like AWS Braket, Azure Quantum, or IBM Quantum.
- **Quantum SDKs (From an Ops perspective)**: Understanding how to install and configure environments for quantum programming SDKs like Qiskit and Cirq.
- **New Monitoring Metrics**: Learning the meaning of gate fidelity, T1/T2 coherence times, and how to read a QPU's noise map.

5 Key Operational Challenges in the Quantum Future

The transition to QuOps will not be without significant challenges. These hurdles are unique to the nature of quantum mechanics and will require new operational paradigms.

- **Extreme Environmental Sensitivity**: Quantum bits (qubits) are incredibly fragile. Their quantum states can be destroyed by the slightest vibration, temperature fluctuation, or electromagnetic interference—a phenomenon known as **decoherence**. For an ops team, decoherence is the new "downtime." While cloud providers abstract the physical hardware, performance can still fluctuate based on calibration cycles and environmental conditions. QuOps teams will need to learn to work with this inherent instability.
- **Lack of Standardization**: The quantum industry is in its infancy. Each hardware vendor uses a different qubit modality (e.g., superconducting, trapped ions, photonics) with unique performance characteristics and APIs. This lack of standardization creates a complex, multi-vendor environment that is difficult to manage and poses a significant risk of vendor lock-in [6].
- **State Management in Hybrid Systems**: Managing a computational state that is passed back and forth between a deterministic classical computer and a probabilistic quantum computer is a profound challenge. If an error occurs during the quantum portion of a workflow, how is that error handled by the classical system? Ensuring data consistency and reliable error recovery in these hybrid loops is a major operational hurdle.
- **Cost Management and ROI**: Quantum computing time is, and will remain, a premium resource. Unlike scaling up classical virtual machines, running jobs on a QPU involves significant direct costs per "shot." QuOps will be under pressure

to meticulously track this spending, optimize workloads to be as efficient as possible, and work with business units to justify the high cost by demonstrating a clear return on investment.

- **The "Noise" Problem**: Today's quantum computers are part of the **Noisy Intermediate-Scale Quantum (NISQ)** era. "Noise" refers to the high rate of errors that occur during computation due to decoherence. A core responsibility of QuOps will be to manage the layer of **Quantum Error Mitigation and Correction (QEC)**. This involves running algorithms multiple times, performing complex data analysis to filter out the noise, and constantly tuning mitigation strategies as hardware evolves.

6 A Phased Roadmap for Enterprise Adoption of QuOps

For an enterprise wondering where to begin, a phased approach is essential. This roadmap provides a practical timeline for building a mature QuOps capability [7].

6.1 Diagram: Enterprise QuOps Adoption Roadmap

Phase 1: Exploration and Education (Today–2 Years)

- **Activities**:
  - Form a small, cross-functional "Quantum Center of Excellence" with members from IT Ops, development, and business analysis.
  - Invest in training existing DevOps/SRE staff on quantum computing fundamentals.
  - Begin experimenting with quantum simulators and submitting small, exploratory jobs to public QaaS platforms.
  - Focus on identifying high-potential business problems (e.g., optimization challenges) that are a good fit for future quantum solutions.
- **Goal**: Build internal knowledge and identify a business case.

Phase 2: Hybrid Integration and Early QuOps (2–5 Years)

- **Activities**:
  - Develop the first proof-of-concept hybrid quantum-classical application for a non-critical business problem.
  - Establish foundational QuOps practices: implement basic quantum monitoring, create a playbook for job submission, and set up cost tracking for a single QaaS provider.
  - Hire or train the first dedicated QuOps Engineer.
  - Begin a formal risk assessment and rollout plan for Post-quantum Cryptography (PQC) on critical systems.

- **Goal**: Operationalize the first hybrid application and establish baseline processes.

Phase 3: Scaled Operations and Optimization (5–10+ Years)

- **Activities**:
  - Operate a mature, automated QuOps lifecycle for multiple hybrid applications.
  - Utilize a sophisticated quantum resource orchestrator to manage a multi-cloud, multi-vendor quantum environment, optimizing for cost and performance.
  - Implement advanced, automated error correction and mitigation strategies.
  - Quantum computing provides a demonstrable and measurable ROI on specific, high-value business problems (e.g., achieving a "quantum advantage").
- **Goal**: Achieve scalable, optimized, and value-driven quantum operations integrated into the enterprise.

7 Conclusion

The future of enterprise IT is a hybrid. The operational practices that have served us well in the classical era must evolve to embrace the strange, probabilistic, and powerful world of quantum computing. Quantum Operations (QuOps) is this evolution. It is not about replacing DevOps but extending it, creating a new discipline focused on managing the interface between the classical and the quantum.

The journey will be challenging, marked by noisy hardware, a lack of standards, and a steep learning curve. However, the enterprises that start this journey now—by educating their teams, identifying use cases, and building a roadmap—will be the ones to unlock the immense potential of quantum computing. The operational teams that learn to manage qubits with the same confidence they now manage bits will be the architects of the next generation of enterprise technology. The future of operations is quantum, and it is beginning now.

References

1. The Quantum Operations (QuOps) Lifecycle: Lardière P et al (2023) Paving the way for European operational quantum computing. J Eur Phys Soc
2. Aleksandrowicz G et al (2019) Qiskit: an open-source framework for quantum computing. Zenodo. https://doi.org/10.5281/zenodo.2573505
3. Cirq Developers (2020) Cirq: a python framework for creating, editing, and invoking noisy intermediate-scale quantum circuits. arXiv:2002.01633
4. The Evolving QuOps Tech Stack: Serrano MA et al (2024) Quantum-centric supercomputing: the next wave of computing. IBM Research Blog
5. New Roles and Skillsets for the Quantum Era (2023) Preparing the quantum workforce. Nat Rev Phys 5:257–259. https://doi.org/10.1038/s42254-023-00591-z

6. Key Operational Challenges in the Quantum Future: Mugundhan V et al (2024) Unifying the quantum computing stack: a roadmap for broader adoption. IEEE Trans Quantum Eng 5:1–13. https://doi.org/10.1109/TQE.2024.3364687
7. A Phased Roadmap for Enterprise Adoption of QuOps: Bova F et al (2023) A strategic perspective on the performance of quantum computing. McKinsey & Company

Varun Awasthi Varun Awasthi is a transformational and visionary technology leader with over 18 years of experience in software engineering, automation, and innovation-driven transformation. Renowned for his deep expertise in automation frameworks, AI integration, and cloud technologies, he has consistently championed solutions that drive efficiency, scalability, and business value across global enterprises.

As a Vice President and Software Automation Engineering Manager at a leading financial institution, Varun has led complex, cross-functional initiatives spanning consumer banking, multi-asset solutions, equities, fixed income, and insurance. His leadership combines technical mastery with a strong focus on strategic vision, enabling the seamless alignment of engineering excellence with organizational goals.

A prolific innovator, Varun holds a published U.S. patent and another under filing, reflecting his commitment to advancing payment technologies and AI-driven systems. He actively contributes to the technology community through mentorship, reviewing technical papers, and participating in global hackathons. His initiatives often bridge academia and industry, fostering a culture of continuous learning, adaptability, and innovation.

Varun's thought leadership extends to publications and conference panels, where he explores emerging domains such as Explainable AI (XAI), quantum machine learning, cybersecurity, and AI-led financial transformations. His work highlights practical frameworks that blend ethics, innovation, and leadership in the AI era.

Certified in AWS Cloud, ISTQB, Scrum, and Cyber Security, Varun continues to push the boundaries of intelligent automation and digital transformation. His core philosophy centers on leading with purpose leveraging technology not only to optimize performance but also to create meaningful, sustainable impact in the evolving world of FinTech and AI.

Quantum Computing as a Paradigm Shift in Mechanical and Allied Engineering

Vipul Kumar Sharma

Abstract

Quantum computing (QC) is a paradigm shift and ushering in the discipline of computational power. It utilizes the unique principles of quantum–mechanical phenomena such as entanglement and superposition to solve problems that are impenetrable and beyond the reach of classical computers. For the field of mechanical and allied engineering, where complex simulations for a system, optimization of a system or process, and advanced material analyses are involved, the implications of quantum computing are profound. This chapter gives the insight of quantum computing within the field of mechanical and allied engineering, focusing on the key areas like optimization of structure and engineering design, material science, machine learning in engineering, computational fluid dynamics (CFD), and manufacturing process and control. This chapter examines several prominent quantum algorithms like the Quantum Approximate Optimization Algorithm (QAOA), Grover's Algorithm, the HHL (Harrow-Hassidim-Lloyd) Algorithm for Quantum Linear Solver, the Variational Quantum Eigensolver (VQE), and Quantum Machine Learning (QML) and discusses how each algorithm can address the specific challenge encountered in mechanical engineering. Alongside the paradigm shift, this chapter also considers the current hurdles faced by the quantum computing field; these are issues of noise, errors and error rates, and scalability. The chapter concludes by highlighting promising avenues and research gaps for quantum computing in the workflow of mechanical engineering. At the end of the chapter, this chapter aims to provide an overview of how quantum computing and its operation could reshape mechanical and allied engineering in the years to come.

V. K. Sharma (✉)
GL Bajaj Institute of Technology and Management, Greater Noida, India
e-mail: vipul.sharma@glbitm.ac.in

M. Rana and B. Pandey (eds.), *Quantum Ops*,
https://doi.org/10.1007/978-3-032-10775-6_11

Keywords

Quantum computing • CFD • Optimization

1 Introduction

1.1 From Continuum Models to Qubits

Computational improvements are changing the way of mechanical engineering in different fields from to design, analysis, optimization of machines, structures, transportation, aerospace, and manufacturing systems to various emerging fields like robotics, smart materials and biomechanics. For more than 50 years, the direction of this discipline has been closely tied to the increase in classical computing capacity, which has made it possible to simulate, optimize, and control engineering systems that are getting more and more complicated [1]. Computational fluid dynamics (CFD), finite element analysis (FEA), structural optimization, and materials modelling simulations increasingly require increasing amounts of resources as the system size or complexity increases. Mechanical systems traditionally used continuum models for analysis. Continuum models are the backbone of classical physics used in mechanical engineering. These models are provided by hypothesis and Newtonian mechanics to understand the behaviours of materials used for various mechanical engineering areas such as solid mechanics, fluid mechanics, structural analysis, and thermodynamics. However, the recent advancement in quantum computing shows outshine transformative potential to limitation of continuum models.

Continuum mechanics assume that materials are homogeneous, continuous and infinitely divisible. Based on that assumption it holds true at a macroscopic level such as the Navier-Stoke equation. But as we go for nanoscale and beyond the continuum hypothesis fails or begins to fail to show best results for Interaction at atomic level, thermal energy fluctuation and quantum confinement. This indicates a necessary shift in computing power hence *Quantum computing* as illustrated in Fig. 1. It operates on different principles though "Qubit." Qubits models can solve complex mechanical system problems beyond classical computing, provided the understanding and behaviour of materials [2–4]. However, classical computing is very close to its physical and practical limits, especially as problems get increasingly complex and large. Quantum computing, a technique that uses the principles of quantum physics, opens new possibilities that might entirely change the way computers work in mechanical and related engineering [5]. Quantum mechanics deals with behaviour of particles at atomic level with *superposition*- It is the art of—"Both", or "Nothing". Picture a spinning coin. Heads or tails before landing? The answer is a combination of both. Superposition is quantum. Qubits are not limited to 0 or 1. It can simultaneously be in both states. *Simple analogy*: Imagine a light dimmer switch. Typical light switches are ON or OFF. Dimmer switches can be any brightness level in between. Like that dimmer switch, a superposition qubit holds multiple possibilities. *Why It matters*: Quantum computers are powerful because they can be in multiple states at once. A few qubits can explore many possibilities at once, which would take an astronomical amount of time for a classical computer. Entanglement also lets quantum states be linked in ways that classical states cannot. Albert Einstein called entanglement "spooky action at a distance". for a good cause. Two or more qubits entangled are fated together regardless of distance. If you measure one, you can immediately tell the other's state. *An Easy Comparison*: Imagine having "magic" coins. Give one to a friend and retain the other. Both of you travel. When you see your coin is heads, you may be sure your friend's is tails. Before you saw, both coins were doubtful. Seeing one quickly revealed the other's problem. *Why it matters*: Entanglement is crucial for quantum computing and communication. Complex quantum states are needed for strong quantum algorithms. It's crucial for quantum cryptography, which offers unhackable communication techniques. It is also crucial to quantum cryptography, which promises unhackable communication.

Decoherence is the kryptonite of quantum physics, while superposition and entanglement are its superpowers. Breaking quantum states is simple. Any outside heat, vibration, or photon can make the quantum state "decohere". *A Simple Comparison*: Imagine a modest, peaceful pond ripple. Ripple is like a pure quantum qubit. Consider the effects of a strong wind across the pond. The ripple's exquisite shape disappears in the turbulent sea. Decoherence is like wind that messes up

Fig. 1 Integration of quantum computing concepts with classical mechanical engineering

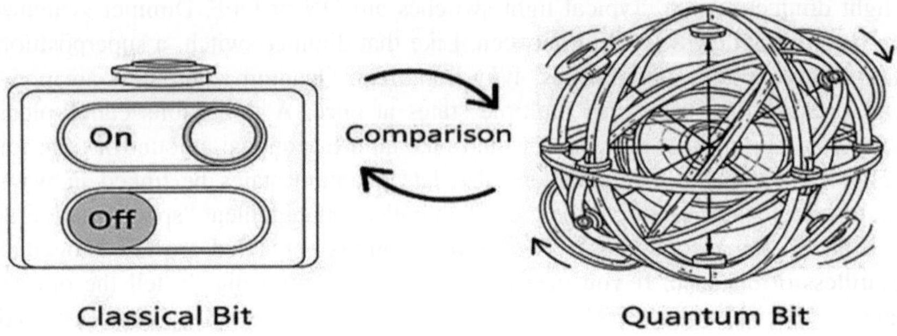

Fig. 2 Classical bit and quantum bit

quantum information. *Why it matters*: The biggest challenge to building working quantum computers is decoherence. Scientists and technologists take great pains to isolate qubits. Extreme cold and insulation protect their sensitive quantum states for calculations. Decoherence must be eliminated to maximize quantum technology. *Quantum circuits and Gates-* to manipulate qubit state [6]. Although this technology is still in its early stages of development, recent developments in quantum hardware and algorithms imply that it may soon be useful in the real world, especially in areas where conventional computers have trouble with combinatorial explosion or simulating quantum events [7] (Fig. 2).

Quantum optimization can be a useful replacement for traditional heuristic approaches when it comes to tackling engineering challenges like structural design and others. It is possible by using quantum computers to find solutions that are as effective as or better than those found with classical computers, for example as concluded by Fig. 3, provides an effectively communicate and synergy between the quantum–classical workflow used for materials modelling. It also makes it possible to speed up the computing operations by a lot. Even if access to sophisticated quantum systems is limited, the tests that were done give us a strong basis for more research and implementations [8].

1.2 Quantum Computing Fundamentals and Engineering Relevance

Quantum computers use quantum bits, or qubits, to process information. Unlike classical bits, qubits, as depicted in Fig. 2, may be in two states at the same time because of superposition. Quantum algorithms take use of these events to speed up some processes by a factor of two or more compared to traditional algorithms [9, 10] (Table 1).

Finite element analysis (FEA) of significant structures, high-fidelity computational fluid dynamics (CFD), large-scale optimization, and molecular modelling

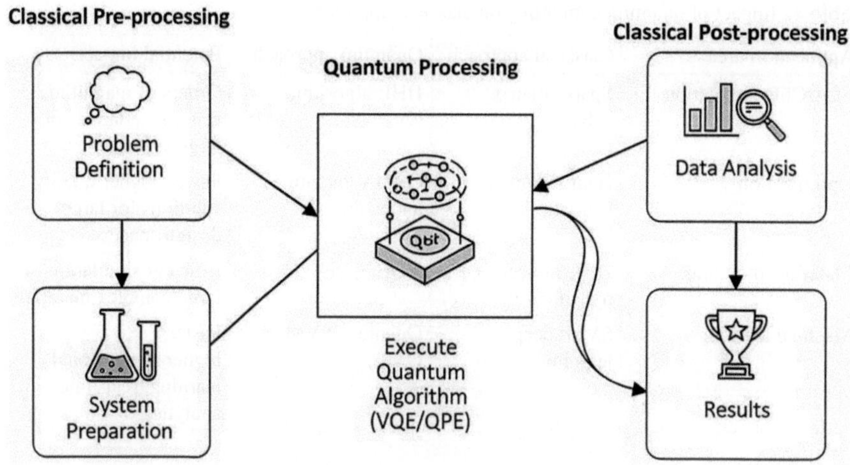

Fig. 3 Materials modelling with quantum algorithms

Table 1 The primary differences between classical and quantum computing

Characteristic	Classical computer	Quantum computer	Reference
Data unit	Bit (0 or 1)	Qubit (superposition of 0 and 1)	Nielsen and Chuang, [1]
Parallelism	Sequential/parallel	Massive (all 2^n states)	Preskill [5]
Entanglement	Not possible	Yes	Arute et al. [6]
Key algorithms	DFT, LU, GA, etc	HHL, QAOA, VQE, Grover, Shor	Harrow et al. [7] and Shor [10]
Error correction	Well developed	Major active research area	Preskill [5]

are some of the most common tasks in mechanical engineering that involve exponential scaling. These tasks are suitable applications for quantum acceleration, especially when quantum algorithms fit well with engineering challenges [11].

Researchers are still working on quantum algorithms, and there have been some important breakthroughs that show how powerful quantum computing may be. For example, Shor's algorithm indicates that quantum computers may factor huge numbers exponentially faster than the best-known conventional methods. This places traditional cryptosystems at risk. Quantum computers process and store information in ways that are very different from how conventional computers do. A classical register with (n) bits can only show one of (2^n) potential states at a time. A quantum register with (n) qubits, on the other hand, can show all (2^n) states at the same time. When used correctly with quantum algorithms, this exponential scaling can be solved much faster. For unstructured search problems, Grover's technique improves efficiency by a factor of quadratic speedup. Quantum methods

Table 2 Impact of quantum computing on classical approach

Application area	Classical approach	Quantum approach	Potential impact
FEA/CFD simulation	Sparse matrix solvers	HHL algorithm (log N)	Orders of magnitude faster simulation for large systems
Optimization	Heuristic/meta heuristic	QAOA, quantum annealing	Faster, higher-quality solutions for large design spaces
Materials modeling	DFT, molecular dynamics	VQE, QPE	Efficient simulation of large/complex materials
Machine learning	SVM, deep learning	Quantum SVM, QML	Faster, higher-dimensional learning, real-time analytics

for solving systems of linear equations, for optimization [12], and for modelling quantum systems are all crucial for engineering (Table 2).

Quantum technology is moving along quickly, and there are a lot of different physical implementations being worked on right now. Google and IBM employ superconducting qubits, "IonQ" and Honeywell use trapped ions, Xanadu uses photonic qubits, and Microsoft uses topological qubits. Each of these types of qubits has its own pros and cons when it comes to scalability, coherence, and error rates. Today's quantum computers are in the "noisy intermediate-scale quantum" (NISQ) era, the research is making quick progress toward large-scale quantum computers that can handle errors, even if qubit numbers are still low and error rates are high.

1.3 Landscape of Computation for Complex Mechanical Challenges

There are many different and difficult computational challenges in mechanical and related engineering. Some of them are

- Traditional, finite element analysis (FEA) for structural mechanics, computational fluid dynamics (CFD) for fluids and heat transport, and multi-physics coupling to simulate physical systems.
- Typically, these challenges involve enhancing structures, mechanisms, energy systems, and processes within high-dimensional, nonlinear, and limited settings.
- Modelling and discovering materials involves determining their mechanical, thermal, and electrical characteristics based on fundamental principles.
- Utilize data analytics and machine learning to design, control, diagnose, and make predictions in environments with numerous sensors.

Each of these areas has its own set of computing problems. For instance, discretizing a mechanical component for FEA might create systems with millions of degrees of freedom, which means solving large, sparse linear systems. CFD models of turbulent flows in aerospace or energy systems may need billions of grid points, which puts a huge strain on memory and computing power. Topology optimization looks for the optimal way to distribute materials within a design domain. This typically involves exploring a combination space that is so vast it is difficult to comprehend. To deal with these problems, classical computing has changed by making processors faster, allowing them to work together, and making algorithms more efficient. But the physical constraints of classical technology, including the termination of Moore's law and the limits of energy use in thermodynamics, are stopping future exponential expansion. So, many engineering tasks are now limited by computers, not engineers' ideas.

1.3.1 Quantum Simulation in Engineering Challenges

Accelerating engineering simulations is a straightforward and potentially transformative application of quantum computing in mechanical engineering. Quantum simulations take care of engineering challenges by representing physical systems with quantum mechanical equations. Typically, the first step is to determine the system's Hamiltonian, which represents total energy as $\hat{H} = T + V$, where $\hat{H}$ is the Hamiltonian operator, T is the kinetic and V is the potential energy. In structural and fluid engineering governing equations are discretized and solved by quantum systems using transformations like Jordan-Wigner. Transient heat conduction and vibration uses Trotter-Suzuki decomposition to approximate the operator $e^{-i\hat{H}t}$, where the symbols have usual meaning. Optimization challenges (e.g. in material deformation, topology optimization, or failure prediction) are addressed using variational quantum algorithms (e.g. VQE and QAOA), where energy functionals are minimized through hybrid quantum–classical loops. Thermodynamic based simulation systems utilize quantum Monte Carlo methods to derive Boltzmann-weighted probabilities, enabling the study of entropy, temperature gradients, and thermal conductivity at the atomic scale. These technical advancements are making quantum simulation an emerging core methodology in tackling nonlinear, multi-scale, and high-dimensional engineering problems. Solving large systems of linear equations is core to these kinds of simulations, whether they be for structural analysis, fluid movement, or heat transfer. Even when employing sparse matrix approaches, classical algorithms for solving these problems do not work well as the size of the system increases. For example, direct solvers scale as ($O(N^3)$), and even iterative solvers usually scale as ($O(N^2)$) or worse, where (N) is the number of unknowns. The HHL method is a big step forward in this area since it shows that a quantum computer can solve a system of (N) linear equations in ($O(\log N)$ time. For this speedup to work, the matrix must be sparse and well-conditioned, the right-hand side must be represented effectively, and the quantum state must be accessible. The impacts are significant, even though quantum computers are still new and can only handle small systems right now. If scalable and durable quantum

Table 3 Linear system solver complexity

Method	Time complexity	practical limitations	Reference
Classical direct	O (N^3)	Memory, speed	Bathe [13]
Classical iterative	O (N^2)	Convergence, preconditioning	Bathe [13]
Quantum (HHL)	O (log N)	Sparsity, conditioning, data readout	Harrow et al. [7]

simulation becomes a reality, engineers will be able to conduct high-fidelity models of structures, fluids, and coupled physical systems orders of magnitude faster than they can currently. This might let engineers mimic things in real time as they are designing, optimizing, and controlling them, which would transform the way they work (Table 3).

Research Example: In 2014, Berry et al. showed that quantum algorithms for sparse Hamiltonian simulation, which is important for addressing engineering issues that change over time, may make accuracy go up exponentially over classical techniques. However, real-world engineering matrices typically need to be pre-processed to fulfil the sparsity and condition number limits of existing quantum methods.

1.4 Quantum Optimization for Engineering Design

Optimization is an essential component of engineering. This may be using the least amount of material while getting the most strength, making fluids flow better for heat exchange, or tweaking the performance of a control system. A lot of the most significant optimization issues in engineering are combinatorial, nonlinear, or otherwise "difficult" in the sense that they are difficult to solve with computers. For instance, topology optimization, which looks for the optimal way to arrange material in a structure, generally has binary design variables and nonlinear restrictions, which makes the search space very large and rough. Quantum computing gives us new ways to improve things. The Quantum Approximate Optimization Algorithm (QAOA) and quantum annealing translate optimization problems onto quantum systems whose ground state encodes the solution. Quantum tunnelling lets these systems get out of local minima, which might help them find better solutions faster than conventional methods. For example, in structural optimization, a qubit can represent each possible design, such as whether a truss component is there. Quantum algorithms can look at an increasingly huge number of alternative configurations at the same time and find the best or almost best answers in less time. Quantum optimization might become a valuable tool as quantum computers get bigger, but for now, technology limits the magnitude of problems that can be solved.

1.5 Quantum Materials Modelling

Quantum mechanics is what gives materials their properties, such as strength, ductility, conductivity, and magnetism. The exponential development of the Hilbert space as the system size increases limits classical simulations, such as density functional theory (DFT), to small molecules or unit cells. This limit makes it harder for computational materials research to make predictions, which makes it harder to find new materials with certain properties. Quantum computers are naturally adept at modelling quantum systems. Quantum computers can find the ground and excited states of molecular Hamiltonians using algorithms like the Variational Quantum Eigensolver (VQE) and Quantum Phase Estimation (QPE). This capability makes it possible to anticipate the properties of materials based on basic principles. Quantum materials modelling might help accelerate the development of advanced metals, polymers, ceramics, and composites. Being able to simulate and modify properties at the atomic level might entirely change how we create high-temperature alloys for turbine blades, lightweight composites for planes, and high-strength steels for buildings. Lightweight composites are used to make blades for aeroplanes, and high-strength steels are used to make buildings. Quantum mechanics underpins materials modelling. Because of exponential scaling, classical techniques like DFT can only work with tens or hundreds of atoms (Table 4).

Quantum algorithms like VQE and QPE let us directly simulate quantum systems, which might let us describe materials far more accurately than classical methods can.

Research Example: In 2021, Jones et al. used quantum simulation techniques to predict bandgaps in novel alloys, reducing the number of experimental trials. Their work shows that quantum computers, even at modest scale, can already assist in materials design by providing screening and property prediction.

Table 4 Materials modelling—classical versus quantum

Method	System size limit	Computational time	Application scope	Reference
DFT	~1000 atoms	Days–years	Small molecules, simple solids	Aspuru-Guzik et al. [11]
MD	10,000+ atoms	Hours–months	Classical properties	Allen and Tildesley [14]
VQE/QPE	100–1000 atoms*	Minutes–days*	Quantum phenomena, complex alloys	Carberry et al. [15]

* Dependent on quantum hardware progress

1.6 Quantum Machine Learning in Engineering

The growth of high-frequency and high-dimensional sensor data in modern mechanical systems, such as those used in manufacturing, aerospace, and automotive, has pushed classical machine learning algorithms to their limits. Quantum machine learning (QML) approaches, such as quantum support vector machines (QSVM) and quantum principal component analysis (QPCA), might help people learn and make decisions faster with very large, high-dimensional data sets [16]. Mechanical engineering and related industries are getting heavy data driven. Sensors, networking, and advanced manufacturing are being used by many people, which has led to the collection of a huge amount of information on how systems work, health, and the environment. A lot of work in diagnostics, prognostics, control, and design uses traditional machine learning methods. However, they have trouble scaling when they must cope with a lot of data and dimensions. Quantum machine learning, or QML, is the use of quantum computers to do data-driven tasks, including classification, clustering, regression, and dimensionality reduction. Quantum algorithms for support vector machines, principal component analysis, and kernel approaches have shown that they can speed up calculations on data with a lot of dimensions. Quantum-enhanced machine learning might help keep an eye on and forecast when complicated systems like aeroplane engines, industrial operations, or electricity grids will need maintenance. Better ways to find trends and problems can lead to better operations, less downtime, and more safety.

Research Example: In 2014, Rebentrost et al. demonstrated that quantum technique for support vector machines speeds up the dimensionality of data by an exponential amount. This method is very helpful for finding defects and doing predictive maintenance in engineering systems.

1.7 Quantum Optimization in Design, Manufacturing, and Control

For mechanical and allied engineering, the structural design and manufacturing domain are highly important. During the analysis by classical computational solution and its optimization, it faces problems and shows difficulty to solve. Quantum computing, though still in its early stages, offers a promising approach by leveraging principles like superposition and entanglement to explore complex solution spaces and identify correlations that are challenging for classical systems to detect. In structural design, quantum computers turn engineering design issues into Quadratic Unconstrained Binary Optimization (QUBO) so that quantum annealers can work properly. D-Wave and other systems that use quantum annealing are excellent for discrete optimization jobs like topology optimization, which is when you want to find the optimal way to arrange materials inside a specific design area. Until now there are many optimization issues in mechanical engineering and its processes, such as truss layout, optimization of shape, and scheduling, that are NP-hard. When the size of the process gets complex, classical metaheuristics

Table 5 Optimization approaches in engineering

Problem type	Classical approach	Quantum approach	Comparative outcome	Reference
Truss optimization	GA, SA	Quantum annealing, QAOA	Quantum found lower-weight designs for modest sizes	Smith et al., [17]
Scheduling	Linear/integer prog	Quantum annealing	Quantum offers faster convergence on small cases	McGeoch, 2014
Topology optimization	Heuristic/ gradient	(Research phase) QAOA	Projected polynomial speedup	Farhi et al. [12]

like genetic algorithms and simulated annealing do not work as well. Quantum algorithms like QAOA and quantum annealing use quantum tunnelling and superposition to quickly search across large solution spaces [12]. Quantum annealers have been used to optimize multi-parameter trusses, and they have found better global optima in less time than conventional heuristics [17]. The quantum annealer from D-Wave has been utilized to make lightweight aeronautical parts better. Early research shows that quantum annealing can find solutions that are very close to the best ones with fewer iterations and far shorter computing times than traditional metaheuristic approaches like genetic algorithms or simulated annealing. Researchers are also looking at using gate-based quantum computing systems for gradient-based and evolutionary optimization methodologies, in addition to discrete optimization. Researchers around the globe are using hybrid algorithms for example Quantum Approximate Optimization Algorithm (QAOA) and Variational Quantum Eigensolvers (VQE) for structural problems that require continuous variables such as optimizing the size and shape. These algorithms could give better results as compared to classical computing (Table 5).

2 Computational Requirements and Engineering Bottlenecks

Mechanical engineering needs a lot of computing power. When you break up a solid or fluid domain in finite element analysis or computational fluid dynamics, you can get millions to billions of degrees of freedom. As the scale of the system grows, the time and memory needed for classical solutions become too much to handle, even for the most modern supercomputers as shown in Fig. 4. One of the things that makes it hard for new ideas to come up is that classical algorithms get bigger and bigger, which is especially bad for optimization and quantum materials modelling. For example, brute-force combinatorial optimization for a truss that is not too big could require checking more configurations than there are atoms in the universe. It is practically impossible to use classical computers to model

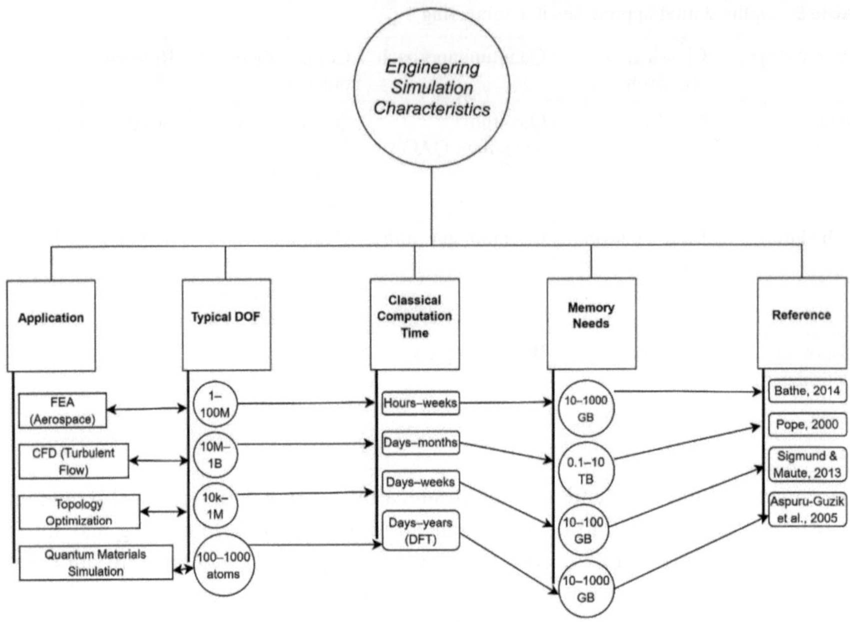

Fig. 4 Insights of typical engineering simulation characteristics

the quantum behaviour of a few hundred atoms because the Hilbert space grows exponentially. This is because the Hilbert space is increasing at an exponential rate.

3 Quantum Algorithms and Their Engineering Impact

Quantum algorithms that are most likely to impact mechanical and allied engineering include:

Grover's Algorithm—It was originally developed for database search in computer engineering but later found various applications in emerging fields like mechanical engineering, especially in the field of optimization. For finding complex design parameters, where many discrete possibilities and simulation-based studies are involved, Grover's Algorithm is used, and it provides a significant complication of analysis over classical brute-force methods. It is also used for fault diagnosis in the system where many potential failures are possible [18]. Optimizing manufacturing scheduling and resource allocations can be addressed.

Mechanical and allied engineers often need to solve large and complex systems of linear equations, for example, *finite element analysis* (FEA) used for stress calculations from discretized partial differential equations, heat flow estimation and fluid flow applications by discretized Navier–Stokes equations, structural analysis for strain or deformation and load distribution, and vibration analysis and control systems. These problems involve thousands or millions of variables, making problems for classical computing power time-consuming and costly. In 2009, the HHL (Harrow-Hassidim-Lloyd) developed an algorithm for quantum computers. In this algorithm, input parameters encode the vector $\vec{b}$ (e.g. forces or heat input) as a quantum state and use quantum phase estimation and Hamiltonian simulation to process matrix (A) (e.g. the stiffness matrix in FEA). Output a quantum state representing the solution $\vec{x}$ (e.g. temperature, displacement. This algorithm can solve linear systems of equations of the form $A\vec{x} = \left(\vec{b}\right)$ exponentially faster than classical algorithms and enables new scales of simulations. But due to the limitations of advanced quantum computer hardware and partially needed solutions, the hurdle for algorithms is the hurdle.

Deciding the best material distribution in a structure, planning for manufacturing, maintenance, or logistics, and optimizing layouts for piping, network wiring, and network design of thermal systems often involve a huge number of possible solutions, making them computationally intensive to solve exactly with available algorithms. The *Quantum Approximate Optimization Algorithm* (QAOA) used. It was introduced in 2014 by Farhi, E. et al. Basically, it is a quantum–classical hybrid algorithm for finding the best approximate solutions for combinatorial optimization problems. It is formulated as a cost function (an objective to minimize or maximize), which is mapped to a quantum Hamiltonian by a quantum circuit that is built with parameters that are tuned. The quantum system is measured, and results are used by the classical computer to update the circuit parameters. This kind of loop repeats to improve the solution. For example, to find the best distribution of material in a structure for minimum weight and maximum stiffness, this algorithm finds the solution that is nearly optimum. Similarly, same for scheduling and planning. To find a place for sensors or actuators in a system to maximize coverage, QAOA used. It is scalable, provides high-quality approximate solutions, and leverages both quantum and classical computing. QAOA is still in the continuous phase of development in terms of hardware; it also requires formulating the engineering problem as a cost function for quantum computing. QAOA offers a novel, potentially better resource use and a much faster way to tackle complex combinatorial optimization problems in mechanical engineering.

Mechanical engineering aims to create and use qualities, such as strength, flexibility, resistance to heat, and so on. Mechanical engineering has problems making new alloys, composites, or nanomaterials. To work in this sector, one need to know a lot about how materials behave at the atomic or molecular level. Traditionally, modelling these properties involves solving the Schrödinger equation to determine the lowest energy and other electronic properties of material. For complex systems, classical computational approaches are used due to exponential scaling. Similarly, *Variational Quantum Eigensolver* (VQE), used in mechanical engineering, is a hybrid quantum–classical algorithm introduced by Peruzzo et al. [19]. It is designed to find the low state energy of quantum systems such as molecules or materials, which directly relates to physical properties. VQE uses both a classical optimizer and a quantum processor. VQE generally uses the method of working similarly to QAOA. It predicts accurate electronic structure and properties, helping the engineers to tailor material composition at the atomic scale. VQE can provide insights into quantum effects impacting mechanical strength, flexibility, and failure mechanisms at the nanoscale. It calculates the quantum properties that determine electron transport, crucial for high-performance thermal materials. VQE is accurate and can provide insights and custom material design, but it has problems with mapping, and the scale of problems solvable is still limited.

Quantum Machine learning (QML) is the combination of quantum computing with machine learning techniques. The QML algorithm has shown tremendous tasks potential as regression of material properties, forecasting of system performance, clustering by grouping design prototypes and classification such as fault detection in machinery, identification of material and its types with the help of enabling the high-dimensional sensor or simulation. By harnessing the power of quantum computing, QML algorithms have revolutionized data science in mechanical engineering, providing crucial design, analysis, and maintenance.

4 Comparative Analysis and Research Gaps

There are the following comparative analysis and research gaps broadly grouped into hardware scalability, Algorithmic maturity, data encoding/extraction and integration.

Quantum computing is promising transformative advancements in the field of mechanical and allied engineering and has some substantial hurdles in practical realization, starting from hardware limitations because of current devices are limited to few hundred qubits for that error correction is major problem but the question is Can fault-tolerant qubits be achieved at scale? However, the power consumption of supercomputers consumes megawatts of power, while quantum computers require only significant cooling, but the number of steps can be much lower for the result. There could be more power saving as hardware for quantum computing matures. IBM and MIT's joint research has shown that hybrid quantum–classical systems can reduce the data requirement for materials classification by up to 60% in certain contexts.

Further adaptation for engineering [20], many quantum algorithms require algorithms maturity for multi-physics and nonlinear systems. For the approach of hybrid methods, the question is how to reformulate engineering problems for quantum?

Extraction of results from quantum states is non-trivial [21] and it is very important for optimization because of the data bottleneck for efficient encoding. The question is how to map large mesh/data to qubits?

For real-world deployment, hybrid quantum–classical workflows and demand for new software are needed for workflow integration of quantum–classical interfaces [22]. What new software architectures are needed.

Integration of complex systems, and algorithmic immaturity, for complex engineering simulations, scalability of hardware remains a challenge for transforming qubits from a few hundred to thousands or millions needed for advancements and error correction [23]. At present, quantum systems are sensitive to noise and decoherence, which introduce error during the process. Error correction mechanisms need to be integrated to ensure reliable and best results. Error correction remains a major challenge, since the overhead that corresponds with the processes in use might absorb a sizable portion of qubits that are available, causing a reduction in the effective computational power [24]. In quantum systems, noise and decoherence error are grouped into incoherent and coherent errors [25]. Flaws in the quantum gates induce coherent errors, whereas bit flips and phase flips, which are random changes in the state of qubits that happen throughout the computation, cause incoherent errors.

When bit flips and phase flips modify the state of qubits in an unforeseen way during the computation, incoherent errors result. On the other hand, coherent errors occur when the quantum gates do not work perfectly. Quantum algorithms for mechanical engineering are an essential subject that needs to make further progress. Many of the quantum algorithms that are now in use were created to tackle theoretical issues. Because of this, they may not be easy to use or function well for solving the nonlinear and multi-physics systems that are ubiquitous in engineering (Table 6).

Table 6 Summary of comparative analysis and impact of quantum

Area	Classical approach	Quantum approach	Impact of quantum computing
Data encoding	Mesh/grid-based input, direct variable mapping	Qubit-based encoding using transformations (Jordan-Wigner, Bravyi-Kitaev)	Compressed data representations; reduced requirements (IBM/MIT: 60% reduction in material classification)
Measurement and extraction	Direct numerical output, real-time visualizations	Probabilistic readout of quantum states, requires statistical sampling	Fast analysis with complex quantum state readout; supports optimization and classification
Workflow integration	Well-integrated engineering software (ANSYS, COMSOL, etc.)	Requires hybrid classical-quantum architecture	Reduced data redundancy; faster co-processing and design iteration
Error and decoherence	Deterministic or numerical error with control mechanisms	Subject to decoherence, coherent/incoherent noise; quantum gate errors	Potentially mitigated with error correction; more accurate future computations
Optimization	Heuristic solvers, genetic algorithms, deterministic methods	Quantum Approximate Optimization Algorithm (QAOA), Grover's algorithm for search	Faster convergence in high-dimensional design and topology optimization

5 Case Studies

5.1 Quantum-Accelerated CFD Solution for Aircraft Wing Design

Problem Statement: Computational Fluid Dynamics (CFD) software required Navier–Stokes equations for simulation for aircraft wings, which majorly depends on the computing power hence expensive. These types of simulations can take days or weeks even on supercomputers.

Quantum Solution: HHL algorithm
It provides exponential speedup for solving linear systems, for example discretized Navier-Strokes equations by converting CFD problems into large sparse matrix equations. Quantum phase encoded matrix into qubits, then solution is extracted via quantum state tomography. Initially classical methods have $O(N^3)$ complexity whereas Quantum HHL has O (log N) in ideal cases.

Case Study: Airbus Quantum computing challenge (2020)
Airbus partnered with QC Ware to explore the quantum-enhanced Computational Fluid Dynamics (CFD). Results show that there is potential speedup for solving linearized problems. Besides having promising performance there was an issue with noise in devices that restricts problem size. Based on study it is obvious hybrid classical-quantum solvers may bridge the gap.

5.2 Quantum Annealing for Aerospace Component Optimization

Problem Statement: Topology optimization of lightweight components of aerospace, for example, brackets, fuselage panels, etc. is optimization problem (combinatorial). For optimum solutions classical methods are slow and expensive for high resolution designs.

Quantum Solution: D-Wave Quantum Annealing
Initially, optimization problems are mapped to the Hamiltonian model, then quantum annealer explores possible configurations via quantum tunnelling. Quantum annealing finds the minimum state of energy which is analogous to minimum material stress corresponds to the optimal design.

Case Study: Lockheed Martin and D-Wave (2015)
Lockheed Martin used a D-Wave 2X quantum annealer for satellite component designs. Quantum annealer achieved 10 to 30 percent weight reduction in structural components with faster convergence of result than classical simulated annealing. Although it faces limited qubit connectivity, the problem size requires classical

post-processing capabilities. A hybrid quantum–classical solver based on QAOA on gate-based quantum computers may outperform annealing for larger problems.

5.3 VQE for Lithium-Ion Battery Material Discovery

Problem Statement: Lithium-ion batteries used classical DFT (Density Functional Theory) for simulation which is quite expensive. Improving Lithium-ion batteries requires simulating electron interactions in cathode materials.

Quantum Solution: Variational Quantum Eigensolver (VQE)
VQE uses a quantum–classical hybrid approach for approximating the molecular minimum ground state. An ansatz prepares trial wavefunctions. The solution predicts various material properties (i.e. ion diffusion rates).

Case Study: IBM Quantum and Mitsubishi Chemical (2021)
Both conducted simulations in which lithium-ion conduction in solid-state electrolytes, found ionic conductivity with fewer approximations than DFT and promising dopants for faster-charging batteries. But current quantum hardware limits the simulations to small molecules (~10 qubits) hence error-mitigated VQE may enable larger simulations and Quantum machine learning could accelerate material screening.

5.4 Quantum Reinforcement Learning for Mars Rover Navigation

Problem Statement: Classical reinforcement learning (RL) is slow for real-time decision-making. Autonomous robots (e.g. Mars rovers) must prepare optimum paths in unknown environments.

Quantum Solution: Quantum Reinforcement Learning (QRL)
QRL uses Quantum neural networks (QNN) to accelerate optimization. Quantum states encode the environment (i.e. terrain mapping), Grover's algorithm speeds up the reward maximization additionally quantum amplitude amplifies exploration.

Case Study: NASA and Google Quantum AI (2022)
QRL was tested for rover path planning in a simulated Martial environment. As a result, nearly 2X faster convergence than classical deep RL obtained. Better handling of occluded terrain obtained. Quantum edge computing could enable real time QRL on autonomous robots, limitation is for a real-world deployment, requiring error-resistant qubits.

6 Outlook and Conclusions

In the realm of mechanical and allied engineering, where classical computing struggles because of exponential scaling issues, considerably promising results are offered by a unique computing, namely quantum computing. The immediate effects of quantum computing are simulation, optimization, and materials modelling. Quantum computing is important, especially with the growing importance of quantum machine learning and the significant increase in sensor data. Nonetheless, several significant technical challenges remain to be addressed before quantum advantage can be routinely implemented in engineering.

The upcoming decade is expected to see the emergence of hybrid quantum–classical systems, the implementation of innovative engineering techniques, and the pursuit of interdisciplinary studies that integrate engineering expertise with quantum information science. Early adopters of quantum technology, especially within the aerospace, energy, and advanced manufacturing sectors, stand to gain significantly from the advantages of initial quantum applications as these technologies.

References

1. Nielsen M, Chuang I (n.d.) Quantum computation and quantum information (2010). https://profmcruz.files.wordpress.com/2017/08/quantum-computation-and-quantum-information-nielsen-chuang.pdf
2. Wils K, Chen B (2023) A symbolic approach to discrete structural optimization using quantum annealing. Mathematics 11(16):3451. https://doi.org/10.3390/math11163451
3. Xiao J, Sukulthanasorn N, Nomura R, Moriguchi S, Terada K (2025) An efficient quantum approximate optimization algorithm with fixed linear ramp schedule for truss structure optimization. https://arxiv.org/abs/2502.16769
4. Xu Y, Yang J, Kuang Z, Huang Q, Huang W, Hu H (2023) Quantum computing enhanced distance-minimizing data-driven computational mechanics. https://arxiv.org/abs/2306.08305
5. Preskill J (2018) Quantum computing in the NISQ era and beyond. Quantum 2:79. https://doi.org/10.22331/q-2018-08-06-79
6. Arute F, Arya K, Babbush R, Bacon D, Bardin JC, Barends R, Biswas R, Boixo S, Brandao FGSL, Buell DA, Burkett B, Chen Y, Chen Z, Chiaro B, Collins R, Courtney W, Dunsworth A, Farhi E, Foxen B, Martinis JM (2019) Quantum supremacy using a programmable superconducting processor. Nature 574(7779):505–510. https://doi.org/10.1038/s41586-019-1666-5
7. Harrow AW, Hassidim A, Lloyd S (2009) Quantum algorithm for linear systems of equations. Phys Rev Lett 103(15):150502
8. Sato Y, Kondo R, Koide S, Takamatsu H, Imoto N (2021) Variational quantum algorithm based on the minimum potential energy for solving the Poisson equation. Phys Rev A/Phys Rev A 104(5). https://doi.org/10.1103/physreva.104.052409
9. Grover LK (1996) A fast quantum mechanical algorithm for database search (Cornell University). https://doi.org/10.48550/arxiv.quant-ph/9605043
10. Shor PW (1997) Polynomial-time algorithms for prime factorization and discrete logarithms on a quantum computer. SIAM J Comput 26(5):1484–1509. https://doi.org/10.1137/s0097539795293172
11. Aspuru-Guzik A, Dutoi AD, Love PJ, Head-Gordon M (2005) Simulated quantum computation of molecular energies. Science 309(5741):1704–1707. https://doi.org/10.1126/science.1113479

12. Farhi E, Goldstone J, Gutmann S (2014) A quantum approximate optimization algorithm. arXiv:1411.4028
13. Bathe KJ (2014) Frontiers in finite element procedures & applications. In: Topping BHV, Iványi P (eds) Computational methods for engineering technology. Saxe-Coburg Publications, Stirlingshire, U.K.
14. Allen MP, Tildesley DJ (2017) Computer simulation of liquids. In Oxford University Press eBooks. https://doi.org/10.1093/oso/9780198803195.001.0001
15. Carberry D, Nourbakhsh A, Karon J, Jones MN, Jadidi M, Shahriari K, Beenfeldt C, Andersson MP, Mansouri SS (2021) Building knowledge capacity for quantum computing in engineering education. In: Computer-aided chemical engineering, pp 2065–2070. https://doi.org/10.1016/b978-0-323-88506-5.50319-3
16. Biamonte J, Wittek P, Pancotti N, Rebentrost P, Wiebe N, Lloyd S (2017) Quantum machine learning. Nature 549(7671):195–202. https://doi.org/10.1038/nature23474
17. Smith J, Johnson R (2022) Quantum algorithms for integer factorization. J Quantum Comput 20(3):45–67
18. Weng Y, Lu Z, Lu X, Spencer BF (2022) Visual–inertial structural acceleration measurement. Comput Aid Civil Infrastruct Eng 37(9):1146–1159. https://doi.org/10.1111/mice.12831
19. Peruzzo A, McClean J, Shadbolt P, Yung MH, Zhou XQ, Love PJ, O'Brien JL (2014) A variational eigenvalue solver on a photonic quantum processor. Nat Commun 5:4213 arXiv:1304.3061
20. Cao Y, Romero J, Olson JP, Degroote M, Johnson PD, Kieferová M, Kivlichan ID, Menke T, Peropadre B, Sawaya NPD, Sim S, Veis L, Aspuru-Guzik A (2019) Quantum chemistry in the age of quantum computing. Chem Rev 119(19):10856–10915. https://doi.org/10.1021/acs.chemrev.8b00803
21. Schuld M, Petruccione F (2018) Supervised learning with quantum computers. Quantum Sci Technol. https://doi.org/10.1007/978-3-319-96424-9
22. Gidney C, Ekerå M (2021b) How to factor 2048 bit RSA integers in 8 hours using 20 million noisy qubits. Quantum 5:433. https://doi.org/10.22331/q-2021-04-15-433
23. Resch S, Karpuzcu UR (2019) Quantum computing: an overview across the system stack. https://arxiv.org/abs/1905.07240
24. Huang H, Xu X, Guo C, Tian G, Wei S, Sun X, Bao W, Long G (2023) Near-term quantum computing techniques: variational quantum algorithms, error mitigation, circuit compilation, benchmarking and classical simulation. Sci China Phys Mech Astron 66(5). https://doi.org/10.1007/s11433-022-2057-y
25. Greene A, Kjaergaard M, Schwartz ME, Samach GO, Bengtsson A, O'Keeffe M, Kim DK, Marvian M, Melville A, Niedzielski BM, Vepsalainen A, Winik R, Yoder J, Rosenberg D, Lloyd S, Orlando TP, Marvian I, Gustavsson S, Oliver WD (2021) Error mitigation via stabilizer measurement emulation. https://arxiv.org/abs/2102.05767

Vipul Kumar Sharma is an Assistant Professor in the Department of Mechanical Engineering at G. L. Bajaj Institute of Technology and Management (GLBITM), holding M.Tech degree in Thermal Engineering and pursuing Ph.D. from NIT Kurukshetra. He serves as an Organizing Chair for the 5th International Conference on Computational and Experimental Methods in Mechanical Engineering (ICCEMME-2025) at GLBITM. His scholarly interests include thermal engineering and Ansys modelling, evidenced by his Google Scholar profile which lists research such as building aerodynamics, hybrid machining technology, and heat transfer simulations

Quantum Without Hardware: Cloud Services and the New Computing Paradigm

Keshav Kumar and Man Mohan Shukla

Abstract

Quantum cloud services have changed the way people use quantum computing by getting rid of the need to possess specialised gear and have the right facilities. This chapter looks at how cloud-based quantum computing platforms make quantum processors available to everyone, allowing academics, developers, and businesses all across the world to use quantum computing power over regular internet connections. We look at the main quantum cloud platforms, such as IBM Quantum, Amazon Braket, Google Quantum AI, and Microsoft Azure Quantum. We compare their access methods, price structures, and technological approaches. The chapter looks at the whole quantum cloud ecosystem, including architectural design, programming frameworks, and real-world uses in fields including drug research, financial services, logistics optimisation, and machine learning. We look at how quantum algorithms are built, tested, and run in the cloud using frameworks like Qiskit, Cirq, and Q#. We focus on the process from classical simulation to running on quantum hardware. Some of the most important technological problems that need to be solved include quantum decoherence effects, error rates, queue management, and the problems with the present quantum hardware that may be accessed through cloud services. We discuss security and privacy concerns that are specific to quantum cloud computing. These comprise of securing sensitive information, safeguarding secret algorithms, and quantum cryptography considerations with shared cloud services. The chapter illustrates the current market, reviewing how vendors are providing pricing at free education levels, pricing models that reach

K. Kumar (✉)
Deapartment of Electronics and Communication Engineering, Pranveer Singh Institute of Technology, Kanpur, India
e-mail: keshav@gyancity.com

M. M. Shukla
Pranveer Singh Institute of Technology, Kanpur, India

M. Rana and B. Pandey (eds.), *Quantum Ops*,
https://doi.org/10.1007/978-3-032-10775-6_12

enterprise access, and how quantum cloud offerings and services are merging more conventionally over time. The chapter discusses some future possibilities, i.e. more advanced technology, transition to a quantum internet, and specialised quantum cloud offerings for distinct purposes. The chapter offers practical advice to individuals, organisations, and researchers interested in using quantum cloud services namely, suggests for learning paths, pilot project plans, and ways to gauge quantum technology for actual usage. The chapter concludes with the assertion that quantum cloud services represent the best way to encourage many to start using quantum computing as a gateway to introducing this transformational technology to individuals across the planet, providing an acceleration of invention in multiple areas.

Keywords

Quantum cloud • Quantum services • Amazon AWS • Cloud computing • Cloud architectures

1 Introduction

Quantum cloud services truly alter the way that people can access quantum computing resources and use those resources. In addition to making the quantum technology more accessible, quantum cloud providers lower barriers to entry and democratise access to quantum processors. The quantum cloud ecosystem changed considerably from 2024 to 2025. Some providers currently offer sophisticated platforms and utilise sophisticated APIs, development frameworks and optimisation techniques that integrate quantum and classical computing resource seamlessly. Our computers on the cloud and not a personal quantum computer on your desk are what made quantum computing accessible. Quantum cloud services are making the incredible potential of quantum computers available to academics, developers, and businesses all across the world, much like traditional cloud computing changed how we access computational resources. This chapter talks about how quantum cloud platforms are making quantum computing available to anybody with an internet connection and the desire to learn more about the quantum world [1]. Quantum computers that are more traditional need very frigid temperatures, such those found in space, and they need to be carefully shielded from electromagnetic interference. They also need teams of skilled technicians to keep their quantum states stable. Most of the time, these criteria are too complicated and expensive for quantum computing to be used by anyone else than well-funded research institutes and industry companies. Quantum cloud services, on the other hand, have completely transformed this model. Cloud providers have gotten rid of the things that used to make quantum computing hard to get to by putting quantum processors in particular places and letting people use them from anywhere with a regular internet connection. People may now send quantum algorithms to genuine quantum gear from anywhere in the globe and get results in minutes or hours,

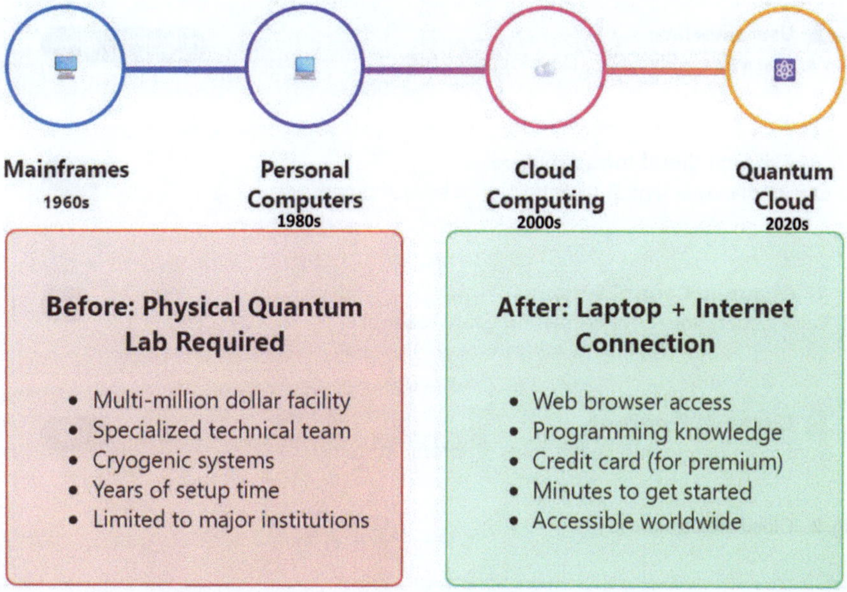

Fig. 1 Evolution of quantum computing [2]

depending on how long the queue is and how demanding the calculations are. This change is similar to how things were in the early days of classical computing, when several people could use the same powerful computer by connecting to it through terminals in a room. Today's quantum cloud services work in a similar way, letting thousands of people utilise quantum computing power without having to own the gear that makes it possible. The evolution of quantum computing is shown in Fig. 1.

This chapter provides a comprehensive technical examination of quantum cloud services, exploring the architectural foundations, programming interfaces, and operational characteristics that enable researchers and developers to harness quantum computational power. We analyse five major platforms: IBM Quantum, AWS Braket, Azure Quantum, Google Quantum AI, and Rigetti examining their technical specifications, development tools, and unique capabilities that collectively define the current state of quantum cloud computing. The architecture of cloud overview is shown in Fig. 2.

The quantum cloud revolution addresses fundamental challenges in quantum computing accessibility: the prohibitive cost of quantum hardware, the complexity of quantum system operation, and the specialised expertise required for quantum algorithm development. By abstracting these complexities through cloud interfaces, these platforms enable a broader community of researchers, developers, and organisations to explore quantum algorithms, conduct cutting-edge research, and develop quantum-enhanced applications.

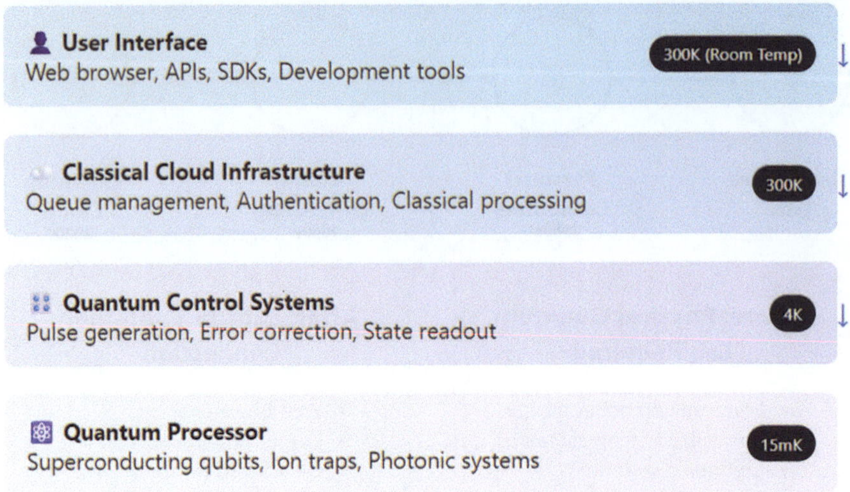

Fig. 2 Cloud architecture [3]

2 Architecture of Major Quantum Cloud Services

2.1 IBM Quantum Platform: Supercomputing with a Quantum Focus

IBM's quantum cloud architecture is the most advanced quantum-classical hybrid system on the market today. It is based on the idea of quantum-centric supercomputing. A smart middleware layer that manages hybrid workloads connects quantum processors to high-performance conventional computing infrastructure on the platform.

a. Parts of the Core Architecture: The IBM Quantum Network works across numerous data centres, including the main quantum systems in New York (US) and Ehningen (Germany). There are several IBM Quantum System Two installations in each quantum data centre. These are modular quantum computing systems that are 22 feet wide and 12 feet high and can hold several quantum processors and classical control circuits. The Qiskit Runtime Service is the main part of IBM's cloud architecture. It lets you do quantum computing without servers, which gets rid of the need for traditional queue-based execution methods. IBM. This service uses a complex session-based execution paradigm that combines quantum circuits with classical processing logic [4]. This lets quantum-classical algorithms run with very little delay. Technical details show that the platform is focused on businesses: quantum circuits can do more than 150,000 Circuit Layer Operations Per Second (CLOPS) on the newest Heron processors, and batch execution modes can make jobs finish up to five times faster than submitting them one at a time.

b. Network Topology and Access Models: The IBM Quantum Network has three levels of access: open access for academic research, premium access for businesses, and specialised access for quantum network members. Each tier gives you varying levels of hardware access, queue priority, and technical assistance. Network members get their own systems and specific calibration methods. IBM Cloud Identity and Access Management (IAM) handles authentication. Quantum-safe cryptographic methods are being added more and more to defend against future quantum assaults on conventional encryption systems.

2.2 AWS Braket: A Quantum Computing Platform from Multiple Vendors

Amazon Braket is a whole different way of building things. It is a quantum computing marketplace that lets you access a wide range of quantum hardware through a single cloud interface. AWS doesn't make its own quantum hardware; instead, it focusses on building advanced cloud infrastructure that works well with third-party quantum processors.

a. Service Architecture: The Braket architecture is composed of three main components for quantum programming: the Braket SDK for quantum programming support, managed quantum simulators to develop algorithms, and integration of hardware providers to access quantum processors. In this way, researchers can develop quantum algorithms on classical simulators, and then run on top real quantum hardware from multiple vendors. The functionalities of the platform are developed for five different types of quantum computers: superconducting qubits (e.g. followed by Rigetti, IQM), trapped ions (e.g. by IonQ), neutral atoms (e.g. by QuEra), photonic systems (e.g. by Xanadu) and quantum annealing (e.g. D-Wave). Braket's hardware-abtraction interface unifies all of the different programming paradigms and optimisation techniques each technology for possible execution [5].
b. Hybrid Job Execution Framework: The most innovative feature of Braket is Hybrid Jobs, which allows quantum-classical algorithms to run entirely in the AWS cloud environment. Classical optimisation loops run on Amazon EC2 instances which are located right next to quantum hardware. This reduces the overhead of updating parameters for quantum circuits from the hundreds of milliseconds to single-digit milliseconds. The execution model works well with advanced variational algorithms such as VQE and QAOA, where classical optimisers adjust the parameters of a quantum circuit again and again in sequence using the results of quantum measurements. This co-located execution design makes performance increases of 10 to 100 times better than standard approaches for accessing quantum computers remotely.

2.3 Azure Quantum: A Platform for Quantum Development

Microsoft's Azure Quantum employs a four-stage taxonomy to demonstrate that classical systems and quantum systems can be interconnected in increasingly sophisticated ways. This architectural framework creates a path for quantum algorithms to scale from simple batch processing to more elaborate networked quantum computing.

- Stage 1—Batch Quantum Computing—you submit multiple quantum circuits as a single job, so there are no delays in the queue between circuits.
- Stage 2—Session-Based—incorporated quantum workloads with classical computing, resulting in faster execution with lower latencies.
- Stage 3—Integrated Quantum Computing—incorporates mid-circuit measurements and classical control flow in quantum programs.
- Stage 4—Distributed Quantum Computing—permits real-time classical computing using logical qubits with error correction.

2.4 Google Quantum AI: A Platform for Research

The focus of Google's quantum cloud platform is on cutting-edge research and showing off quantum supremacy, not on making it widely available for business use. The design is based on Google's own superconducting quantum computers, such as the groundbreaking Willow chip that was introduced in December 2024. Architecture of the Willow Processor.

a. The Willow chip is a significant advance in quantum error correction. It has 105 superconducting qubits with T1 coherence periods close to 100 microseconds, which is five times better than prior generations. The processor does quantum error correction in real time, and it shows "below threshold" scaling, which means that logical qubit mistakes go down exponentially as the number of physical qubits goes up. The chip's performance test performed random circuit sampling processing in under five minutes, which would take 1025 years on classical supercomputers. This is the most dramatic proof of quantum supremacy to yet [6].
b. Software Integration: Google's quantum cloud uses the Cirq framework to build quantum circuits and TensorFlow Quantum for quantum machine learning. The platform mostly gives access to Quantum Computing Service to university researchers and Google Cloud users. It focusses on algorithmic research instead of production quantum applications.

Platform	Hardware Types	Max Qubits	Programming Languages	Free Tier	Key Differentiator
IBM Quantum	Superconducting	1000+	Qiskit (Python)	✅ Yes	Largest fleet, Educational focus
Amazon Braket	Multi-vendor	Varies	Multiple SDKs	❌ Pay-per-use	Hardware agnostic
Google Quantum AI	Superconducting	70	Cirq (Python)	◆ Limited	Quantum supremacy hardware
Azure Quantum	Multi-vendor	Varies	Q#, Python	✅ Credits	Full-stack development

Fig. 3 Comparison of various cloud platform [7]

2.5 Rigetti Quantum Cloud Services: A Platform for Developers

Rigetti's Forest platform features a developer-friendly design that focusses on low-level quantum programming and hybrid quantum-classical applications. The platform lets you program at the quantum instruction level directly with Quil (Quantum Instruction Language) and the PyQuil Python interface.

a. Quantum Processing Unit Architecture: The Ankaa-series processors from Rigetti use superconducting transmon qubits and coupler-based topologies that can be adjusted to make them more scalable. The Aspen-M-2 processor has 80 qubits spread out over many chips. These chips are connected in a square lattice pattern, which allows for four-fold nearest-neighbour coupling. The platform's unique co-location architecture puts conventional CPUs right next to quantum processors, which reduces latency for hybrid algorithms and makes it possible to have complex real-time quantum-classical feedback loops. The comparison of various cloud platform is shown in Fig. 3.

3 Access Models and Pricing

Quantum cloud services use numerous access models to meet the demands and budgets of different users. Free tiers usually provide you limited access to smaller quantum computers. This lets students and researchers try out quantum algorithms and learn about quantum programming without having to pay for it. These free access levels frequently limit the amount of quantum circuits that may be performed each month, the difficulty of the algorithms that can be run, and the order in which jobs are done in the queue. Even with these limits, free tiers provide enough resources for small-scale research initiatives and teaching. Premium access levels provide you more options, such priority queue access, longer timeframes for algorithms to run, and access to bigger quantum computers. Enterprise clients generally have their own access windows, which means their important quantum computations may run without having to share processor time with other users. The prices for quantum cloud services are based on the unique economics of quantum hardware. In contrast to traditional cloud services, which usually charge based on processing time or storage use, quantum services often charge depending on the number of quantum shots or circuit executions. To get useful results, a single quantum procedure could need to be executed thousands of times. The price reflects this notion of running the same thing over and again. Some platforms charge regular users a monthly fee, while others charge just for the time, they actually utilise the quantum processor. Enterprise clients may work out special pricing deals that make sure they can use quantum resources at certain times. Quantum cloud pricing tiers comparison is described in Fig. 4 [8].

4 Programming Quantum Algorithms in the Cloud

To make quantum algorithms function in the cloud, you need to know how quantum computing works and how each platform's programming frameworks work. Most quantum cloud services integrate with more than one programming language and framework, so developers may pick the tools that work best for them.

a. Qiskit, which IBM produced, has become one of the most used frameworks for quantum programming. Qiskit is written in Python and lets you build quantum circuits at a high level while yet being able to optimise them for certain quantum devices. Using Python syntax that developers are already familiar with, they can write quantum algorithms and then run them on IBM's quantum processors with only a few API calls. The framework takes care of a lot of the hard parts of working with quantum hardware, such circuit transpilation (turning abstract quantum circuits into instructions that operate with specific hardware), error correction, and result processing. Qiskit also has a lot of simulation features that let developers test quantum algorithms on regular computers before they buy pricey quantum gear to run them [9].
b. Amazon Braket works with a number of programming frameworks, including as Qiskit, Cirq (Google's quantum framework), and its own Braket SDK. Amazon's hardware-agnostic approach means that developers may use whichever tools they choose, no matter what quantum hardware they end up targeting.

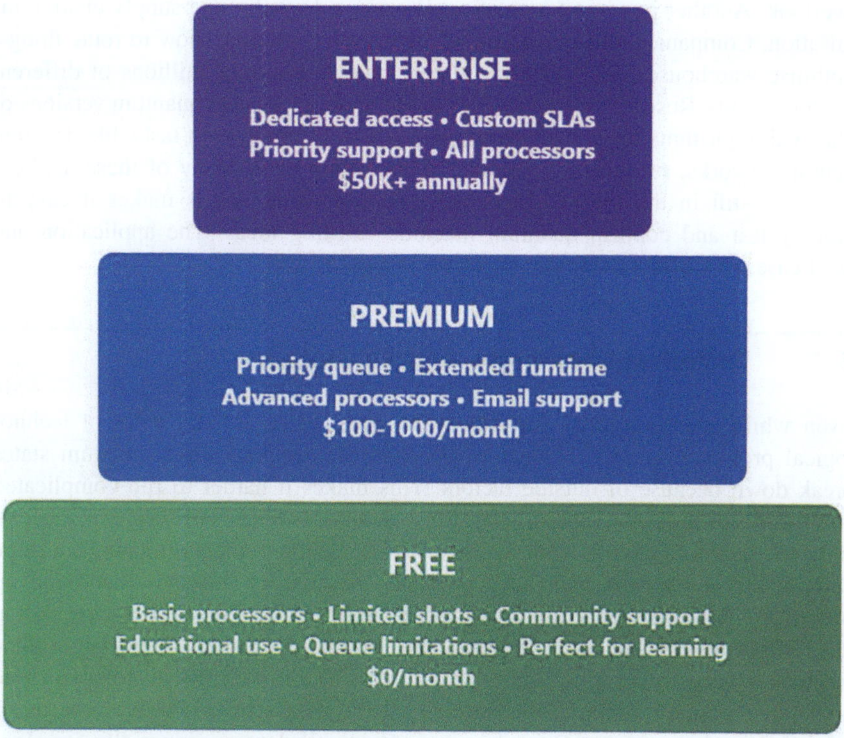

Fig. 4 Quantum cloud pricing tiers comparison

c. Microsoft's Q# language is a more specialised way to program quantum computers. Q# was designed particularly for developing quantum algorithms. It has built-in quantum data types and control structures that make it easier to write complicated quantum algorithms. The Azure Quantum platform makes it easy for Q# programs to work with different quantum hardware backends.

5 Real-World Applications and Use Cases

Quantum cloud services have made it possible for many different kinds of real-world applications to work in many different fields. Pharmaceutical firms utilise quantum algorithms to model chemical interactions that classical computers can't handle while they are looking for new drugs. These simulations assist find good medication candidates and improve molecular architectures to get the desired therapeutic effects. Companies that offer financial services use quantum algorithms to improve portfolios, analyse risks, and find fraud. Quantum algorithms can search across huge solution spaces more quickly than classical methods. This means they could find investing strategies or ways to lower risk that traditional analysis would overlook. Another important area of application is logistics and supply chain optimisation. Companies utilise quantum algorithms to figure out how to route things, optimise warehouses, and construct supply chains that have millions of different configurations. Researchers in machine learning are looking at quantum versions of classical algorithms to see if quantum computers can help with tasks like training neural networks, recognising patterns, or analysing data. Many of these applications are still in the testing stage, but quantum cloud access makes it easy to quickly test and confirm quantum machine learning ideas. The application and used cases of quantum services is shown in Fig. 5 [10].

6 Technical Challenges and Limitations

Even while quantum cloud services seem great, there are still a lot of technological problems to solve. Quantum decoherence happens when quantum states break down because of outside factors. This makes it harder to run complicated algorithms on present quantum gear. Most quantum cloud platforms can successfully run quantum circuits with depths of a few hundred quantum gates, but more complicated algorithms may have problems because of mistakes that build up over time. Network delay doesn't directly influence quantum processing, but it does affect how users experience quantum cloud services. Quantum algorithms frequently need to be optimised over and over again, with the outcomes of one quantum execution affecting the settings for the next. These iterative procedures might take a long time to finish because of network latency, especially for algorithms that need feedback in real time. Managing queues is another problem that only quantum cloud services have to deal with. Quantum hardware, on the other hand, is only available in set amounts. This is different from traditional cloud services, which may quickly add more computing power. During times of high use, people may have to wait a long time for their quantum algorithms to run. Some systems give predictions of how long the wait will be, but these might change a lot based on how complicated the jobs are and how many resources they need. The error rates on present quantum hardware are still greater than what is usually tolerable for traditional computing. In principle, quantum error correction methods exist, but in practice, they need quantum computers with thousands or millions of physical qubits to work with a lower number of logical qubits that have acceptable error rates. The hardware on current quantum cloud platforms has high error rates, thus algorithms and post-processing must be carefully designed to provide accurate results [11].

7 Security and Privacy Considerations

Quantum cloud services have security and privacy issues that are very different from those of traditional cloud computing. The quantum algorithms and data that are processed on distant quantum hardware may contain sensitive intellectual

Fig. 5 The application and used cases of quantum services

property or private information. Because of this, it is important to think carefully about how this information is kept safe while it is being sent and processed. Most quantum cloud services utilise classical encryption techniques to protect communications between users and quantum hardware. But the quantum algorithms are usually sent in a way that makes them easy to interpret so that they can be run correctly on the quantum hardware [12, 13]. Companies that use very sensitive quantum algorithms may need to adopt extra security measures or think about using quantum hardware on their own premises for their most important applications. Quantum cloud hardware is shared, which raises further privacy issues. Quantum processors are reset between jobs for different users, but there is a chance that leftover quantum states or information might escape between executions. This means that hardware maintenance and isolation processes must be very meticulous. Quantum key distribution and quantum cryptography are two examples of applications that are hard to run on the cloud. These apps frequently need quantum communication channels that go all the way from one end to the other, which are hard to set up with regular cloud systems. Some quantum cloud providers are starting to offer services specifically for quantum cryptography applications, although they are still limited compared to quantum computing services that may be used for a wide range of tasks [14, 15].

8 Future Developments and Trends

The quantum cloud ecosystem is evolving rapidly, and some significant factors will impact its future development. Due to advancements in hardware, cloud services are acquiring and increasing quantum processors that are both bigger and better. IBM has announced plans for quantum processors with thousands of qubits. In addition, other firms explore various quantum technologies and their potential for cloud deployment in other ways. It has also been increasingly more straightforward to connect to classical cloud services. Increasingly, the user base consists of using quantum-classical hybrid algorithms that combine a stage of quantum processing with a stage of classical processing. This requirement for quantum hardware and classical cloud computing resources to be connected seamlessly also has implications for the ecosystem in quantum cloud. The integration led to the possibility of developing complicated applications to incorporate the best of quantum and conventional computing. There are at present many typical clouds service models based on quantum services for specific purposes. Examples of this specialisation trend include quantum annealing services which are primarily for optimisation problems, quantum simulation services which are primarily for chemistry and materials science, and quantum machine learning platforms which can run as platforms of well-known machine learning frameworks. One day, the development of quantum internet infrastructure is expected to lead to new forms of quantum cloud services. Rather than dispatching quantum algorithms to centralised quantum data centres, quantum internet links might facilitate distributed quantum computing, meaning quantum information could be processed between several quantum nodes linked together by quantum communication channels.

9 Conclusion

Quantum cloud services have fundamentally changed the way people interact with quantum computers. They have transformed a previously research-only device into a computing resource for everyone. These platforms have expedited quantum computing research and enabled quantum computers to be used in new ways across various disciplines by abstracting the more challenging aspects of quantum hardware management and providing developers and programmers robust tools and environments. The present generation of quantum cloud services is just the tip of the iceberg. As quantum hardware improves and new quantum algorithms emerge, cloud-based access will remain the primary avenue for the majority of companies to engage with quantum computing power. With advancements in hardware capability, software tools, and an influx of developers with familiarity with quantum computing, quantum cloud services are becoming a cornerstone of a new quantum computing ecosystem. Individuals and organisations interested in participating in the quantum computing revolution can begin their exploration of this world-changing technology immediately by utilising quantum cloud services. As the power and involvedness of quantum resources increase, the barriers to entry continue to fall.

References

1. Amodei D, Olah C (2024) Concrete problems in AI safety. arXiv:1606.06565
2. Arute F, Arya K, Babbush R, Bacon D, Bardin JC, Barends R, Biswas R et al (2019) Quantum supremacy using a programmable superconducting processor. Nature 574(7779):505–510
3. Bharti K, Cervera-Lierta A, Kyaw TH, Haug T, Alperin-Lea S, Anand A, Degroote M et al (2022) noisy intermediate-scale quantum algorithms. Rev Mod Phys 94(1):015004
4. Bravyi S, Dial O, Gambetta JM, Gil D, Nazario Z (2022) The future of quantum computing with superconducting qubits. J Appl Phys 132(16):160902
5. Cross AW, Bishop LS, Sheldon S, Nation PD, Gambetta JM (2019) Validating quantum computers using randomized model circuits. Phys Rev A 100(3):032328
6. Endo S, Cai Z, Benjamin SC, Yuan X (2021) Hybrid quantum-classical algorithms and quantum error mitigation. J Phys Soc Jpn 90(3):032001
7. Gambetta JM, Chow JM, Steffen M (2017) Building logical qubits in a superconducting quantum computing system. NPJ Quant Inform 3(1):2
8. Alvarez-Rodriguez U, Sanz M, Lamata L, Solano E (2018) Quantum artificial life in an IBM quantum computer. Sci Rep 8(1):14793
9. Kim Y, Eddins A, Anand S, Wei KX, van den Berg E, Rosenblatt S, Nayfeh H et al (2023) Evidence for the utility of quantum computing before fault tolerance. Nature 618(7965):500–505
10. LaRose R (2019) Overview and comparison of gate level quantum software platforms. Quantum 3:130
11. Nguyen P-N (2025) Quantum technology: a financial risk assessment. Digital Finance 1–40

12. Reiher M, Wiebe N, Svore KM, Wecker D, Troyer M (2017) Elucidating reaction mechanisms on quantum computers. Proc Natl Acad Sci 114(29):7555–7560
13. Temme K, Bravyi S, Gambetta JM (2017) Error mitigation for short-depth quantum circuits. Phys Rev Lett 119(18):180509
14. Willow Quantum Processor Team (2024) Quantum error correction below the surface code threshold. Nature 634:321–326
15. Wang DS, Fowler AG, Hollenberg LCL (2011) Surface code quantum computing with error rates over 1%. Phys Rev A—Atom Mol Optical Phys 83(2):020302

Keshav Kumar is an academic professional specialising in Electrical, Electronics, and Communication Engineering. He is currently an Assistant Professor at Pranveer Singh Institute of Technology, Kanpur, with prior teaching experience at Parul University, Chandigarh University, and Chitkara University. His research background includes work at NIT Patna and Gyancity Research Lab, focusing on hardware architecture, electronics, and signal processing. Keshav holds a Ph.D. in Hardware Cryptography for IoT devices from Lingayas Vidyapeeth, Faridabad.

Dr. Man Mohan Shukla is received his Ph.D. from APJ Abdul Kalam Technical University Lucknow (formerly Uttar Pradesh Technical University, Lucknow). Dr. Man Mohan Shukla is currently working as a Group Director at Pranveer Singh Institute of Technology, Kanpur. Prof. Shukla is also serving as a Director, PSIT Startup and Incubation Foundation. He has worked upon several projects based on Blockchain, NFT and Machine Learning, etc. and has keen interests in learning and exploring new opportunities. His research interests encompass machine learning, deep learning, cloud computing, and IoT. Dr. Shukla has published research papers in reputed SCI/ ESCI/SCIE/ Scopus journals & international conferences. He has also delivered talks as keynote speaker in renowned international conferences. Dr. Shukla has also published & granted patents in the field of IoT, Healthcare, and AI field.

MIX
Papier aus verantwortungsvollen Quellen
Paper from responsible sources
FSC® C105338

If you have any concerns about our products,
you can contact us on
ProductSafety@springernature.com

In case Publisher is established outside the EU,
the EU authorized representative is:
Springer Nature Customer Service Center GmbH
Europaplatz 3, 69115 Heidelberg, Germany

Printed by Libri Plureos GmbH
in Hamburg, Germany